The Day the World Turned Blue

THE DAY THE WORLD TURNED BLUE

a biography of Gene Vincent
by britt hagarty

Talonbooks · Vancouver · 1983

copyright © 1983 britt hagarty

published with assistance from the Canada Council

Talonbooks
201 1019 East Cordova
Vancouver
British Columbia V6A 1M8
Canada

This book was typeset by The Typeworks, designed by
David Robinson and printed in Canada by Hignell
for Talonbooks.

First printing: September 1983

Canadian Cataloguing in Publication Data

Hagarty, Britt, 1949-
   The day the world turned blue

   ISBN 0-88922-214-2

   1. Vincent, Gene, 1935–1971.   2. Rock
musicians – United States – Biography.
I. Title.
ML420.V55H34 1983   784.5'4'00924   C83–091365–3

for Donna Big Eyes

America I've given you all and now I'm nothing.
— Allen Ginsberg, "America" (1956)

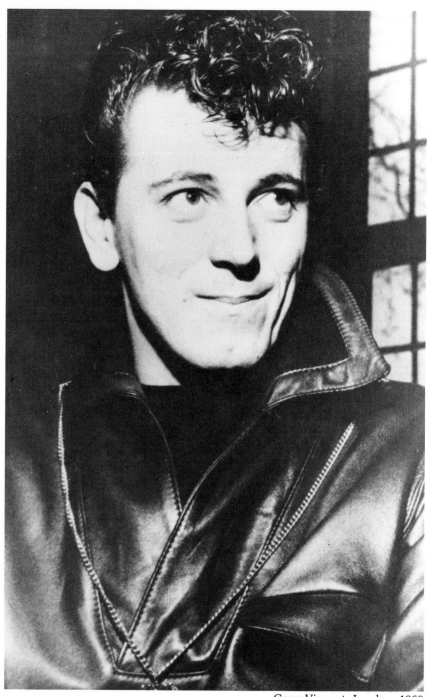

Gene Vincent, London, 1960

Rock'n'Roll Legend

Few other performers in the history of rock'n'roll have left behind a legend as great as Gene Vincent's. He was one of the originators of the progression from blues and country to rockabilly to pure rock'n'roll, and never strayed far from his chosen path. He never went country and western like Jerry Lee Lewis, never went pop like Elvis Presley, and never turned to gospel like Little Richard. Gene lived fast, died young, and never stopped rockin'.

His first record, *Be-Bop-A-Lula*, released in 1956, sold millions of copies, and throughout the late fifties he toured the United States to packed houses of wild screaming fans. But it wasn't until he toured Britain in the early sixties that he reached the peak of his career. He put on such a consistently frantic stage show, few people realized that his left leg was crippled as result of a motorcycle accident he had when he was an unknown young sailor in the U.S. Navy. On stage Gene was the very essence of wild rebellion. Hunched over the microphone in his black leather jacket, with his dark curls cascading over his brow, his leg held in a metal brace and stretched out behind him, he gave himself completely to the music he loved and lived for. His voice was phenomenal and ranged from haunting falsettos to deep rasping growls. More than any other rock'n'roller, Gene Vincent used his voice as an instrument and wrenched from it every bit of emotion possible. His career spanned only sixteen years, yet he left behind an enormous legacy: twenty-one different original albums, and at least twenty anthologies.

In the mid-sixties, Gene left Britain and returned to the United States. His crippled leg had developed osteomyelitis, a disease of the bone marrow, and he was in and out of the hospital during the rest of his career. In the late sixties, he tried in vain to make a comeback, and though his later albums were as good in their own way as his earlier work with the Blue Caps, he never attained the success he deserved. The late sixties were years of hippiedom and flower power, and there was little interest left for a greasy rocker with a ducktail haircut and black leather jacket.

Gene Vincent died in 1971 at the age of 36. Few people mourned him at the time, but today he is revered. The 'image' he actually lived has become a pop culture cliché, used by countless punk, new wave and neo-rockabilly bands. If only Gene could be around to witness the revival of interest in his music and his style. As an old friend and fellow rocker Johnny Carroll sang in a recent tribute:

> The Black Leather Rebel is now in the ground –
> But his spirit goes around and around and around.
> The deejay leeches are still cuttin' him down,
> But Gene keeps a rockin' to the Wildcat sound.

Gene's career was one long continuum of a style he created almost single-handedly: rock'n'roll lunacy. He lived out of a suitcase and toured all over the world: the United States, Canada, Australia, Japan, Britain, France, Germany, Belgium, South Africa, Italy, Switzerland and Israel.

Everything he did – his music, his personal relationships, his drinking bouts and his antics on and offstage – was marked by excess. His friend and former road manager Henry Henroid once said, "Gene was a colossal drinker.... But once he hit that microphone he'd still be the greatest rock'n'roll singer ever! Sex, drugs and rock'n'roll... Gene Vincent invented it!"

Gene's drinking was in large part due to the pain of his leg, but it also had a great deal to do with his emotional make-up. According to Gene's friend Adrian Owlett, "If you were a rock'n'roll fan and saw Gene in his black leathers doing hard rock, you loved him. But when you got a little closer, you realized that he was mad, completely over the top!"

He was married four times and had three children, yet he died on his knees, in terrible pain, alone except for his mother and father. Gene Vincent was a musical genius, but he was also a tortured man. This is his story.

Gene Craddock, U.S. Navy

1

Gene Craddock, U.S. Navy

*There was lots of coloured folks around there and they'd
sit on the porch and sing and sometimes Gene would
play his guitar for them. That's where his sound came
from.*

— Louise Craddock

Dick Thomas, who toured with Gene for several years in Sounds
Incorporated, once remarked, "Gene was *always* in dispute." Dick
was referring to Gene's rocky relationships with managers, promoters, musicians and his wives, but the same can be said about all
the facts of Gene's life: they're in dispute.

According to various album covers, books and magazine articles,
his full name was either Eugene Vincent Craddock or Vincent
Eugene Craddock. His gravestone and his naval records indicate
that his first name was Vincent, but from childhood on he was always called Gene. February 11th, 1935 is usually quoted as his
birthdate, but his sister Evelyn says he was born on George Washington's birthday, February 22nd. Gene's mother, Louise Craddock, says he was born on February 17th and that when she applied for his birth certificate her handwriting was misread. "Gene
was *always* in dispute."

His parents, Mary Louise Cooper and Ezekiah Jackson Craddock,
were from farming families in North Carolina. Both families eventually moved to the nearest big city, Norfolk, Virginia, a large sea-
port and naval base just across the North Carolina line. They were
neighbours in the Brambleton district and married in May, 1934.
Three years after Gene's birth they had a second child, a daughter,
Evelyn.

In 1942, when Gene was seven, they moved out to the country

near Munden Point and opened a store. Previous to this move, Gene had heard only country music, like the Grand Ole Opry that his mother played on the radio, but there were lots of blacks around Munden Point and here, for the first time, Gene was introduced to blues and gospel. According to Evelyn, "We'd leave the house and sneak over to the black church and look through the window. They did a lot of hand music, clapping, very active with their hands and their hallelujahs. . . . And later on we used to jitterbug to the radio." Like all true rock'n'roll, Gene's music would grow out of equal portions of black music and country music. Mrs. Craddock remembers Gene sitting on a fence in their back yard and singing a song called *A Little Sir Echo*. A neighbour said to her, "Did you know your little boy could sing?" In his third or fourth grade Gene sang in a school play. "I made him a little sailor suit for his play in school and he had six little girls on either side of him looking just like paper dolls."

Gene's upbringing in the paternal society of the post-war South, where little boys were dressed as sailors and girls were dressed as paper dolls, would contribute to Gene's lifetime of frustrating relationships with women, relationships that he was not prepared to understand or deal with. This fascination with "paper doll" women began at an early age, and later became one of his more destructive obsessions. Mrs. Craddock recalls: "Every afternoon there'd be a crowd of girls waiting for Gene to get off school," and according to his father, "Gene always was a ladies' man. He liked his girls."

As much as young Gene Craddock liked girls, he liked music more. Impressed by both the Grand Ole Opry and the neighbourhood gospel singers, he bugged his parents for so long they finally got him a guitar and arranged for lessons. He spent his afternoons on the porch of their country store and soon people in the neighbourhood began to take notice of the little white kid with the big guitar. Says Evelyn, "A black man lived down the street and he'd come to the store, an old country store, and we had chairs there and he sang while Gene played. And then we'd all sing." Mrs. Craddock agrees: "There was lots of coloured folks around there and they'd sit on the porch and sing and sometimes Gene would play his guitar for them. That's where his sound came from."

When Gene was thirteen, his parents had another child, Tina, and a year later his third sister, Donna, was born. About this time they gave up their store and moved back to Norfolk. Kie Craddock started working in the Navy shipyard and Gene attended junior high school. He was small and trim for his age—"He'd eat like a hayhand and never gain an ounce." Perhaps because of this and his envy and resentment of the larger boys, Gene began to develop the temper he'd become famous for in his later years. Evelyn remembers Gene having "a nasty temper, a vicious temper. He was like a little bantam rooster. Most of the kids his age were bigger than him and they tended to pick on him a little, so he had to be tougher than most. He had his share of fights and hassles at school."

Gene attended South Norfolk High but he didn't stay long. Mrs. Craddock insists that Gene never failed any grades, in spite of his naval records indicating that he only finished grade eight. Not doing too well academically probably had little to do with Gene's sudden departure. His mother comments: "Gene wanted to make the football team, but he was too small. It broke his heart." Gene was in grade nine and almost seventeen years old, yet he weighed only 110 pounds and stood only five foot six. He was frustrated by his experiences at school and wanted to assert himself in some way, and since Norfolk was a sailor's town, Gene decided to join the navy. Evelyn remarks: "Mother didn't want him to go, but dad thought it would be good for him." Kie Craddock, who'd enlisted in the Coast Guard during the World War II, signed the papers giving Gene permission to join.

In June of 1950, U.S. President Harry Truman had ordered American military forces into Korea. U.S. Commander-in-chief in the Far East General of the Army Douglas MacArthur headed the combined forces of the U.S., South Korea, and the ground forces of the participating members of the United Nations. By 1951, the conflict had become a war of attrition, and in April MacArthur was removed from his command for repeatedly requesting permission to attack military bases in Red China, and for making these views public.

The U.S. had suffered over 100,000 casualties so far, and in January of 1952 alone had lost over fifty fighter bombers. Almost thir-

15

teen million tons of explosives had been shipped to American forces in Korea. At the beginning of February *Newsweek's* cover story read 'Should We Bomb China?' The answer, this time from retired General of the Air Force Carl Spatz, was yes.

1952 was a year of high patriotism in the United States, and a frenzied anti-Communism was sweeping the nation. In the Senate, where he was safe from legal suits for damages, Joe McCarthy continued to accuse prominent government officials of being Communists, spies, infiltrators and 'fellow travellers.' This obsession with exposing imagined Communist conspiracy, 'McCarthyism,' was defined by Harry Truman as "the corruption of truth, the abandonment ... of fair play ... in the name of Americanism and security." Graham Greene was refused entry into the United States because of his month-long flirtation with Communism in the thirties, and ironically, two big new books of the season were Erich Maria Remarque's *Spark of Life* and Bertrand Russell's *New Hopes for a Changing World.* America's most successful film actor at the time was John Wayne, whose screen roles exemplified the doctrine that whatever dilemma you found yourself in, you could always shoot your way out of it.

In the midst of all this blind nationalism and paranoid anti-Communism, something else was beginning to happen in America. Johnny Ray was at number one on the radio and every jukebox with his blues-influenced lament, *Cry.* Although he was also number two on the rhythm'n'blues charts, he never made the country charts where Polish-American Pee Wee King from Wisconsin was at the top with an accordion-instrumental, *Slow Poke*, while Hank Williams' *Cold, Cold Heart* was number nine. Hank, whose next release was *Honky Tonk Blues*, had less than a year to live.

Gene Craddock must have felt very much in the mainstream of American society at the time. There was a shooting war in Korea, but negotiations were taking place. Gene almost certainly wanted to get in on the adventure before it was over. His mother remembers his fascination as a child with hundreds of toy soldiers, and later in his career he would exhibit some fairly peculiar behaviour with knives and pistols. And he was wild about the movies, especially war films and shoot-'em-up westerns.

On the 19th of February, 1952, in Richmond, Virginia, Gene

made a solemn oath: "I, Vincent Eugene Craddock, do solemnly swear that I will bear true faith and allegiance to the United States of America; that I will serve them honestly and faithfully against all their enemies whomsoever...."

The same day he was transferred to a Naval Training Centre at Bainbridge, Maryland, near Baltimore, and by the 6th of June had completed Recruit Training. The Korean War was just entering into its third year and would end in July, 1953. His parents came up north for his graduation ceremony and Gene was proud. He felt good in his tight new sailor suit.

In September, 1952, he was assigned to the tanker *USS Chuckawan* and commenced sea duty as a deck hand. In May of 1953, after a two week course on the *USS Amphion,* he was advanced to the position of boilerman and transferred back to the *Chuckawan.* In January, 1954, this ship began a four-month tour of the Mediterranean, and when Gene returned he was entitled to wear both the National Defense Service Medal and the Navy Occupation Service Medal (Europe). On the *Chuckawan* in the fall of '54 Gene met Ed Butler, who was to become one of his closest friends. Ed remembers Gene singing and playing his guitar on board: "You get all those hillbillies together and a jam session would happen. Gene would sing country songs and spirituals. Did pretty good too."

Gene was happy in the navy and got along well with both the officers and the men. In March of 1955, although he had almost a year of his original enlistment to go, Gene decided to sign up for a further six years. Gene had changed in the three years he'd been in the navy. He stood five foot nine, weighed 131 pounds, and had developed a passion that would irrevocably change the course of his life: motorcycles.

At first he bought a small bike, but soon he wanted a bigger one, and this could have been the reason for his early re-enlistment. Gene received a $642.12 re-enlistment bonus and $300.00 mustering-out pay, as well as 26½ days accumulated leave. He promptly bought a big Triumph. Says Ed Butler: "It was a horse to go, the hottest thing on the road!" Evelyn agrees: "That motorcycle was mean. It'd go right out from under you! He took me for a ride once. But never again after that. It was too fast! When he took off, he almost

17

lost me off the back!"

According to Mrs. Craddock, a number of Gene's fellow sailors had motorcycles and planned to start a club, and she also says that Gene was probably influenced by Marlon Brando's portrayal of a rebellious leather-clad biker in the film *The Wild One*, which had been released the year before.

Now that Gene had grown up physically and could wear a few medals on his sailor suit as he roared around Norfolk on his big motorcycle, he was less interested in sea duty. He arranged for a transfer to a 'tender', the *USS Tutuila*. According to Ed Butler, Gene transferred because the *Tutuila* stayed in port more often than the *Chuckawan* and "Gene wanted to ride that motorcycle and see his girls."

On a weekend in July of '55, Gene jumped on his Triumph and headed off to see a girlfriend. He didn't get far. In Franklin, a small town close to Norfolk, a woman in a Chrysler ran a red light, smashed into Gene and crushed his left leg. Gene's parents say that the police claimed the accident was Gene's fault, and that it was settled out of court after Gene had signed some papers while under the influence of heavy medication. Evelyn remembers visiting Gene. He was in pain and only semi-conscious: "He was out of it, babbling and carrying on. They scooted me out." She doesn't think there was ever any settlement. "There was a lot of discrepancy about it, a lot of hard feelings. He was in and out of the hospital forever, it seemed."

The doctors wanted to amputate Gene's leg, but when his mother visited, Gene made her promise not to sign the papers giving them the required permission. She did as he asked, but years later said, "I tell you, when I looked into his eyes, I knew I couldn't do it. . . . But now I wish I had."

The accident had cost the U.S. Navy an average sailor, but the world was about to gain a great rock'n'roller.

Gene, 1956

2

Be-Bop-A-Lula

He came up wearing a cast and sang Be-Bop-A-Lula
and all the chicks went berserk!
— Willie Williams

Gene Craddock spent approximately six months in the Portsmouth Naval Hospital, some of it as an out-patient, and he had plenty of time to think about his past and his future. The United States had come through the depression of the thirties, the World War of the forties, and the Korean War of the early fifties, and now it was the richest, most powerful country in the world. Though the fifties in the States was an era of right-wing politics, anti-Communist witch-hunts and Hollywood blacklisting, it was also a period of cultural renaissance.

In film there was the disquieting presence of Marlon Brando, whose performances in *A Streetcar Named Desire* (1951), *The Wild One* (1954) and *On the Waterfront* (1954) introduced a new type of social realism and a new type of hero, or anti-hero, to the American public, much different from the macho stereotypes popularized by John Wayne *et al*. This new type of protagonist was further popularized by James Dean, whose performance in *Rebel Without a Cause* in 1955 seemed to epitomize America's burgeoning rebellious youth.

In literature a new style of writing, and living, seethed below the surface and the writers of the Beat Generation were soon to transform not only literature, but the sense of America itself. Between 1951 and 1955, though they weren't published until the late fifties and early sixties, Jack Kerouac wrote *On the Road, Visions of Cody, Doctor Sax, Book of Dreams, Maggie Cassidy, The Subterraneans, San Francisco Blues* and *Tristessa*. In poetry, Allen Ginsberg was working on *Howl* and Lawrence Ferlinghetti had just published *Pictures of the Gone World*. In music, one saw even more radical changes, and this, naturally, had the strongest effect on young Gene Craddock.

In jazz, the swing of the forties gave way to the Be-Bop of the fifties, and though the progenitor of this modern jazz, Charlie Parker, died of an overdose of drugs and alcohol in March of '55, the wildness of his Be-Bop solos had a strong influence not just on progressive jazz, but on rockabilly (including Gene's early work with the Blue Caps, especially on some of the wild guitar breaks of his first lead player, Cliff Gallup). The acoustic blues of the Mississippi Delta, called 'race music' in the forties, had given way to the electrified Chicago blues of Muddy Waters and Howlin' Wolf and the more sophisticated rhythm'n'blues of Roy Brown and Joe Turner.

In country music, both Appalachian-style Old-time music and Blue Grass gave way to Western Swing, as played by Bob Wills and his horn band the Texas Playboys, and Country Boogie, as done by piano extemporizer Merrill Moore. But it was probably the honky-tonk laments and hillbilly dance tunes of Hank Williams that had the strongest influence on Gene. Hank Williams had overdosed on booze and pills on New Year's Day, 1953, yet his music lived on and Gene was to sing and record Williams' songs for the rest of his life.

In the apparently complacent America of the mid-fifties, all these diverse styles came briefly together in a new social phenomenon: rock'n'roll. In July of 1955, as Gene lay in the hospital, Bill Haley and the Comets were at number one nationwide with *Rock Around the Clock*, a song that typified America's *lebensfreude* at emerging victorious from a depression and two wars, and other rock'n'roll hits of '55 were Chuck Berry's *Maybelline* and Little Richard's *Tutti Frutti*. It seemed a revolution had begun, and it would have a direct effect on Gene.

His parents had brought him his guitar to play in the hospital, and at first he merely amused himself by singing country songs by Hank Williams and Red Foley, like *Red Sails in the Sunset* and *Rockin' Chair Daddy*. But with the advent of rock'n'roll, Gene began to write songs of his own, the best-known being *Race with the Devil* and, of course, *Be-Bop-A-Lula*. According to most sources, 'Lula was inspired by the comic strip 'Little Lulu' and was co-written by

22

another patient. Ed Butler says that a marine from Michigan helped write it and that Bill Davis, who later became Gene's manager, paid the marine $25 for his half of the rights. Louise Craddock adds, "I told that boy not to do it. But he did it anyway." She came to see Gene with her brother Will Cooper, who later worked as Gene's chauffeur, and Gene sang 'Lula for them. Cooper apparently thought that the song was a joke but Gene told him, "Don't laugh! This'll be on a record someday!"[1]

Eventually, Gene was released from the hospital and his sister Evelyn remembers him coming home on crutches: "Gene was hurtin' when he got home. Everybody was glad to see him and glad that he was alive. It could have been worse. . . . But that leg of his wasn't nothin' but a big mess of pain for him. I imagine it would be like having one big bad toothache all your life." Luckily for Gene, he was still technically in the navy, so he received medical benefits as well as partial pay. But his mother knew that his crippled leg would hinder Gene in getting a good job or re-joining the navy on a permanent basis, so she encouraged him to pursue a musical career.

In the fall of '55, a local country music staion, WCMS, brought a package show, Hank Snow's All Star Jamboree, to the Norfolk Municipal Auditorium. It featured Elvis Presley and the Blue Moon Boys (with Scotty Moore on electric guitar and Bill Black on acoustic bass, but no drums) as well as Cowboy Copas, the Louvin Brothers and Jimmie Rogers Snow. The Jamboree was in Norfolk for two days, September 11th and 12th, and Gene went. WCMS had been playing Presley's Sun records and Gene had been impressed. Now he could see the adulation that Presley's live performances generated. He once said, "I wasn't influenced by his voice, except that he was obviously young like me and I was encouraged by this, 'cause I was just a shy kid."[2]

Gene's friend Ed Butler had been dating Evelyn Craddock and in October they married. Gene was best man, and apparently pleased that his buddy was marrying one of his sisters. About this time, Gene started a romance with a fifteen-year-old high school student,

1. Rob Finnis and Bob Dunham, *Gene Vincent and the Blue Caps* (London: Mimeographed edition, c.1972).
2. Ibid.

Ruth Ann Hand. After only going out for a few months, and in spite of Gene's parents' objections, they were engaged. Kie Craddock felt that "Gene was too young to get married, and Ruth was too young too." Louise Craddock adds, "Ruth Ann was a very nice girl, but she was only fifteen. And Gene was just starting his career." Evelyn remembers Ruth Ann: "She was very quiet, a shy girl. Not gorgeous but pretty.... Gene's romances were always whirlwind. He more or less went steady with her for three or four months. He was engaged *a lot*. But this one he *did* marry."

Louise Craddock was the dominant influence on Gene during his formative years, and she kept an even stronger hold on him when he returned home. Naturally enough, Gene, though he loved his mother very much, wanted to assert his independence. For the past three years in the navy, he'd had a taste of independent adult life. Now, after his traumatic accident, he was living at home again with his three young sisters. His impetuous marriage to fifteen-year-old

Gene and Ruth Ann, 1956 (courtesy of Ruth Ann Holloway)

Gene and Ruth Ann (courtesy of Ruth Ann Holloway)

Ruth Ann was a break with his family, and more than that, with his past and his childhood.

On February 11th, 1956, legally Gene's 21st birthday, he and Ruth Ann Hand were married with a large church ceremony. Gene wore his naval uniform. Unfortunately, Mrs. Craddock didn't give Gene's marriage her blessing. Ruth Ann explains: "She didn't seem to like me. But it wasn't just me. Gene was her only boy and I don't think she wanted him to marry *anybody*."

Gene and Ruth Ann spent their honeymoon at the apartment of some friends in nearby Chesapeake, because, as Ruth Ann remembers, "Gene wasn't making that much money. He was just getting started as a singer." Around this time, radio station WCMS advertised on TV that they were looking for local talent for a new show, Country Showtime. It was to be broadcast from a local club, the Carnival Room, which belonged to the station's owner, Sy Blumenthal. Louise Craddock suggested that Gene go down to the station and audition, and despite his shyness, Gene went to try out. The judges were station manager Roy Lamear and deejays Joe Hoppell and Bill 'Sheriff Tex' Davis. Gene sang *Heartbreak Hotel* (Elvis Presley's current hit, his first national one), and Davis says, "I never heard such sweet sounds. He was great!" Over one hundred people auditioned, but Gene Craddock was the obvious choice. Along with nine other finalists he played at the Carnival Room in Norfolk and was backed by the WCMS staff band, the Virginians, led by a native of Maine, Willie Williams. Williams recalls vividly his first night playing with Gene: "He came up wearing a cast and sang *Be-Bop-A-Lula* and all the chicks went berserk!"

During these shows a metamorphosis took place in Gene Craddock. While offstage, he was usually shy, quiet, polite and reserved, but in front of an audience he became a consummate performer and seemed almost possessed. "He played guitar and fell on one knee and slammed the mike against the floor and broke it.... He went everywhere with that guitar, probably slept with it. Then on stage he'd throw it all over and step on it.... But he could sing like a bird! An unbelievable boy!"[3]

Gene became so popular so fast that he soon became the major at-

---

3. Bill Davis.

'Sheriff Tex' Davis (courtesy of Bill Davis)

traction on Country Showtime, and he became well-known around the Norfolk area because people either saw him live at the Carnival Room or heard him on the radio. As WCMS deejay Joe Hoppell recalls, "Gene was getting all the crowd reaction. It was supposed to be a family show, but he was certainly getting all the teenage reaction. He had something special and they really went for him. We began thinking, *maybe we do have something here!"*

A Chevrolet dealer named Wilkins hired Gene and the Virginians to play at his car lot on the weekend, and in return Gene was given a special deal on a brand-new cherry-coloured Chevrolet convertible with a continental spare. Gene, Ruth Ann and Gene's friends cruised around Norfolk with the top down and the radio blaring.

Country Showtime, mostly because of Gene's sensational performances, was proving increasingly popular. It relocated to a larger venue, the Gates Theater in downtown Portsmouth, just across the Elizabeth River from Norfolk. Evelyn Craddock recalls: "It was packed. And the people went crazy! They loved him. And there was always lots of girls!" This sudden adulation was probably the beginning of the end of Gene's recent marriage to Ruth Ann. According to Joe Hoppell, "Gene was mobbed by girls even *before* he made records. We had to get a Chevy convertible to take him to the shows and the girls used to crawl all over him!" Though Gene continued to live with Ruth Ann at her parents' house, she began to hear that Gene was going out with other girls.

Meanwhile, WCMS station manager Roy Lamear and deejay 'Sheriff Tex' Davis had decided that they wanted to make some money out of Gene Craddock who, after all, was only a naive young sailor with no experience in show business. Lamear managed a booking agency with Sy Blumenthal called L & B Talent Management, and they handled local acts as well as bringing in better known singers.

Lamear, Blumenthal and Davis had all watched the meteoric rise of Elvis Presley, another young Southern boy. Presley was only one month older than Gene, and he sang the same kind of strange music that people were only beginning to call rock'n'roll. Presley had recently changed labels, going from the small independent Sun to RCA Victor, and his first single on RCA, *Heartbreak Hotel*, was a huge success. Following in the tracks of Chuck Berry, Little

Richard, and Bill Haley and the Comets (who had actually been the first white rockers with *Crazy, Man, Crazy* in 1953), Presley attained phenomenal popularity. In early '56 he appeared on the Dorsey Brothers television show four times. Sun Records had recently released Carl Perkins' *Blue Suede Shoes* and it was roaring up the charts. Rock'n'roll was definitely the big seller that year, but no one knew how long the fad would last. To cash in on the craze, Lamear, Blumenthal and Davis decided to form a rock'n'roll band around Gene. Bill Davis knew a lot of musicians around Norfolk, so he arranged for Gene to rehearse with Willie Williams (acoustic rhythm guitar), Jack Neal (acoustic bass), Cliff Gallup (electric lead guitar) and Dickie Harrell (drums). Gene was twenty-one years old, Williams was twenty, Jack and Cliff were twenty-six, and Dickie, who was still in high school, was only fifteen. They got together at the WCMS studio on the top floor of the Halina Building in downtown Norfolk.

Initially, they just practised two of Gene's own songs, *Be-Bop-A-Lula* and *Race With the Devil*, and the sounds were impressive. Davis called Ken Nelson, producer for Capitol Records in Los Angeles, and asked him if he was interested in a rock'n'roll singer, saying "I've got this kid and, boy, is he great!" Nelson replied that Davis must have had his office bugged because that very morning he had been discussing with other executives how much they wanted a rock'n'roller to counteract RCA's Elvis Presley. He told Davis, "If you have anything by that boy on tape, send it to me right away!"

On April 9th, after rehearsing one or two more times, Gene and the band made a demo of *Be-Bop-A-Lula*, a one-sided acetate, and sent it to Nelson in L.A. Three weeks went by and Gene continued to play at the Gates Theater, but there was no word from Capitol Records. Gene's disappointment showed, so Davis took him aside and told him not to worry; if Capitol wasn't interested, they'd try another company. Then, on a Friday afternoon, Ken Nelson phoned Davis at WCMS and said, "I don't know where you got him from, but he's perfect! Can you get those people down to Nashville on the next plane?"[4] That night, Gene was headlining Country Showtime. Just before he went on, Bill Davis went to the mike and

---

4. Finnis and Dunham.

said that he had an announcement to make: Capitol wanted to sign Gene to a contract. "At first the crowd was silent, then all of a sudden it sounded like a party. Everybody was yelling and clapping. . . . I looked at Gene and he was so happy he was about to cry. . . . Later that night I spoke with his mother and she was crying and could hardly speak. This, I believe, was the happiest night of my life."[5]

left to right: Willie, Dickie, Gene, Cliff, Jack

On the 3rd of May, Gene and his band flew to Nashville and stayed at the Andrew Jackson Hotel. Jack Neal, Cliff Gallup and Willie Williams took time off from their day jobs and Dickie Harrell had to be excused from school. The next day they caught a cab to Owen Bradley's studio. (A few months before, Buddy Holly had done his first professional sessions there, but these hadn't produced any hits.) Gene was nervous. The studio was a two-storey house with the second storey removed, so it had a high ceiling. Next door was a quonset hut attached to the studio by a stairway. The engineer was Mort Thomasson, who had devised an echo chamber that utilised a 'slapback' machine, a form of 'delay echo.' This machine was a decided influence on Gene's sound and his initial success. The back-up engineer was Charles Bradley, the brother of the studio's owner.

Gene and the band arrived about six p.m. and sat in the quonset

5. Dickie Harrell, quoted in Finnis and Dunham.

hut watching television until Nelson and Thomasson arrived. Thomasson recalls: "I got two impressions, one when I got in, and one when I heard them play. We walked in and they were sitting around in black coats and hats and they looked like a motorcycle gang. I said to Ken Nelson, 'Are you sure we're in the right place?' Then they started playing and all hell broke loose! It was hectic! They didn't know nothin' except to play loud and fast!" Cliff says that "rock'n'roll was something totally new. Nobody knew what it was supposed to sound like, so we just went into the studio and did our thing." Charley Bradley: "I didn't know what we were going to get into. We'd been doing a lot of country stuff. I personally didn't think that rock'n'roll would go. So it was different for me to try to adapt to that music at the time. But I got along with the people. They *were* unusually dressed, kinda like zoot suits, but not *too* flashy. It was different music, so we had to treat it differently. But Gene was very likable. He put you at ease and appreciated every-thing you did. He was an easy guy to work with and he knew what he wanted. And Cliff, he was just fabulous!"

Nelson was unsure of Gene's band, so he brought along some of Nashville's best session musicians (apparently Grady Martin, Hank Garland, Buddy Harmon and Bob Moore). But Cliff Gallup was one of the finest rock guitarists of the fifties, and the first song they recorded, *Race With the Devil*, started with a succession of fast runs on the bass strings of Gallup's pancake-model Gretsch. According to Davis, the session musicians were astonished and knew right away they wouldn't be needed: "They knew it was all over. When they heard Cliff go off on all those runs, they turned to each other and went, 'Whaaat! Whaaat!'"[6]

The band played so loudly that Thomasson had trouble getting the levels balanced. "We kept moving Gene around and finally I said, 'You're going out, boy!' We had to put him in the stairway 'cause that band just played so loud! I didn't know whether I liked rock'n'roll or not. All I knew was that it was damn loud!" The musi-cians were grouped in a semi-circle in the studio and Gene was left in the stairway with the door held partly open by a Coke box. Gene's quiet voice was also a factor in this move, and he was given

---

6. Finnis and Dunham.

31

headphones so he could hear the band without being drowned out by them.

The next song was *Be-Bop-A-Lula*, and by now Ken Nelson must have realized he wasn't dealing with an Elvis imitator but a real artist with a unique voice and a hot band:

> She's the gal in the red blue jeans,
> She's the queen of all the teens.
> She's the woman that I know....
> She's the woman that *loves* me so!

As Gene reached the end of the first verse his voice suddenly became quivering and breathless, and as they went to the chorus Dickie did a build-up on his snare drum and threw in a piercing scream. When Nelson asked what that was for, Davis replied, "I don't know. He's a fifteen-year-old kid. He's liable to do anything!"[7] According to Dickie, the scream wasn't on the original version. "But one time we were with Mister Nelson, listening to the tapes, and I felt like screaming. So I did. Then Gene turned and said, 'Hey, man. That sounds good. Let's leave that in there.' So we did. And that was the beginning of 'The Screaming End'."

Next they did a song that Nelson had chosen, *Woman Love*, written by Jack Rhodes.[8] Gene gave the arrangement a whole new sensual treatment, using his voice like an instrument:

> I went to see my doctor not too long ago,
> Was walkin' round in circles and moanin' low.
> He took one look at me and said, 'Good Lord above!
> You shore be needin' you some Woman Love!'

The final song was *I Sure Miss You*, a ballad written by a friend of Davis. Gene sang it in his inimitable manner and showed Nelson that he was capable of handling various styles with a wide range of notes and inflections.

---

7. Finnis & Dunham.
8. *Woman Love* was banned in Britain later in the year by the BBC as 'too provocative.'

clockwise from top: Jack, Dickie, Gene, Willie, Cliff

While they played back the tapes, Davis asked Dickie why he'd screamed on *Be-Bop-A-Lula* and he said, "Man, I want my family to know I'm on the record!" Nelson asked them what they thought of the tapes and they replied, "Yeah, that's boppin' stuff, man!" Nelson picked *Woman Love* as the best take and Gene was, as usual, agreeable: "Yeah, that's a good song. Anything you say.... I'm just glad to be on a record." He asked what they'd put on the flip side and Nelson replied, "Let's put on that crazy thing that you guys wrote, " meaning *Be-Bop-A-Lula*.[9] Nelson also suggested that Gene call himself Vincent instead of Craddock and that the band should come up with a name. Dickie, who wore his hat even while drumming, suggested the Blue Caps and everyone agreed. Says Dickie, "I had been wearing them caps for years. But I don't know why we chose blue. I used to wear a hat like that all the time when I went to school. I'd wear a windbreaker with no shirt, roll the sleeves up on my jacket, and dungarees and blue suede shoes. And my little hat. Then later I said to Gene, 'Man, a good name for the group would be the Blue Caps.' And it was a good idea, 'cause later on those hats caused many a riot. We would throw them into the audience at the end of the show and the kids would go crazy!"

The session was over and Gene and the 'Blue Caps' went to a restaurant for dinner. Willie Williams recalls: "We had a good time, laughing and acting loud like typical tourists." Afterwards, they walked around Nashville and on their way back to their hotel room they stopped and listened to a black street-band playing for tips. The guitarist used a pencil and a rubber band for a capo, and the drummer played on pots and pans.

The next day they flew back to Norfolk to await the release of their record. Little did they know they'd made musical history. Twenty-five years later, the songs they recorded that day are still available all over the world. But Gene and his band were unaware of what lay ahead. According to Williams, they were proud of their efforts, but didn't have any great expectations: "The most that any of us thought was that it might get some local airplay and we might get some bookings around Norfolk." Though the band had no great expectations, Gene almost certainly did. Jack Neal, the bass player,

---

9. This conversation reported in Finnis and Dunham.

confirms this: "Gene had a strong personality and knew exactly what he wanted. He wanted to be a star."

Ruth Ann had just turned sixteen and Gene began to introduce her not as his wife, but as his cousin. He explained to Ruth Ann that his contract with L & B Management insisted that his marriage be kept secret because a large percentage of rock'n'roll fans were teenage girls. Jack Neal agrees: "Promotions at that time probably looked better for a young rock'n'roll star if he was not married, so I guess that was the reasoning behind the big mystery." Ruth Ann recalls one incident when the band was on the road and Dickie Harrell unexpectedly walked into Gene's hotel room and saw him on the bed with her. "Ah, kissin' cousins," he said with a wink. Dickie has this to say about Ruth Ann: "In this business you meet a lot of people who aren't too friendly, people that think a lot of themselves. But Ruth Ann seemed really nice. She was very down-to-earth."

For a while Ruth Ann and Gene continued to stay with her parents in Chesapeake, but every day Gene would leave for a band practice and often wouldn't show up till late at night. Soon she was seeing less and less of Gene and hearing more and more about his flirtations with other girls. Finally, Gene moved back in with his parents, and Ruth Ann sued for divorce. Mrs. Craddock says that it was Ruth Ann's idea to split up: "She asked for a Cadillac and a thousand dollars. And Gene gave it to her. . . . But Gene wasn't going out with other girls. He didn't have time for that." Dickie Harrell says, "All I know is that one time they were together and the next time they were broken up. But Gene never talked about his personal life." According to Gene's brother-in-law, Ed Butler, "I don't think Gene was too tight with Ruth Ann. Actually, I don't think Gene ever got along with anyone for long."

Gene waited for the release of his record and continued playing at the Gates Theater to enthusiastic crowds. But he was no longer billed as Gene Craddock and the Virginians. Now it was Gene Vincent and the Blue Caps. He was on the threshold of a new life that would take him far from the bucolic serenity of the South and the docks and naval yards of Norfolk to Hollywood, London, Paris, and beyond.

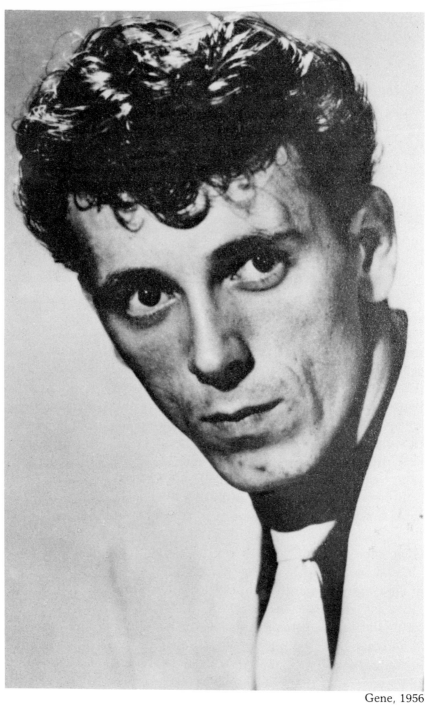

Gene, 1956

3

Rockabilly Rebel

Gene done a lot of crazy things. He popped a lot of pills. . . . But he was a real showman. He'd break his cast in almost every town. Then in the next town we'd have to hunt up a doctor and get a new cast.

— Red Gwynn

Woman Love b/w *Be-Bop-A-Lula* was officially released on June 2, 1956, and special copies with a picture sleeve were sent to various deejays. Included with the single was a press release: 'Sparkling the rock'n'roll roster with what he terms "Rockabilly" is lively Gene Vincent from Norfolk, Virginia. . . . "Rock'n'roll is a young person's music," he says. "I had a feeling for this kind of music and the more accepted kinds didn't move me."' *Be-Bop-A-Lula* was described as "a novelty dreamed up by Gene with Sheriff Tex Davis."

Gene got a copy and took it over to the navy barracks near the hospital where he was still technically an out-patient. "Hey, I just cut a record. Wanna hear?" he said to his friends. Apparently they weren't too impressed. "The barracks was full of guys. . . . At the end of the record there were only about two guys left. They thought it was terrible. I played it to aunts, uncles, parents and they all thought it was terrible. They'd all been used to country music and this was a long way from that."[1]

Capitol placed a half-page ad in *Billboard* magazine advertising Gene's record and describing him as 'The Screaming End.' In this issue there were several rock'n'roll songs on the Honour Roll: Presley's *Heartbreak Hotel* (number two), Carl Perkins' *Blue Suede Shoes* (seven), Little Richard's *Long Tall Sally* (ten), Fats Domino's *I'm In*

---

1. Finnis and Dunham.

Love Again (fifteen), and Frankie Lymon and the Teenagers' *Why Do Fools Fall In Love* (sixteen).

At first, Gene's record attracted no attention at all. Gene described his disappointment: "It took about two weeks really. And I think those were the longest two weeks I've ever waited for anything. I just kinda sat around and nothing happened. Then a disc jockey up in Baltimore picked it up and started playing it. About a month after that, it went."[2] The deejay had ignored the "A" side, *Woman Love*, and instead played *Be-Bop-A-Lula*, probably because *Woman Love* was considered too suggestive, though *'Lula* was as thoroughly sensual. On June 16th it entered the Billboard Top 100 at 78, but in the category 'Coming Up Strong' it was listed as third. In the column 'This Week's Best Buys,' *Billboard* wrote:

> Not many of those trying to move in on the money-making tracks of Elvis Presley are succeeding. Vincent is a notable exception; his Capitol record has shown much of the sales excitement that Presley stirs up and is already listed on Atlanta's and Pittsburgh's Top 100 lists. Other cities reporting very good sales are Nashville, Durham, St. Louis, Milwaukee, Cleveland, Minneapolis, Baltimore and Boston. It is selling to customers in all categories. The flip is *Woman Love* which is also sparkling good action.

By the following week *'Lula* was number three in both Atlanta and Pittsburgh and four in Minneapolis/St. Paul. It came in at 43 in Billboard's Top 100, but for sales in stores it was 24 (The Top 100 also reflects radio and jukebox play, and this accounts for the difference). By June 23rd, *'Lula* had sold 200,000 copies and Capitol Records realized they had a monster smash on their hands. Ken Nelson rushed Gene back to Nashville for more sessions.

Except for Country Showtime, where he usually did only two or three songs, and his brief gig at Wilkins Chevrolet, Gene had no professional experience. His repertoire was limited. He'd appar-

---

2. From a recorded interview by Jim Pewter, included in the four record set, Rock'n'Roll Legend (Capitol Records).

ently signed a management contract with Lamear and Blumenthal, so the deejays at WCMS went through their record collection to try to find some songs for him to record. According to Joe Hoppell, "Gene had no experience and would do anything that was suggested to him." Unfortunately, since it was a country station, they didn't have the kind of material that Gene needed. They should have given Gene some rhythm'n'blues songs like the ones Bill Haley and Elvis Presley were doing. Presley's first album was number one on Billboard's LP charts and featured a lot of R & B standards such as Ray Charles' *I Got A Woman*, Little Richard's *Tutti Frutti*, Clyde McPhatter's *Money Honey*, plus Carl Perkins' *Blue Suede Shoes*. This is exactly the kind of material Gene would have been able to use his talents on.

On June 24th, Gene and the Blue Caps went back to Bradley's studio and cut four more tunes. Three were pop standards, but one, *Crazy Legs*, was a real rocker:

> I got a little woman called Crazy Legs,
> She's the queen of the teenage crowd,
> Just give her lots of room and a rock'n'roll tune
> And she'll do the bop till the cows come home.
>
> Crazy Legs, Crazy Legs, she's boppin' all over the joint.
> Crazy Legs, do the bop, Crazy Legs!
> She's my baby and I don't mean maybe,
> She's mine, mine, all mine!

The next day they returned and did another three standards, as well as *Gonna Back Up Baby*. On the third day Gene and the band really started rocking. The pop songs chosen by the WCMS staff were out of the way and Gene did three of his own tunes, *Who Slapped John, Jumps, Giggles and Shouts*, and *Blue Jean Bop*, as well as Bobby Carrol's *I Flipped*. The Caps were back in the groove and on their fourth session they kept rockin' with *Bop Street* and *You Told A Fib*, both by Cliff Gallup, as well as *Jump Back, Honey, Jump Back* and *Well, I Knocked, Bim Bam*. This last song features one of Cliff's wildest guitar solos, combining savage fury with technical excellence.

A few days after Gene and the Caps returned to Norfolk, *Be-Bop-A-*

Lula was number one in Milwaukee, two in Pittsburgh, three in Atlanta, and fifteenth in sales nationwide. A week later, offers for shows came pouring in. Gene phoned Dickie and asked him if he wanted to go on the road. "When I heard this I fell right out of bed onto the floor."[3] Gene came over in his cherry-coloured Chevy and took Dickie down to see Bill Davis, who told them he'd booked them on a three-week tour, as well as a spot on the Perry Como television show. Says Dickie, "I knew right then that we had got a very big break."[4] Dickie left school and Jack Neal and Cliff Gallup quit their jobs. Davis was to be the road manager and he and Willie Williams took leaves of absence from WCMS. The radio station put up the money for band uniforms (black jackets and pants, with yellow shirts) and a big Cadillac.

The first gig was in Folly Beach, just outside of Charleston, South Carolina. Jack says, "Gene was all over the stage and put on a tremendous show. Gene was never shy. He was the kind of guy who couldn't stay still to save his life. He was nervous and energetic. But his leg never seemed to bother him. On stage, he wore a black outfit and had a black sock over his cast. Later, he got a shoe that fit over the cast. You'd only notice his leg when he got offstage. He took medicine for the pain, and he never complained. But it itched him all the time and he'd get a coat-hanger and push it down inside. . . .

"Gene would talk to anybody about anything, but mostly it was about music. All he was interested in was, 'Let's go out and play!' He loved rock'n'roll. For him there was nothing else like it. . . . He wouldn't hog the spotlight, but you knew he was the star. He didn't have to remind you."

From Folly Beach they headed up north to New York state for a series of fair dates organized through the GAC booking agency of New York City. They played Binghamton, Hamburg, Whitney Point, Watertown, Syracuse and Baldwin. The chauffeur was Red Gwynn, a 36-year-old former shipyard worker who'd been hired by WCMS. Willie Williams: "There was sure no nonsense in that car. And that included Vincent. Red was tough. You didn't mess with him. But a nice guy." Red and Gene didn't get along very well, as

---

3. Finnis and Dunham.
4. Ibid.

Red recalls. "Gene was very temperamental. One time in Pittsburgh he demanded that he use the Cadillac to run around with some girls and I wouldn't do it. He got up and demanded the Cadillac and I jumped up and said I'd punch his face clean off. Sherriff Tex Davis jumped between us... but I got along with Gene most of the time." On another tour, in Philadelphia, they were booked into a Polish club and Gene had another hassle with Red. According to Williams, "They hired us because we had a hit record. Then all they wanted us to play were polkas. Man, they hated us! We played a couple of rock songs and they just stood there and said, 'It's too loud.'" Gene stomped off the stage, punched his fist through a wall and refused to perform. Red Gwynn phoned Davis in Norfolk and got him to talk Gene into going back on stage. Red says, "The management was mad 'cause Cliff was too loud. He was blasting the people in front of the stage. But Gene refused to turn down!"

Ever since Gene's motorcycle accident, his attitude toward authority had changed. Drastically. He probably felt he'd been shafted; perhaps by the police, the Navy, some insurance company or lawyer, the woman who hit him, or even the doctors. Gene would carry a chip on his shoulder for the rest of his life, if only because of his injured leg. Even though his relationships with musicians were usually good, Gene would quarrel with agents, managers, chauffers, road managers, record company executives, policemen and anyone else who seemed to represent authority of any kind. Red Gwynn says, "Gene was his own worst enemy," and adds, "Gene done a lot of crazy things. He popped a lot of pills.... But he was a real showman. He'd break his cast in almost every town. Then in the next town we'd have to hunt up a doctor and get a new cast."

Another of Gene's traits emerged on this first tour: his ability to squander money. Gene had just gone from his naval pay of $136.39 per month to very substantial money. Jack Neal remembers him walking into a shoe store and buying red and blue suede shoes and never asking the price: "He might get them in three or four colours. Gene could spend money, brother." Red Gwynn agrees: "Money meant nothin' to Gene! And he was the kind of guy who wanted things done for him. He didn't like to do things himself. He got Dickie to look after his clothes and Dickie'd go through his jackets

Gene, 1956

and find tens and twenties and stuff and keep them." (Years later, Gene saw this humourously and used to tell an apocryphal story to the members of Sounds Incorporated about how Dickie constantly bummed money for hamburgers, saved the cash, then years later drove up in a Cadillac and said, "Thanks, Gene.")

Willie Williams takes a bit more charitable view of Gene's sudden success and sums it up quite articulately: "Vincent was easy to work with and knew exactly what he was doing. From the minute I met him I found him to be agreeable. There was no arrogance or egotism. He was a guy from relatively humble beginnings who was a little bewildered by his sudden success. I thought he handled it pretty well. Though I seem to recall that he spent a lot of money!"

Gene himself admitted that it all happened a little too quickly for him: "Listen, I never meant to make money. I never wanted it. I'm a singer, man. My only thought was just to make a living singing. But all of a sudden I was getting $1500 a night. And you take a kid and put him in those circumstances. . . . I had a Cadillac and all. It was a bad scene. It shouldn't have happened on that first record. I just didn't know how to handle it."[5]

By the end of July, *Be-Bop-A-Lula* was in the top ten of the pop charts, the rhythm'n'blues charts and the country and western charts. *Rolling Stone* magazine once estimated that it eventually sold about nine million copies, though this is probably an exaggeration. In any case, Gene Vincent and his Blue Caps were a big attraction (perhaps in spite of an appearance on the Perry Como show where they sang '*Lula* in something vaguely resembling a submarine), and continued touring through the northeast. For a while they were part of a six-week package tour with the Johnny Burnette Rock'n'Roll Trio. This was certainly an historic tour since it featured two of the greatest singers of the fifties, two of the greatest bands, and definitely the two greatest guitarists, Cliff Gallup and Burnette's lead man, Paul Burlison.

Burlison remembers the tour fondly: "I knew Gene real well and he hung around with us a lot. Offstage, Gene was kinda shy. Then on stage he'd cut up a bit. He was handicapped and he limped when he walked, but he had a tremendous voice and he didn't seem bit-

---

5. Finnis & Dunham.

ter about his leg, although he mentioned a couple of times that he wished he didn't have the cast on so he could move around more on stage. He had a pretty good sense of humour. I remember him laughin' a lot, but he wasn't usually the one tellin' the jokes. He seemed pretty serious until he got on stage, then he got wild. He had to limp to the mike sometimes, but I didn't feel sorry for him at all 'cause he went over so well, the screamin' teenagers and all that. But because of his leg he really couldn't express himself as well as he wanted.

"I remember the Blue Caps pretty good too. Jack used to ride with us and I got to know him pretty good. He didn't know any chords, but he'd still hit the notes right on. We'd be fooling 'round on some tune and tell him to go to D. But he didn't know D. He just knew the sound. And he'd get it just right.

"Wee Willie was fun. He'd move around and cut it up a bit on stage. Cliff was a very good musician and did a lot of finger-pickin'. But he wasn't too happy on the road. He had his wife with him and he was talkin' about quittin' and goin' back home. And Dickie, he had to have a tutor with him 'cause he was too young to leave school!

"For a while we toured with Frankie Lymon and the Teenagers and some other black groups that did dance routines. And we were with Lavern Baker and Chuck Berry for a while. And Carl Perkins too, I think. We left the tour to make the movie *Rock, Rock, Rock* and joined them later. I think we finished the tour in Norfolk and for a finale we all did *Hound Dog* together and Gene and Johnny'd point at each other when they sang, 'You ain't nothin' but a Hound Dog!' But I never saw Gene after that, though I know he visited Johnny in L.A. in the early sixties."

By then, Johnny Burnette had abandoned rock'n'roll for pop music, but not before writing some songs for Gene, including *My Heart*. Burnette died in a boating accident in 1964, but at least one famous photograph survives of his historic tour with Gene in 1956. Gene had just bought a new '56 T-Bird and he, Johnny, Paul, and Johnny Black are leaning against it with their shirts off and they all look sickly pale. The interesting feature is that Gene is smirking and giving the finger to the cameraman. Paul Burlison explains: "That picture was taken in Reading, Pennsylvania. We'd played an open-air date at some race-track and were sort of sunbathing and hangin' around. I asked Tex Davis to snap a picture and he said something like, 'Well, let's see some muscles, Superman.' And that's when Gene gave him the finger. But I don't think he expected Tex to snap the picture just then." Johnny Black played bass for Burnette on this tour. "We did *many* shows with Vincent. And he was a good showman. Absolutely! He had a way with a crowd. They just loved him. The most impressive thing about Vincent was that he would play his heart out, fall on his knees, or whatever it took to get the crowd going. . . . We were the show-openers. Vincent was *always* the headliner. People might be out buying popcorn or soft drinks while we were playing. And we didn't have a big hit. We'd brush our tails trying to steal the show from Vincent, but it was mighty difficult.

"Gene always had a good crowd and they'd be just screamin'. He had crowd appeal. The kids would dance, scream, whatever they felt like doing. And Gene was mobbed after *every* show! He was a tremendous performer in his own right.

"Sure, the fame might have gone to his head a little bit. He'd just got out of the service and there's no way a man can have a huge hit like that and not be affected. But Gene wasn't any different than anybody else. He was a pretty cool boy. He knew what he wanted. He wanted to be a star. And he had everything it took.

"Unfortunately, music changed a lot in the late fifties. And some artists just couldn't make that change. Look at Carl Perkins. And he was a big star! But by 1958 or '59, they were getting away from the hardcore rockabilly. If music hadn't changed so rapidly, who knows how big Gene could have been? He had everything going for him, that voice, his act, looks, everything!"

Although most people still thought of Gene as a polite young man, he seemed to be developing a streak of devil-may-care-arrogance. Willie Williams tells a story about a drive back to Norfolk in Gene's new T-Bird. Williams had taken over the wheel when they were passed by a Buick Roadmaster with a bunch of black men in it. Gene immediately ordered Willie to catch up and pass it. He did. But the Buick gained speed and was about to pass them again. Gene yelled out, "Hit it! Let's go man! Let's blow 'em off the road!"

Willie got the T-Bird up to 120, but said to Gene, "Man, they're gonna drive *us* off the road!"

Gene answered, "Man, you worry too much. To hell with them!"

"Hell is where we're gunna be, all right!"

Gene's response was, "Don't worry. It's only a car. I'll buy another one."

Then Willie asked him, "But what about our bodies?"

Gene shrugged his shoulders nonchalantly. But Willie gave up and let the Buick by.

Ed Butler says that Gene's obsession with cars became stronger as he made more money: "That '56 T-Bird was too small and aggravated his leg, so he got a '56 Cadillac Coupe de Ville, lavender with a white top. Later he traded it for a black convertible Coupe de Ville."

By now, rock'n'roll was sweeping the United States and most other western countries. On July 7th, *Be-Bop-A-Lula* hit *Billboard's* number eleven position and the next week it entered the top ten at number seven. It stayed in the top ten for another eight weeks before dropping back to number eleven in mid-September. *Time* had already featured two articles on rock'n'roll: one in May, with a picture of Elvis Presley; and one in June with a picture of Bill Haley. In August, *Life* did a huge spread on rock'n'roll, mostly about Presley, but it also featured large pictures of Carl Perkins and Gene Vincent with this comment: 'the closest facsimile of Presley is shouter Gene Vincent who recorded the fast-selling single *Be-Bop-A-Lula.*' Gene and the Blue Caps were still on the road, and in Shamokin, Pennsylvania, Gene was mobbed when he went outside to sign some autographs after the first show. Teenage girls crowded around him, stealing his tie and tearing his clothes. Gene had to be rescued by the police and escorted back into the theater. The local paper published an article entitled "Local Teenagers Mob Rock'n' Roll Artist."

Bill Davis recalls a fair date in New York State where Gene shared the bill with Pat Boone. Boone was supposed to be the head-liner, but Davis tried to persuade him to go on first. Boone wouldn't agree and, as Davis says, "Nobody could follow Vincent in those days...nobody!" Gene went on and about 2,000 kids went wild and tried to swarm the stage. Policemen tried to hold them off, but some of the kids ran up and tried to grab pieces of clothing for souvenirs. When Gene finished his set all the kids left. Pat Boone sang

clockwise from top: Dickie, Paul, Jack, Gene, Russell
(courtesy of Capitol Records)

to an empty house.

All through August, Gene and the Caps toured the Northeast. *Be-Bop-A-Lula* was entrenched in both the pop and country top ten, and broke into the top twenty in England. Following RCA Victor's lead – RCA released Presley's *I Want You, I Need You, I Love You* while *Heartbreak Hotel* was still in the top ten – Capitol released a new single by Gene, *Race With the Devil* b/w *Gonna Back Up Baby,* easily as good as his first release. Capitol placed a full-page ad with a large picture of Gene in *Billboard,* but the record did poorly, and made only a brief appearance on the charts. Perhaps it was Gene's breathless sinister treatment of the almost indecipherable lyrics or its frantic beat and wild guitar that doomed this self-penned hot-rod song. Presley's first RCA releases, in contrast to his earlier Sun records, had moderate rhythms. Moreover, their lyrics were romantic, thus marketable. Instead of romantic mush like Elvis' *Love Me Tender,* Gene sang lines like:

> I was goin' pretty fast, looked behind.
> Here comes the Devil doin' 99...!
> Move fast, yeah, move, man!
> Let's drag again...!

In September, 1956, Capitol released his first album, *Blue Jean Bop,* plus a single featuring the title tune and *Who Slapped John.* Both were written by Gene and were breakneck-paced. *Who Slapped John* is a wild rockabilly number about a barroom brawl:

> The lights went off!
> Then went on!
> John got slapped
> Tryin' t' hold his own!
> Who? Who? Who slapped John?

The guitar solo is characteristically frantic and punctuated by screams from the Blue Caps, one of whom yells, "Go, cats! Go! All you cats, boot it!" This single also fared poorly in the United States, but it was a big hit in England. Luckily for Gene, the *Blue Jean Bop* album did better than the single, yet only six or seven of the songs could be properly classed as rockabilly or rock'n'roll, the rest being slow standards. Both *Blue Jean Bop* and *Who Slapped John* were superior to Presley's saccharine *I Want You, I Need You, I Love You,* which soon broke into the top ten. Presley intended from the beginning to become a pop singer, and his idol was Dean Martin. And although Presley had performed, and would perform, many rock'n'roll classics, he wasn't sufficiently dedicated. As early as the beginning of July, 1956, when Presley played on the Steve Allen Show wearing a tuxedo and appearing lamely bourgeois, teenagers had paraded in front of the TV station with protest signs saying 'We Want the Real Elvis.' This incident was written up in *Billboard* under the title 'You Can't Do That To Elvis': 'A painfully subdued Elvis... was presented on the Steve Allen Show.... He rolled not, nor did he rock.'

Vincent's image as a greasy punk, wearing a black shirt with up-turned collar, black pants, and dark grease-soaked curls falling over his pale forehead, was no match for Presley's startling pretty-boy looks that were causing girls all over the world to swoon with ecstasy.

Gene and the Caps continued to tour, but problems began to develop. Gene had apparently signed a contract with Lamear and Blumenthal of WCMS, then decided that Bill Davis should be his sole manager. While the group was in New York, a letter was sent to WCMS informing them of this new deal. Davis says that his arrangement with Gene was only verbal, sealed with just a hand-shake, but according to Kie and Louise Craddock, Gene signed con-tracts with both Davis and L&B Management. At any rate, Lamear and Blumenthal rushed up to New York and argued with Davis and Vincent. Litigation was initiated and Davis was fired by WCMS. He continued to manage Gene and the Caps, and they kept touring.

Joe Hoppell comments on this turn of events and Gene's character at the time: "He was a very shy guy and very bashful. That was his undoing, so much success so fast. It went to his head.... I'll never forget him standing in the station hallway with tears in his eyes thanking the WCMS staff for all they had done for him.... Then three weeks later he sued us!" Joe also comments, as does almost every person who ever knew Gene, that he "wasn't the easiest guy in the world to live with."

In the middle of this dispute, the Caps were about to go through some personnel changes. After a gig in Fredricksburg, Virginia, Willie Williams quit because, as he says, "I was looking at a picture of my wife in her bathing suit. And she's a fine looking woman. Then I looked around the room at all those hairy-legged guitar pickers and I said to myself, 'Man, I must be crazy!' Besides, I was close to Lamear, and my wife ran the staff band in my absence, and I knew I'd have a job there when I got back. I knew the Blue Caps were a 'foray' and that WCMS was a career."

Willie still has fond memories of his days with the Blue Caps: "Gene was very friendly. People were always looking for someone who'd act outrageous, but he didn't. He was just a good guy. On stage, Gene was a stylist and a communicator. And very exciting. Offstage, Gene would have a beer or two, but he was more interested in the ladies. Cliff was quiet, the kind of guy you wouldn't fool with. He was a no-nonsense person. But Dickie was my favourite. He was an innocent, a thoroughly fine young man, a good cat."

Cliff Gallup also gave notice; he'd stay for the next gig, then leave. He didn't like road work either and, like Williams, missed his wife: "I enjoyed playing the music, but I didn't like being away from home. I was sick of travelling. We stayed on the road all the time. . . . I got along fine with Gene. He was a good singer, and, just like all the rest of us, he was always beating on a guitar. Gene was a typical rock singer; he moved around a lot. He had a little problem with his leg, but I doubt people could notice it. He was a little stiff-legged, but he had a cast and a black sock, then he got that special shoe made for it. . . . We'd sit around the dressing room and sing and play; jam sessions, sometimes with Carl Perkins when we were part of a troupe together. We played a lot of fairs and the kids were always screaming. But Dickie was too damn loud! Rock drummers are always loud. Jack was a good bass man. Bill Davis was a jolly guy, a lot of fun. He had a good sense of humour. I just looked at him as one of the gang. Gene went along with whatever he said. . . . Ken Nelson was a mighty fine person. He probably impressed me more than anybody I ever met. No question about it, Ken Nelson helped. He told me how I ought to set my guitar. And I was satisfied with the sound. We cut some good stuff and I always looked forward to going into the studio. After I quit Gene, Nelson offered me a mighty fine contract, but I turned it down. I was tired of travelling."

When Willie Williams quit, it didn't much matter and a guitarist named Teddy Crutchfield came up from Norfolk to replace him. But it was going to be difficult to find a lead player anything like

Cliff Gallup. Red Gwynn, who quit as chauffeur about the same time, says, "Gene knew damn well that if he lost Cliff, then he'd had it."

Their next gig was at a swank supper club in Washington, D.C., the Casino Royale. The Craddocks were there and Louise was especially impressed. "If you've ever seen Dickie Harrell play drums, then you've really seen something. People were sitting at long tables and clapping their hands. Then Dickie held his snare drum in his hand, beat on it, then jumped up and walked along the table, still playing! People were grabbing their plates out of the way and Dickie never missed a beat! Dickie was a show all by his self! A real clown!" This was supposed to be Cliff's last gig and as soon as it was over the Caps were to appear in the film *The Girl Can't Help It*. So another call was made to Norfolk and a young player named Russell Willaford agreed to go with them to Los Angeles for the film.

During their stay at the Casino Royale, Bill 'Sheriff Tex' Davis happened to meet Paul Peek in the street outside their hotel. Peek was playing steel guitar for a country singer named Red Redding in a bar called the Metropole across the street, and he invited Davis and one of the Caps to come in. They mentioned that they were looking for a rhythm guitarist and Paul said, "I can play some rhythm." Years later he admitted, "I kind of took a chance on that, 'cause I was really a steel player. But they invited me to audition so I went over to the Casino Royale and ran through some songs for them. I remember Cliff showing me the chords to *Jezebel*. I had a little trouble with that one. Afterwards they all went into the back and had a little meeting, then they came back and handed me a cap and said, 'You're a Blue Cap now, man.' So I just lucked out, that's all. And within a couple of days of my joining we all flew out to LA and did the filming for the movie. I just happened to be in the right place at the right time."

The Girl Can't Help It starred Jayne Mansfield, Eddie Cochran and Little Richard. For their spot, the Blue Caps did *Be-Bop-A-Lula*. Gene gave a great performance, looking skinny, gaunt-cheeked, pale and almost tortured. When he reached the second chorus, with Dickie screaming behind him, Gene threw his head back and his blue cap fell off. He let go of his guitar and clenched his fists as

51

he hit the famous line, "She's the woman who *loves* me so!" (Apparently, some of the best footage remained on the cutting room floor. According to Bill Davis, as the Caps all screamed at the end of the song, the framed portraits of Beethoven and Rachmaninoff, hung on the wall behind them, suddenly fell to the floor with a BOOM!)

TOM EWELL · JAYNE MANSFIELD · EDMOND O'BRIEN in THE GIRL CAN'T HELP IT with Guest stars JULIE LONDON · RAY ANTHONY · BARRY GORDON and featuring HENRY JONES

left to right: Russell, Dickie, Gene, Jack, Paul

In Los Angeles, the Caps played at the Palladium with the Coasters and the Diamonds. Jack Neal recalls the next show, in San Diego: "Vincent and Bill Davis wanted me to get real wild. So I did.... At the end I was twirling my bass around, then I picked it up and slammed it down. But it broke the peg and then the bridge fell off.... So that was the end of that gig!" Paul Peek remembers the San Diego gig, mostly because he and some of the other Caps spent a day in Tijuana: "We went over to some of the 'houses' and had a good time."

On October 15th, Gene and the Blue Caps went back to Nashville for more sessions. Cliff Gallup was working at his previous job as a plumber, but agreed to play lead. Paul Peek played rhythm. They did two of Gene's songs, *Teenage Partner*, a dynamic rocker (unfortunately never released in Gene's lifetime) and *Cat Man*, a *pièce de résistance* of frantic rockabilly:

> Catman's a-comin', you better look out!...
> Better hide your sister, man!
> C is for the crazy hair-do that he wears around.
> A is for the arms that he'll sneak around your waist!
> T is for the taste of the lips belong to you!...
> M is for the mean things that this mean man does!
> A is for all the hearts that he has ever broke!
> N is for the names of the list you may be on!
> Catman...!

Dickie thrashes violently on the snare drum while Gene wails in high, tense roars of sensuality, ending with, "Better watch out 'cause *I'm* the Catman!" The strong sensuality of Gene's music aroused the ire of a good many parents, politicians and clergymen who thought that rock'n'roll was eroding the moral fibre of America's youth, and this eventually had a negative effect on Gene's career.

At the same session they did *Blues Stay Away From Me*, an old Delmore Brothers country standard, and a Mel Tillis song, *Five Feet of Lovin'* (another hot rocker that wasn't released until after Gene's death). The Catman session was definitely the best work they'd done since the initial recording of *'Lula* and *Race with the Devil*. "It was quite a riot. Gene kept going off mike in his excitement and I had to keep telling him to stay still because he'd start shouting and moving about. He'd changed quite a lot since the first session when he sang very quietly."[6]

The following day they returned to Bradley's studio and did three more songs: two rockabilly classics, Gene's *Hold Me, Hug Me, Rock Me* and *Double Talkin' Baby*; and the slow standard, *Unchained Melody*. The third day they started with a song that Nelson sug-

---

6. Ken Nelson, quoted in Finnis and Dunham.

gested, *B-I Bickey Bi, Bo Bo Go*, a rocker with lyrics that range from the nonsense of the title to verses typical of Vincent's rockabilly numbers:

> I grabbed a chick an' hit the floor
> The roof was shakin', so was the door!
> We danced down the aisle, just a ziggin' an' a zaggin'
> She's a real cool doll an' I'm not braggin'!

In *Pink Thunderbird*, written by Paul Peek, Gene brags in his high boyish voice:

> I got a pink Thunderbird with a red plush seat.
> Well, baby... it's mine.
> I got a new brick house with a two carport.
> Well, baby... that's mine too.
>
> I got a bank account, baby, filled with green
> Well, baby, it's all mine.
> Anything I got, babe, you can have,
> If you only say 'I do. I do... I do! I do!'[7]

On their fourth session they started with a slow song by Gene, *Important Words*, and continued with *You Better Believe* by Cliff Gallup, who'd written it in his hotel room the night before. *Red Blue Jeans and a Pony Tail* and the bluesy semi-ballad *Five Days, Five Days* followed. The Jordanaires added background vocals to this and two other songs. Ken Nelson was probably trying to emulate Presley here, but the Jordanaires weren't very well- suited to Gene's style. Dickie Harrell remembers being introduced to the Jordanaires and hearing them ask Gene what he wanted them to do. Gene replied, "Put on whatever you think fits in there. Just whatever you feel like."

---

7. *Pink Thunderbird* reflects a strategy of economic manipulation in which wealth and possessions are equated with sexual virility. The image of a 'Pink Thunderbird' is a vivid phallic symbol. This strategy is pervasive today, though in a more subtle form.

Gene and Paul

After recording fifteen songs in four days, Nelson must have known he had enough material for another LP and several singles. As it was, Gene needed another hit to sustain the excitement of his first big smash. His second and third singles had fared poorly, and in the last week of November, 'Lula finally fell off the Billboard Top 100 after being there for twenty weeks.

Gene's name was still well enough known to bring him work and Bill Davis got him a week-long gig at the Criterion Theater in Toronto, the first time that Gene had been booked outside the U.S. According to Bill Davis, "Gene owned Canada when *Be-Bop-A-Lula* was at its height. They had a parade one Saturday for him. They had a big thirteen-storey building and on the tenth floor they had a big banner saying 'Gene Vincent Day'."

Paul Peek says, "The Criterion was just a big ol' theater and we played a week's stand there with the Flamingos. We were billed at the top, but the Flamingos had a pretty big hit right then. We had picked up a guitar player in Boston. He was a real nut and did this act where he played the guitar behind his head and stuff. Gene met a girl named Monique up there. She was a singer on the show and they spent a lot of time together. Gene would go up to her dressing room to rest or get away from the band. Later on, he phoned her just about every day. I was usually the one to room with Gene, and one time he woke me up about three in the morning. He was troubled a lot. And this time he wanted to go see Monique way up in Canada. So he talked me into coming with him and we went outside and got into the Caddy and headed up to Canada. Gene wasn't drinking. He was just troubled and wanted to see Monique. But we only got as far as Pennsylvania and we hit a snowstorm. I was sleepin' in the back and all of a sudden the car started skiddin' around. Gene wanted to keep goin', but I finally talked him out of it. We were just skiddin' around and couldn't git no further. But that Gene, he'd do *anything!*"

The next gig was several weeks at the Sands Hotel in Las Vegas, but Gene didn't like it. He was billed with the Mary Kaye Trio and the Four Lads and they each played only twenty-minute sets, starting around midnight. They were playing in a gambling lounge with almost no teenagers in the audience. Gene told Davis, "This ain't my bag, man!"[8] Dickie Harrell: "We were the first rockabilly band to play there and this was all very new to them. The people in Las Vegas weren't like the kids. They didn't go crazy or anything. It was more of a settled crowd. And Gene wanted to play for the kids.

---

8. Finnis and Dunham.

I did too. We could put more out then, and it was more exciting."
Bill Davis remembers it much differently, and claims that Gene
was so good that people stopped gambling and the promoter
became angry; he was losing money because everybody was listening to Gene. Davis also maintains that Lena Horne and Liberace
came to hear Gene and were much impressed, and that Gene
Krupa was wild about Dickie's drumming and sat in with him for a
twenty-minute duet.

The first time Paul Peek noticed Gene seriously drinking was at
the Sands, and this gig was the end of the original Blue Caps. Dickie
Harrell and Jack Neal were the only originals left, and Jack decided
to quit. His wife and kids were back in Norfolk and the road work
had worn him down. He also thinks the band was being mis-
handled: "Bill Davis was horse-crazy. If you wanted him and he
wasn't around, you'd just have to go to the race-track to find him.
And who takes care of the money? Davis does!"

According to Paul Peek, the Sands gig was eventually cancelled
because Gene had re-broken his leg: "We were supposed to be there
for three or four weeks, but Gene slipped on the spotlights and hurt
his bad leg. He used to get down with one leg held out stiff behind
him and slide the other back, do a kind of dip with one leg bent. But
he slipped on the spotlights. Nobody in the audience noticed it, but
he hurt his leg and afterwards blood started seeping out of the cast,
so we cancelled the rest of the show."

After the Sands, Gene and Bill Davis decided to part company.
Dickie says, "I don't think Davis got fired or anything. But Gene
never talked about it. He never discussed business. I think Davis
just wanted to go home to his family. It gets tiresome on the road
after a while. Him and Gene didn't always get along, but they got
along pretty good." Paul Peek tends to disagree: "As I recall, it
wasn't too friendly." And Davis has this comment: "Let's just say
that we agreed to disagree. . . . That boy was always in pain. It seemed that he had to see a doctor in every town. But all he ever cared
about was music. He worked hard on stage, harder than anybody
I've ever seen. He was a good ol' boy."

left to right: Bobby, Dickie, Bubba, Gene, Paul, Johnny, Hollywood, 1957
(courtesy of Capitol Records)

4

The New Blue Caps

Playing with Gene was probably the most versatile experience you could have because he went either way. One week we might be playing the Ozark Jubilee in Springfield, Missouri, or the Louisiana Hayride with all the C&W artists. The next week we might be playing nightclubs. Then we might be playing rock'n'roll or R&B shows. Every week it was something new.

— Bubba Facenda

Gene went back to Norfolk and stayed with his parents for Christmas. In January, 1957, he went to the naval hospital in Portsmouth to have his leg treated and his cast replaced. Paul Peek visited Gene and saw some of the X-rays of Gene's leg. "There were three or four metal screws in it. The doctors had grafted on a piece of sheep bone, but Gene had broken it or cracked it at the Sands Hotel." When he got out, Gene rented his family a two-storey colonial-style house on the corner of Leckie and Peninsula, only a few blocks away from the hospital.

On January 7th, Capitol released *Crazy Legs* b/w *Important Words*. The single got very little airplay and did poorly, possibly because Capitol didn't indulge in payola. Play-for-pay dated at least as far back as the vaudeville era and was an established way of doing business by the fifties. However, it was generally practised only by the small independent companies. Though it hadn't really surfaced yet, payola would become one of the major factors in the decline of rock'n'roll. Just as mainstream culture assimilated various facets of the hippie movement in the sixties and early seventies, as early as 1956 rock'n'roll was starting to go soft. Producers began promoting 'rock'n'roll-like' music, a homogenized travesty of rock'n'roll deemed palatable for the masses.

If the struggle between real rock'n'roll and 'pop' music can be represented by the careers of Vincent and Presley, then, in a like way, in the all-important world of radio and television this struggle can be personified by two important characters, Alan Freed and Dick Clark. Alan Freed had started his deejay career in the early fifties at WJW in Cleveland, where he had a rhythm'n'blues spot called the Moondog Show. In the spring of '52 he sponsored a Moondog Ball that drew 25,000 racially-mixed teenagers. Freed began calling his rhythm'n'blues records by a new term to avoid the racial stigma attached to black music; he called it rock'n'roll. Freed claimed that he coined the expression, but it was a common phrase in R&B songs as far back as the late forties. In 1954, Freed moved to New York and worked for WINS. During his radio show, Freed drank whiskey from a bottle in his hip pocket and pounded out the beat on a telephone book. He held live rock'n'roll shows at the Brooklyn Paramount and would dance on stage in a plaid sports coat and blow kisses to the audience. Freed's response to his critics was, "Anyone who says rock'n'roll is a passing fad or a flash-in-the pan trend along the music road has rocks in his head, dad!"

In stark contrast to Alan Freed was Dick Clark, who hosted a local television show in Philadelphia called American Bandstand. It didn't become a network show until the summer of 1957, but was certainly a portent of what was to come. Dick Clark dressed like a teacher – white shirt, sports jacket and tie – and the kids on American Bandstand had to follow strict fashion rules: jackets for the boys and skirts for the girls; no jeans, t-shirts or tight sweaters. Singers who appeared on his show were not allowed to play their music live, but had to mime to their records, a process which destroyed the essence of rock'n'roll: the excitement of live performance.

Unlike Freed, who identified with his audience and behaved like one of them, Clark acted like a wooden puppet; a school-teacher looking after a class of obsequious suckholes. Both Dick Clark, and the payola scandal – they emerged contemporaneously – were to be jointly responsible for the annihilation of rock'n'roll's early flowering.

Gene Vincent knew none of this. He only knew that he loved

60

singing and wanted to keep performing. However, in January of 1957, Gene not only didn't have a band, but performances were forbidden by the courts until his contractual dispute with Lamear and Blumenthal was settled. Gene didn't need to play any gigs for financial reasons. Ed Butler saw his tax return for 1956 and says that he grossed $330,000. Not bad for a busted-up sailor who previously earned only $136 a month in sick pay.

Soon after he left the hospital, Gene got together with Dickie and looked around for suitable musicians to form a brand new set of Blue Caps. Influenced by many of the R&B singing groups that he'd toured with, Gene decided to include background singers (later called the Clapper Boys), and Paul Peek was switched from rhythm guitar to vocals. Paul sang the high parts and the other singer was Tommy 'Bubba' Facenda, a seventeen-year-old friend and neighbour of Dickie's who quit school to join the Caps. Bubba was flattered to be chosen by the band: "Gene had a voice like a bell and he could sing in a room and sound just like his records. He didn't need any echo or special effects." They needed a lead guitarist and a bass player, so Paul Peek suggested they go to his home town of Greenville, South Carolina, where he'd played with Country Earl and the Circle E Ranch Boys. Country Earl was a local deejay and a popular singer around Greenville, and he had a guitarist named Johnny Meeks. Gene and Paul drove down to one of Earl's gigs and auditioned Meeks, who at that time was a country musician, though he liked rock'n'roll: "Yeah, I liked rock. I'd heard Elvis' Sun records and I'd seen him in Spartanburg. At the time I'd thought, "My God, that son-of-a-bitch gets into it! He ain't country! What's he doin' up there!' I didn't know what to think." Johnny quit the Circle E Ranch Boys and joined the Blue Caps right away, though the Caps weren't yet working. Country Earl, oddly enough, wasn't upset at losing such a fine guitarist: "I wasn't sore at all. In fact, I was a bit flattered that a big star like Gene wanted one of my boys. I thought it was a real big break for Johnny." Gene and Paul recruited another young man from Greenville, Bill Mack, who played electric bass rather than acoustic. Johnny Meeks comments, "Gene liked it better than the ol' doghouse bass, probably 'cause of the volume, and also 'cause of the space."

Dickie and Bubba each stayed with their parents in Portsmouth, and Johnny Meeks, Paul Peek and Bill Mack moved into the house on Leckie Street with Gene, his parents and his three sisters. Evelyn was there because her husband, Ed Butler, was away at sea. The new Blue Caps spent all day rehearsing in the parlour and Evelyn remembers it well: "They practised a lot, and very loud. But we had a corner house and the neighbours never complained. Gene had a real keen ear and could hear if one teeny thing was wrong. They also did a lot of horsing around and wrestling. Sometimes they'd just sit around and listen to rock'n'roll records. I thought they were great. They all had a lot of personality. And talent to go with it. Bubba was always combing his hair. And Paul had such a Southern drawl. It took forever for him to get a story out. He was a real joker, a prankster. Dickie would twirl his sticks around, then throw them up and catch them."

Kie Craddock also has a vivid recollection of the practices at Leckie Street: "The music was always poundin' in your head, some-times as you were having breakfast, sometimes the last thing at night. Gene was hard on them boys. If one of them was a little bit off, he'd stop and make them git it right. He'd make 'em do the whole thing over. It's something I wouldn't want to do again, but I'm glad I never missed it."

On March 4th, 1957, Gene's second album, *Gene Vincent and the Blue Caps*, was released. This album was far superior to the *Blue Jean Bop* LP and featured some of Gene's finest rockabilly per-formances: *Cat Man, Red Blue Jeans and a Pony Tail, Hold Me, Hug Me, Rock Me, Cruisin', Double Talkin' Baby, You Told a Fib* and *Pink Thunderbird.* The only standards were *Unchained Melody* and *Blues Stay Away From Me.*

On the 25th of March, Capitol released another single, *Five Days, Five Days* b/w *B-I Bickey Bi, Bo Bo Go,* but it never even made the charts. By now the contractual dispute with Lamear and Blumen-thal had been settled out of court — Ed Butler says Gene had to pay over $20,000 to get out of his contract. Gene was anxious to try out his new band and re-create his earlier success. The Clapper Boys had mastered their harmonies, as well as some dance step routines, and Johnny Meeks had changed from a country picker to a rocker, but a much different one than Cliff Gallup. When Johnny first joined the Caps, Gene played his records for him, and Johnny said,

"I don't know if I can play that way." Gene replied, "I don't want you to." So Johnny was given a free hand to develop his own style.

left to right: Bubba, Johnny, Gene, Dickie, Paul, Bobby, the Midwest, 1957

The new Blue Caps' first gig was a ten-day tour of Ohio with Roy Orbison, Carl Perkins and Sanford Clark, and it was billed as a Rockabilly Spectacular. Their repertoire in early '57 included *Be-Bop-A-Lula*, *Blue Jean Bop*, *Woman Love*, *Crazy Legs*, *Jumps*, *Giggles and Shouts* and *Gonna Back Up Baby*, as well as some Little Richard songs, *Long Tall Sally*, *Tutti Frutti* and *Rip It Up*, plus some Bo Diddley numbers. Paul Peek remembers that the three singers usually shared a microphone: "We'd sing together into one mike and we had our little routines and did our little dips down to the floor and sometimes Gene would dip down with us. There was one thing where Gene would actually get down and sit on my leg and Bubba would be on the other side leaning back at the same angle and singing into the mike. And sometimes Gene would actually fall on the floor and sing lying down, a real soul thing." Sanford Clark, who had a big hit at the time with *The Fool*, remembers: "Gene was crippled, you know, but he'd get down on the floor with his leg out straight and the kids loved him. Afterwards we'd have a few drinks in the hotel room. Yeah, we tipped a few. Gene drank pretty good, and we were pretty wild. We popped a lot of pills in those days, dexadrine and dexamils. We were travelling a long ways to each show, and sometimes we'd go on stage straight from the car. It was a terrible strain."

The tour was a success, and Gene was happy with his new band, but there had been personal differences with Bill Mack and he was replaced by Bobby Lee Jones, another one of 'the Greenville Boys.' About this time, Gene went back into the hospital, had his cast removed, and his leg was fitted with a metal brace. Bubba comments: "Gene had skin grafts and everything. But that leg was terrible. It was *never* gunna be right. Seems like it was dead to me." One time one of the Caps bought some expensive shoes but left one behind in a motel room, so someone cracked, "Well, maybe you can sell it to Gene. He ain't got but one good foot anyways!" Johnny Meeks says that Gene's injury never got in the way of his stage show: "Gene'd just work around his leg. He learned to manipulate it and do all those crazy antics. He hobbled a bit, but he put on such a great show that you never noticed. He hollered and sweated and the crowd roared like crazy."

One of their first gigs after the Ohio tour was the week-long Rock'n'Roll Jubilee of Stars at the Mastbaum Theater in Philadelphia. It featured a cast of fifty people and Gene topped the bill along with Al Hibbler, an R&B singer, and Eddie Cochran, who'd just had a hit with *Sittin' in the Balcony.* Cochran had been in the film *The Girl Can't Help It* and may have met Gene then, but it was probably this week-long gig in Philadelphia that cemented their friendship. Dickie Harrell: "Eddie was just down-to-earth and really good people. He really was. He and Gene had a lot in common. They were a little bit like each other and seemed to understand each other. So they started to pal around together." As it turned out, in the history of rock'n'roll the names Gene Vincent and Eddie Cochran are forever connected.

At the end of April, Gene and the Caps went up to Chicago and played on the Howard Miller Show before an audience of around 30,000 teenagers. According to Bubba, "That was the wildest show we ever did. The kids just went crazy!" Dickie Harrell confirms this. "They had a real riot and everybody was screamin' for their life. I know it scared me. The police were holding back the crowd, arm to arm, but they broke through, about 5,000 of them.

Bubba was jumping from car to car, tryin' to get away, but they got him and pulled him down and ripped his clothes off. They knocked down Gene and tore his clothes off too. They trampled him and he lost his car keys. Mister Nelson was there presenting Gene with his gold record for *Be-Bop-A-Lula* and *he* got mobbed too. It was a mess!" For bass player Bobby Jones, the newest member of the Caps, this was his first rock'n'roll riot: "They were pullin' out Bubba's hair and tryin' to rip off his clothes. They sneaked Gene out in a cab later and he had to hide by crouchin' down on the floorboards. Two policemen came and took me down to the basement. That's how I got away."

Since Gene was without a manager, Ken Nelson set him up with Ed McLemore's 'Artist Service Bureau' in Dallas, Texas. McLemore managed several big stars, including Sonny James and Buddy Knox, and he also ran the Big D Jamboree, which was broadcast from a local hall, the Sportatorium, over Dallas station KRLD every Saturday night. Except that it featured both rock'n'roll and country acts, it was similar to both the Louisiana Hayride and the Grand Ole Opry. McLemore's Artist Service Bureau provided Gene with a road manager, Larry Thacker, a bald middle-aged fellow, and bought the Caps new uniforms: red jackets and black pants for the musicians; green jackets and black pants for the Clapper Boys. They still wore blue caps and Gene just dressed as he pleased (usually, black shirts and white pants, or colourful satin shirts and black pants). McLemore also supplied them with a Chrysler Windsor nine-passenger sedan and a half-ton equipment trailer. To be close to his booking agency, Gene bought a big modern house on Dykes Way, in the suburbs of Dallas, and moved his whole family in with him.

Gene and the Caps played a few gigs around Texas, including one in Beaumont billed as the Top Record Stars of 1957, which featured Sonny James, Johnny Cash, Jerry Lee Lewis and Wanda Jackson. Then they drove out to Hollywood for their first session at the Capitol Tower. On June 19th they recorded four songs: *I Got It*, a hard rocker; *Wear My Ring*, a rather saccharine ballad; and *Lotta Lovin'*, another tough rocker. *Lotta Lovin'* is a two-minute, seven-second classic, a raunchy synthesis of voices, instruments and percussion.

The fourth song was *Rollin' Danny*, a takeoff/variation on various R&B hits of the past few years, such as *Work With Me Annie* and *Annie Had a Baby* by Hank Ballard and the Midnighters and *Annie Met Henry* by the Cadets:

> Everybody's talkin' 'bout Workin' Annie,
> But nobody's talkin' 'bout Rollin' Danny.
> Rollin' Danny, he's a rollin' man, uh man, uh man...!
> Dan walked into the ol' dance hall,
> Told the women that he loved 'em all.
> He lined six women up against the wall,
> Well, I'm tellin' you, man, he f-fooled 'em all!
> Rollin' Danny, he's a rollin' man... Rock!

The image of Gene as a child in his sailor suit on stage with six little girls dressed as paper dolls, and all that this implies, recurs in a more obvious form in the lyrics of this song. *Rollin' Danny* may seem sexist today, but in the late fifties it was lewd, rebellious and sinister.

The next day they recorded four more songs. The first three were ballads, *Time Will Bring You Everything* and *True To You*, both by Gene, and *In My Dreams* by Bernice Bedwell (who also wrote *Lotta Lovin'*). The last song was a rocker, *Dance to the Bop*, and the lyrics are typical of Gene's dance songs:

> Well, there's a little juke joint
> On the outskirts of town
> Where the cats pick 'em up
> And they lay 'em down.
> Now you get your gal
> And I'll get mine,
> And we'll get together
> And have a good time!
> And we'll dance a little bit to the bop!
> Do the bop!

The vocal counterpoint in this number, between Gene and the Clapper Boys, was now one of the main ingredients of the Blue Cap sound.

Ken Nelson decided that Gene's next single should be *Lotta Lovin'* b/w *Wear My Ring*, probably hoping that if the deejays didn't like the raunchy rocker, they might go for the ballad. *Lotta Lovin'*, Gene's first record with his new band, was released on July 22nd and in the meantime, Gene and the Caps toured through the Midwest and the Northwest mostly on the strength of *Be-Bop-A-Lula*, which was still fresh in most teenagers' memories. But they were also doing their new material, *Lotta Lovin'*, *Wear My Ring*, *Rollin' Danny* and *Dance to the Bop*, as well as some of the old rockabilly songs. They not only played rock'n'roll concerts and teenage dances, but country shows as well. Bubba Facenda comments: "Playing with Gene was probably the most versatile experience you could have because he went either way. One week we might be playing the Ozark Jubilee in Springfield, Missouri, or the Louisiana Hayride with all the C&W artists. The next week we might be playing nightclubs. Then we might be playing rock'n'roll or R&B shows. Every week it was something new. . . . We used to work on routines where we really had a lot of good precision work down. Gene would keep telling us that we had to outdo this or that act. The wilder we were, the better he liked it."

Bobby Jones remembers that when they played dances, the Blue Caps would do a set of their own, mostly instrumentals like *Raunchy* and *Honky Tonk*, and Johnny Meeks would sing a few songs like *Johnny B. Goode* and *Sweet Little Sixteen*: "Gene wouldn't let Paul and Bubba on stage until he went on because it made a bigger impression when they came out together. The kids would scream and go crazy and we'd turn everything wide open. But sometimes you still couldn't hear the music that good if the crowd was really with us."

Johnny Meeks: "We'd be on the road for two or three months, then back for a week. Sometimes there'd be thousands of screaming kids. And Gene liked it that way. The guitar was very much a part of Gene's sound. He was a pretty easy-going guy. Nothin' really bothered him. He wasn't that hard of a boss. He might have appeared to be screwy, but he was all right. Nobody was a real business head, a Colonel Tom Parker or anything. Thacker took care of business. He was there to oversee Gene, to

Gene, St. Paul, 1957 (courtesy of DiAnne Kaslow)

keep him on his allowance. We just wanted to rock'n'roll. They'd give us the bookings and we'd do 'em. I don't know what ever happened to all the money. I don't think Gene ever saw much of it. I must have bought him a million cheeseburgers. We'd go to get something to eat and he'd say, 'Shit! I got no money! Hey, Thacker, give me some money!' And Thacker'd say, 'You've already had it this week!' Money just had a way of disappearing around Gene!" Bubba says that Gene was overly generous and would leave waitresses twenty dollar tips at truck stops and restaurants, "Then, as soon as Gene got up to leave, me or Dickie would grab the twenty and leave a one instead!" Johnny Meeks adds, "Gene was a very generous person. He'd give you anything he had. He'd give you the shirt right off his back." According to Paul Peek, this was literally true: "Gene had a shirt fetish. He had a whole closet of them. He'd buy two or three a day, flashy shirts. Some of them he wouldn't wear but once. On the road, rather than do laundry, he'd just go shopping. There was no way he could have worn all those shirts!"

After touring together for so long, the Caps became good friends. "We were just like brothers. Paul was just a down home guy. Johnny Meeks was a wild guy, a fun guy. He only had two interests, guitars and women. All the Blue Caps were lucky with women. Though Bobby didn't fool around much. He was married and sometimes he'd bring his wife along. I remember one time in California when Paul got a Dear John from his girl back home. So he got drunk and he wanted to cut cards for money. Then I cleaned him out and he was even more depressed. He asked me, 'What else could go wrong?' So he finished off the whiskey and threw the bottle over his shoulder... and right through the television screen!... But I can't think of one argument we ever had. We'd argue with Gene. He must have fired us a hundred times. He'd throw our money on the floor and we'd take it 'cause we knew he'd hire us back in the morning. Gene wanted to fit in with us, but he was always Gene Vincent, *the star,* the boss. And sometimes he'd get moody. Gene was a poor kid who'd never had nothin'. And here he was a star overnight. It was probably hard for him."[1]

Bobby Jones comments: "Gene was a nice guy, but he was a bit on Cloud Nine because of his big success. Yet he wasn't any more swell-headed than anyone else would be who was in his position. He was a fun-loving person and he liked to kid around and be one of the guys. Like all of us, he drank a little too much. When you're on the road you have to find some way to spend the time."

Bubba remembers that at first Gene didn't drink excessively, but indulged more as the grind of constant touring got to him: "And his leg bothered him. He'd drink and take aspirins. And prescriptions too."

Throughout the summer of 1957, Gene and the Blue Caps toured almost every state in the union, sometimes by themselves and

---

1. Bubba Facenda.

Gene and Eddie Cochran (courtesy of Steve Aynsley)

sometimes in package tours with the likes of Jerry Lee Lewis, Wanda Jackson and Eddie Cochran. They also toured Canada. "All the Canadian gigs were good. I can't really remember any bad ones. . . . One time we went way up there and it wasn't nothin' but Indians. I couldn't believe it. It was called Moose Cow or something."[2] The Canadian police arrested both Bubba and Paul Peek for suspicion of statutory rape, after an underage girl had accompanied them to a few gigs. The talked their way out of it somehow, but Gene was still furious and said, "I knew this would happen! I knew it!" He threatened to fire them, but soon forgot about it.

On August 19th, *Lotta Lovin'* entered the *Billboard* Top 100. Number one was Presley's *Teddy Bear*, 17 was Jerry Lee's *Whole Lotta Shakin' Goin' On*, 18 was Little Richard's *Jenny, Jenny,* and Buddy Holly's Crickets were at 38 with *That'll Be the Day*. There was a lot of competition in the rock'n'roll field, but *Lotta Lovin'* did well, climbing to 8 by the middle of September. *Wear My Ring* was also getting airplay and broke into the Top 100. By the end of the month *Lotta Lovin'* was thirteenth in sales and in the top ten in Florida and Ohio. The gigs started picking up and the Caps were getting more money. Bubba says, "It was Gene's second biggest hit. It was really a shot in the arm." That same month, September, 1957, probably unknown to Gene, a similar artist, though in another field, published a book that would have as great an effect on youth as rock'n'roll: Viking Press brought out *On the Road* by Jack Kerouac, an individual whose sudden popularity, personal excesses and tragic fate would run strangely parallel to Gene's. Both *Lotta Lovin'* and *On the Road* hit the number 11 position on their respective best-seller lists, and both men drank excessively. Vincent and Kerouac were both initiators of mass movements, the Beat Generation and rock'n'roll, which would, in a few years, amalgamate and become the 'counter-culture'.

At the end of September, Gene and the Caps flew to Australia with Little Richard and Eddie Cochran. It was one of their most successful tours and they played to some of their biggest crowds yet. In Brisbane they played two shows; 5800 attended the first one and 5400 were at the second. In Sidney they played two shows

2. Bubba Facenda.

Australia, 1957

before a total of 22,000 rock'n'roll fans. A newspaper clipping says that 'pandemonium broke loose.'

"It was just great. The fans tried to grab Gene and drag him off-stage. Several times they almost got me. The audience was really wild. They were more exuberant than the audiences in the States. It was more like America had been a year or so earlier. Rock'n'roll was just something new to them and they were really appreciative."[3]

It was during this tour that Little Richard decided to give up rock'n'roll. The whole troupe travelled from town to town on a chartered plane and Paul Peek remembers Little Richard's religious fervour: "This was right after the Sputnik had gone up and we could see it in the sky over Australia. And somebody had reported seeing a fireball in the sky and Little Richard took that as a religious sign. And one time in the plane, as we were preparing to take off, Little Richard got down on his knees and started praying. The stewardess asked him to get back in his seat, but he just kept praying. He was always expounding about religion and carrying a Bible around. This was supposed to be his last tour anyway. But one time we were on a school-type bus on a ferry and Little Richard got in a little argument with his half-brother who played sax in his band and his brother said, 'If you really had religion you wouldn't wear those flashy rings and clothes and be showin' off.' And Richard said, 'Well, I'll show you.' And he rolled the window down and threw the rings into the water. Then we all stood up and said we were gunna dive in the water and get them. They were probably worth about four or five thousand each. And that's when Richard gave everybody on the tour a little something. He gave Gene some of his flashy suits. And he gave me some really expensive shoes, purple ones with glitter on them. They were worth about $40, and that was a lot of money then."

When Gene and the Caps got back to the States, *Lotta Lovin'* was still thirteenth in sales and number 8 in the R&B charts (and in the top ten in New York, Detroit, Philadelphia, Chicago and Ohio). Gene Vincent and the Blue Caps were on top again. At this point, Dickie Harrell quit to go back to Norfolk and see Bubba's sister, whom he'd been dating, and he was replaced by Dude Kahn, a young Texan who'd played with Sonny James. Gene also hired a seventeen-year-old Dallas musician named Max Lipscomb: "I was gonna be a background singer, but that didn't work out, so they switched me to rhythm guitar... then I ended up on piano."[4]

---

3. Paul Peek.
4. Finnis and Dunham

Johnny Meeks comments: "Max wasn't that great a musician. Gene was doing him a favour by hiring him. Really, Max should have paid Gene!" Max agrees: "By the time Gene knew I wasn't any good he liked me so well he kept me around anyway."[5]

Gene and the Caps went out west and toured north through California and into Oregon. The gigs were booked by McLemore's agency and Pat Mason, a promoter in Seaside, Oregon, who later became Gene's personal manager.

Ever since Gene had broken up with Ruth Ann, he'd had only two relationships that were at all serious. The first was with the French-Canadian singer Monique whom he'd met in Toronto, but this hadn't lasted long. According to Paul Peek, "Monique just sort of faded into the background." Gene had also had a relationship with a girl from New York named Jacqueline, and this was more serious. Gene's family thought quite highly of her, and his sister Evelyn thinks Gene should have married her. Mrs. Craddock comments, "She was a really nice girl. . . . But she was a little too smart for Gene! . . . Gene would go so far as to even buy them engagement rings. I don't know whether he meant to hurt them or not, but he'd do it."

At a gig in Klamath Falls, Oregon, Pat Mason brought along a young attractive divorcee to work as a ticket-taker at the auditorium. Darlene Hicks was from Vancouver, Washington, and had a young daughter. Darlene remembers the show vividly: "A local band played first, then Gene came out. It was wild. The girls were all screaming and hollering and all that, flipping out. It was crazy!" Darlene admits that she'd actually had her eye on Johnny Meeks, who she thought was "pretty slick," but it was Gene who paid the most attention to her, and as Pat Mason remarked, "Darlene had a figure that just wouldn't quit!"

The following night, the Caps played in Eugene, and Darlene was again the ticket-taker. Gene came over and asked her to stand at the front of the stage, and when she did he dedicated *Wear My Ring* to her, then in the middle of the song he leaned over and held her hand. "I was so embarrassed, just mortifed."

This tour lasted about two weeks and the Caps played at the

---

5. Finnis & Dunham.

Gene and Darlene (courtesy of Darlene Norton)

Gene, Debbie and Darlene (courtesy of Darlene Norton)

Division Street Corral in Portland, the Wagon Wheel in Camus, and in Longview, Tacoma, Bremerton and other towns. Darlene was there for most of the shows. Bonnie Lund, who was like a mother to Darlene and, later, to Gene too, remembers Darlene's initial infatuation with Gene: "She came home all excited and was talking all about him. Then he left, and for the next week the house was filled with flowers and telegrams and she was getting long distance calls."

On November 4th, Gene's newest single was launched with an advertisement in *Billboard* that proclaimed, 'Gene Vincent and his Blue Caps follow up on his triple-market smash *Lotta Lovin,* with *Dance to the Bop* b/w *I Got It.*'

Gene and the Caps went up to Vancouver, Canada, for a concert at the Georgia Auditorium, and before the gig, Gene was interviewed by a local deejay Red Robinson who asked him about the ride up and if it was a drag. Gene answered very softly, "It was. It was raining all the ways, you know." When asked if he'd had any trouble at the border, he laughed and said, 'Shore did. I stayed there about two hours." He talked to Robinson about where he got his big break, saying that Capitol had had a contest and 243 of the 250 entrants did Elvis Presley songs and he won with *Be-Bop-A-Lula*, and he mentioned that his next release would be *Rollin' Danny*. Gene was asked it he thought rock'n'roll was slipping down at all and replied, "Well, if anybody thinks it's slippin down, you look at *Billboard's* top thirty." About his background, he said, "I was born in Virginia and I come from Dallas, Texas." Then Red Robinson asked Gene if he was married and he answered "No," with a laugh, and explained, "Well, you know how this world is, Red. You never hardly meet anybody long enough to know them that well."

Red remarked, "You never stay in one spot long enough."

"That's the difference," said Gene.

Gene said he'd been on the road since the 10th of July and added, "The travelling is mostly what gits you down. It gits horrible sometimes." Red asked him if he ever got to go home and Gene said, "Once in a while." He laughed and repeated softly to himself, "Once in a while." Then he added, "I've been off about eight days since July 10th."

Red asked about Elvis Presley and Gene mentioned Presley's gig in Norfolk, probably the one in the fall of '55: "He came in with Hank Snow. That was when I first met him."

When asked about the show that night, Gene said, "Well, the first two numbers will be just ordinary rock'n'roll. Then, as you probably know. . . rock'n'roll was derived from the ol' blues records, you know. And I'll do a blues song for them about then. Then I'll carry on with the show."

Gene was asked to give some advice to budding performers and said, "Well, sir, I'll tell you. I've heard people set around and say, 'Boy, I wish I had a break,' and this, that, and the other. You can make your own breaks. 'Cause there's no record company today that if you take them a dub record they won't listen to it. And if they like it, they'll record it."

Red asked Gene if he thought rock'n'roll would be around a

while, and Gene said, "I think it's gunna be around for an awful long time." Red mentioned that ballads were coming back and asked Gene if he could sing them. Gene said, "Have you heard that song on my album... *Unchained Melody?* Well, the guitar work on that is beautiful.... If you get the right instruments, you can do ballads."

Red wanted to know who Gene thought was the greatest pop guitarist, and Gene said, "Well, there's been lots of arguments between Sugarfoot Carlin and Chet Atkins. I tell you, I think Chet Atkins.... It's funny for a guitarist to play his own rhythm. And he does."

When asked what he would do if his singing career caved in, Gene said, "I'm one of the lucky ones that's got something to fall back on in the industry. I've done pretty well and I've saved my money. And I've got something to fall back on... radio. I own some interest in radio. I own some in Peoria, Illinois, and I own a third of one in Lubbock.... Jimmy Bowen is the manager. That's how we all got in together."[6]

That night, Gene and the Caps put on a riotous show in Vancouver. The supporting act was Bonnie Guitar, a country singer who'd just had a big hit, *Dark Moon,* but her manager made the mistake of insisting she go on last. Gene and the Caps did a wild show, and at the end they threw their hats into the audience: "It was just bedlam when the kids tried to get hold of the caps. ... Bonnie went out with just her guitar and tried to follow that, and by the end of her first song there wasn't more than half a dozen people in the audience!"[7]

Red Robinson says, "It was fantastic! Vincent jumped around all over the place. He slid over the piano. It was like an acrobatic show with music. This was really show business. Vincent was on stage for a good hour and a half and the kids were dancing in the aisles. Then when Bonnie Guitar came out, at least half the kids left to go outside and wait by the stage doors for Vincent and the Blue Caps. It was an incredible show!"

6. From a recorded interview by Red Robinson, on Great North-West Records, GNW 4016.
7. Pat Mason.

Next, Gene and the Caps went to New York City and performed *Lotta Lovin'* and *Dance to the Bop* on the Ed Sullivan Show. Max Lipscomb played rhythm, and Dickie Harrell replaced Dude Kahn on drums. Since Vincent was a highly visual performer, this should have been a great opportunity for him, especially since he and the Caps were playing live. But Gene's main prop, a mike-stand, was denied him. Instead, he had a microphone on a cord slung around his neck, just as Buddy Holly did when he played on the same show a month later. At least Gene and the Caps didn't dress in tuxedos and bow ties like Holly and the Crickets.

Johnny Meeks was a bit disappointed by the whole atmosphere of the show: "It was kind of a joke really. It was just this old theatre, like an old high school auditorium. It was disillusioning." Paul Peek remembers the show a bit more fondly: "We had a ball on the Ed Sullivan Show. We were prepared for that one. It was really a thrill at the time. It came off well and we gave a good presentation. We were probably more worried about the studio audience than the TV audience. Gene was a little bit uptight, but I think he performed well."

Gene, Dickie, Bobby (courtesy of Bonnie Lund)

The truth is that the public was beginning to drift away from real rock'n'roll. In the November 4th, 1957, edition of *Time* magazine there was a paradoxical article called 'The Rock is Solid' that served up some interesting opinions on the new music. First it was noted that Elvis Presley was as popular as ever, then they quoted a Chicago deejay, Marty Faye: "The kids have accepted this twanging guitar, this nasal, unintelligible sound, this irritating sameness of lyrics, this lamentable croak. . . . We'll have to live with it until the kids find a new sound." *Time* mentioned that ballads were becoming more popular and quoted Boston deejay Bill Marlowe: "Rock'n'roll has had it. The teenagers are beginning to look to better music." (This same deejay was one of the first to be fired when the payola scam eventually surfaced.)

After the Sullivan show, Gene phoned Darlene and said he wanted to see her, but first he had to return to Los Angeles for more recording sessions. He asked her if she'd come out to Dallas and spend Christmas with him if he sent her a plane ticket. Darlene was in love with Gene and agreed to go.

Gene and the Caps went back to Hollywood, and Ken Nelson, impressed with the success of *Lotta Lovin'*, intended to bring out another single as well as a third album. For these sessions, Gene wanted to add a piano, probably because he'd been touring with Jerry Lee Lewis. Bobby Jones comments: "Gene really liked Jerry Lee's music, and if we were in a restaurant he'd go to the jukebox and play *Whole Lotta Shakin' Goin' On*. He really liked that."

In the first week of December, Gene and the Caps went back to the Capitol Tower in Hollywood and recorded fifteen songs in four days, including some of their hottest numbers such as *Baby Blue* (written by Gene and Bobby Jones), *It's No Lie, Flea Brain, Brand New Beat, Yes, I Love You Baby* (by Gene, Paul, Bubba and Max), *Right Now,* and *I Got a Baby.* During these sessions, *Dance to the Bop* broke into the *Billboard* Top 100 at number 43.

After the sessions, the Blue Caps all went home, but Gene flew to Philadelphia where he mimed some of his songs on Dick Clark's American Bandstand, now seen coast to coast on over 100 stations. In retrospect, it seems fitting that Gene's last appearance of '57 was on such a sterile bourgeois show. According to Dickie Harrell, Gene thought a lot of Dick Clark, but years later, when Gene was touring England, he used to tell a story about how he played a dee-jay convention for Dick Clark and had to sign his cheque over to Clark right after the show. Later, at another deejay convention, Gene got drunk, stood up, and said over the microphone, "Well, if you're all assholes like Dick Clark, then you can all go get fucked!" Then he walked out.[8]

Rock'n'roll was giving way to the era of teen idols, usually protégés of Clark who were bland enough to be sold to a broad spectrum of the masses, *especially the parents*. Even Elvis Presley, who had helped start the whole movement, and who'd once had the toughest image of all, had recently gone into the RCA studio in Hollywood and recorded an album of Christmas songs such as *Santa Claus is Back in Town, White Christmas, Silent Night* and *Oh Little Town of Bethlehem*.

Things were changing radically, and although Gene Vincent was at the height of his career, the bottom was precariously near. It would be a long hard fall.

---

8. This story was repeated by three members of Sounds Incorporated. Its accuracy is questionable as Gene was known for making up stories about himself.

St. Paul, 1958 (courtesy of DiAnne Kaslow)

5

Be Bop Boogie Boy

At the height of the riot a cop grabbed Juvey and shouted,
"Get behind your bass drum and hide your head!" Juvey
thought to himself, "So this is what it's like to play for
Gene Vincent."

— Juvey Gomez

Gene returned to his big five-bedroom house in Dallas to see his family for Christmas. He bought bicycles for his youngest sisters, Tina and Donna, and a watch studded with diamonds for his mother. Darlene Hicks flew out with her baby daughter Debbie, and Gene lied to his parents, saying they were already married. Actually they couldn't marry for another four months, until he got his divorce from Ruth Ann. (According to Gene's original bass player, Jack Neal, a year earlier Ruth Ann had gone to court and had Gene's assets frozen. Jack found out that Ruth Ann was Gene's wife and not his cousin when his pay cheques bounced.)

At the beginning of 1958 it must have seemed to Gene that he and his band were finally on top. He'd just recorded enough tracks for a third album and he had two singles in the Top 100. *Lotta Lovin'* had been there for nineteen weeks and *Dance to the Bop* for three. Gene's popularity and career were at their peak in America, and two of his chief rivals were about to abandon rock'n'roll. After the Australian tour, Little Richard had re-converted to Christianity and enrolled in a Bible school in Huntsville, Alabama, vowing to sing nothing but gospel music. More significantly, just before Christmas, Elvis Presley had received his draft notice telling him to report for induction into the army on the 20th of January, the same day that Capitol released Gene's new single, *I Got a Baby*, b/w *Walkin' Home From School*. Gene had picked out the song himself: "I thought *I Got a Baby* was going to be a great big smash 'cause it was such a great session with everybody going like crazy. But it didn't do a thing."[1]

While still in Dallas, Gene and the Caps played at the Sportatorium with Johnny Carroll and Joe Poovey, then they went back out on the road. Problems had been developing, and while gigging around the Midwest, the Clapper Boys decided to quit. According to Paul Peek, "We were getting on each other's nerves. Things had been building up for some time. Gene was drinking a bit too much and gettin' orn'ry. We were arguin' in a hotel room and it almost came to blows. I didn't really think we'd go through with it, but we did, and Bubba and I quit." Both Paul and Bubba wanted to begin singing careers of their own and this probably helped with their decision to leave. Paul went to Atlanta, Georgia, and saw Bill Lowery, whose publishing company owned the rights to *Be-Bop-A-Lula*. Lowery had just started a new record company called NRC. He signed Paul up, and his first record, *Skinny Jenny* b/w *Rockaround* was the label's first release. It took Bubba longer to get a contract, but in 1960 he had a fair-sized hit with *High School U.S.A.* b/w *Give Me Another Chance* on Legrand Records.

At about the same time as the Clapper Boys quit, Gene's chauffeur left. Gene's best friend and brother-in-law, Ed Butler, had recently got out of the navy, and he and Evelyn were staying at Gene's house in Dallas. Gene asked Ed to join the Caps as one of the Clapper Boys, but Ed was a country music fan and didn't want to sing. However, Ed did need a job, so Gene hired him as his chauffeur. At the time, Gene had a '57 Chrysler New Yorker with lake plugs and fender skirts. As Ed says, "It was a hellascious car! This machine would run!" Gene also had a Cadillac and a Lincoln Continental. Because McLemore wanted Larry Thacker, the middle-aged road manager, to do the driving, Gene paid Ed out of his own pocket: "I never got a cheque from McLemore. My money always came straight from Gene." Gene would rather pay a friend to do the driving and have someone he felt he could trust, than have a chauffeur imposed on him by either managers or agents. It seems Gene and Thacker often quarrelled, and Ed Butler says that

---

1. Finnis and Dunham.

"Thacker was your picture of a used car salesman."

At this point, the Caps consisted of Dickie Harrell on drums, Johnny Meeks on lead guitar, Bobby Lee Jones on bass, and a new member, Clifton Simmons, on piano. Simmons had previously played with Peek, Jones and Meeks in Johnny Earl's Circle E Ranch Boys and fitted into the group perfectly.

They toured through the South, and in Austin, Texas, they did a gig with ten other acts, including Ray Campi. Natually, Gene topped the bill. They also played the Louisiana Hayride in Shreveport and Gene did some country songs, including Johnny Cash's *Rock Island Line* and some Hank Williams numbers. Darlene came along for the first part of the tour, then she flew back to Dallas to look after her daughter, Debbie.

After a gig in Biloxi, Mississippi, while Gene and Ed were in a restaurant, a musician from another band came in and complained that nobody had gone to his own gig: "Everybody went to see that creep Gene Vincent." Gene took exception to this and made a "rude comment." The other guy turned and said, "Well, if you feel froggy...jump!" As Gene got up Ed intervened, saying "If you wanna jump...jump with me!" The other guy decided not to bother.

When they got outside Gene was still indignant and insisted they go back to their hotel room and get one of his pistols: "Let's go get the piece and come back and lighten up their lives a little!"

Ed tried to dissuade him: "No, Gene. We'll end up in jail."

"That's okay. I'll just pay the bail and we'll be back in Texas in the morning."

Ed wasn't convinced: "No way I'm doing time in Mississippi! In a civilized place maybe.... But not in Mississippi!"

Gene was becoming more aggressive and relied on friends and employees to back him up in potentially dangerous hassles which he'd usually instigated himself. As Henry Henroid, his road manager in England, later remarked, "Gene was only satisfied when he'd succeeded in creating havoc." Gene's growing fascination with weapons, especially handguns, would increase commensurately with the steady disintegration of his personality from the pressures of show business, alcoholism and constant touring.

Paul Peek had also noticed Gene's obsession with weapons:

Gene and Johnny (courtesy of Di Anne Kaslow)

"Gene pulled a gun and clicked it at us once. We were leavin' the hotel early in the morning and pilin' into the car. There'd been a party the night before and we were all laughin'. Then Gene swung around and said, 'Laugh, will you, you bastards!' So he pulled this gun out and clicked it at us. Thacker yelled at him, 'You stupid son-of-a-bitch! Put that damn thing away!' Afterwards Gene felt quite sheepish about it, 'cause it turned out that there was a damn bullet in the gun! Gene did it just in fun, but it could have been serious. It could have been fatal!"

Gene and the Caps kept touring the South and hit Tallahassee, Florida; North Carolina; and Richmond, Virginia. They joined a package tour with Ferlin Husky, the Champs, and Bill Justis. Dickie Harrell remembers that they also toured with Sonny James, Jerry Lee Lewis, Buddy Knox and Jimmy Bowen: "We'd run into them for three or four days, then we wouldn't see them for a while. Then we'd run into them again. We did a lot of fairs and things. It went on for three or four weeks and it was a pretty good tour."

While out in Nebraska, Gene decided that they needed a rhythm guitarist, and McLemore's agency sent out Grady Owen, a musician who'd played both bass and lead guitar in various Dallas bands. Owen recalls a show they played with Ferlin Husky: "Husky was supposed to be the headliner and Gene was supposed to be next. But Ferlin didn't want to follow Gene's act, so we got the headline spot. . . . We had a pat show down. We'd do the same thing every time and the MC would introduce Gene and we would start a heavy riff leading into 'Lula, just a slow blues beat, real heavy though. Everybody, including the drummer and the pianist, were standing. And when Gene would start singing 'Lula, everytime it brought the house down! Everyday it was a thrill for me to hear the roar of applause as he started 'Lula! . . . I'm pretty sure we closed with *Lotta Lovin'*, and he did several Little Richard songs. And we always used to do one bit, the Jerry Lee Lewis song, *Whole Lotta Shakin'*. During that we would do these acrobatics on stage. We'd get on the floor and we'd jump in the air and swing our guitars around."[2]

In Milwaukee they did one of their wildest gigs. "It was a great show. They rioted and 'bout tore the place down! Gene did Little Richard's *Can't Believe You Wanna Leave* and the kids grabbed him and tore his shirt off and got a shoe too! The dance floor was a mess with kids screamin' and goin' crazy!"[3]

Grady Owen: "We always got a wild reaction. And the little girls would try to touch Vincent and drag him off stage. Quite often they did. In fact, one time in Milwaukee; I think it was a place called the Million Dollar Barn, packed with thousands of kids. . . we had to have a line of police escort us in from the dressing room to the stage. And he got a little close to the front of the stage and they got him and were passing him from one to another over their heads and. . . when he finally made it back he had scratches all over his face."[4]

Afterwards, Gene flew to Philadelphia and did his second spot on American Bandstand, miming his songs without the Caps. Ed and the band members drove up to Green Bay, Wisconsin, and Gene flew in to meet them. They worked their way southwards through South Dakota, Iowa, Nebraska, and Kansas. Then back to Dallas.

It had been quite a tour, but by then Ed felt he'd had enough. "Gene and I had a good relationship. We were very blunt and very honest with each other. He wanted me to stay, but those drives were just too long. The money was righteous, but it was three or four hundred miles to each show! It was just a crude way to live! But Gene didn't seem to mind too much. He'd sit in the back seat and strum his guitar and write a song, or maybe nip on a bottle. But it wasn't my kind of life!. . . Rock'n'roll was never my kind of music."

Dickie Harrell missed his girlfriend, Bubba's sister, so he quit for the second time and went back to Norfolk. Dude Kahn replaced him. Johnny Earl promoted a Blue Cap gig at the armoury in Greenville, and Paul Peek and Bubba Facenda rejoined, supposedly just for that one night, but after the gig Gene approached Paul and told him that he was going to be in a film, *Hot Rod Gang*, and about to

2. Finnis & Dunham.
3. Ed Butler.
4. Finnis and Dunham.

cut a new LP. Paul told Gene of his own record, *Skinny Jenny,* and Gene said, "Well, why don't we get back together for this movie and my new album. We can do some shows together and it'll be a good chance for you to promote your own record."

St. Paul, 1958 (courtesy of DiAnne Kaslow)

Gene Vincent Rocks and the Blue Caps Roll, (recorded in June and December of '57) was released on March 8th and it was his best album yet. It features rockers like *Brand New Beat, Flea Brain, Rollin' Danny* and *It's No Lie;* soulful ballads like *Should I Ever Love Again* and *In My Dreams;* and Gene's rocked-up treatment of the standards *By the Light of the Silvery Moon, Frankie and Johnny* and *Your Cheatin' Heart.* However, Gene's most recent single, *I Got a Baby,* hadn't even made the charts, though it did fairly well in Britain. Although rock'n'roll was also going soft in the U.K., there was still a strong cult following of Teddy Boys and rockers who were true to hard-driving rock'n'roll. This point was made especially clear during the British invasion of the mid-sixties, based as it was on original rock'n'roll, and by the rise of punk rock and neo-rocka-billy in the mid-seventies.

In the meantime, Ken Nelson was sure he could come up with some more hits and booked Gene into the Capitol Tower for the last week in March. This coincided with Gene's spot in *Hot Rod Gang,* which McLemore had arranged.

Before leaving for Los Angeles, Gene and the Caps played in Dallas at the Will Rogers Coliseum before about 8,000 fans. The warm-up band, the Vikings, had a fifteen-year-old drummer named Juvey Gomez who, as Bubba says, "played a carbon copy of Dickie Harrell's drumming." Gene was obviously impressed because he got Larry Thacker to phone Juvey and ask him if he wanted to join the Caps and cut an album. For Juvey this was a big break, but he was still in school and had to get his mother's permission. She agreed to let him go if Thacker promised to get him back right away. Juvey recalls the gig at the Will Rogers Coliseum: "Gene was great! I didn't know how to take it at first, but I was curious about why a person would look and act that way. He wore a shirt with billowy sleeves and he walked out with a limp. He said a few words, then he went straight into the music. Gene wasn't putting anybody on. He was an individual and an innovator. And the girls were wild about him and screaming and stuff."

To prepare for the sessions and *Hot Rod Gang,* the whole band including Paul and Bubba as back-up singers, stayed at a motel in Dallas and practised at Gene's big house on Dykes Way. By this time Mr. and Mrs. Craddock had left and only Gene, Darlene and Debbie were staying there. Juvey remembers that "Darlene was sweet and quiet. And obviously crazy about Gene." Paul Peek adds, "Darlene really loved him. I think she was tryin' to help him. And she was very good for him at the time."

They rehearsed for two or three days, then drove to Los Angeles, stopping on the way in Globe, Arizona, to play at the National Guard armoury. This was another wild gig and it soon erupted into a full-scale riot. A fight broke out when Gene was dragged from the stage by the local sheriff. Bubba says, "They had to shoot tear-gas into the joint. Navahoes and Apaches were all goin' at it!" Grady Owen recalls: "The sheriff had arrested Gene for wrecking a motel room, being drunk around minors and doing a lewd show. They dragged him off stage bodily, and took him to jail.... And so they started to fight. The whole thing erupted, and so the sheriff came back and shot tear-gas bombs in the place and cleared it! In the meantime, somebody tried to punch Juvey. Somebody jumped up and down on the trailer and smashed it! That was Juvey's introduction!"[5]

At the height of the riot a cop grabbed Juvey and shouted, "Get behind your bass drum and hide your head!" Juvey thought to himself, "So this is what it's like to play for Gene Vincent!"

Paul Peek remembers it a bit differently: "We'd played a hop that afternoon at some school gym to promote the show that night. But some Pachuccos mouthed off to me and Bubba and I'd said a few things back, which maybe I shouldn't have. But they swore they were gunna come back and get us that night. So they brought their gang and we were lookin' out for them and a little nervous. A sheriff and some deputies were there to protect us. We were on stage doin' *Lotta Lovin'* and we were down on our knees singin' and the place was goin' crazy! Then a fight broke and suddenly everybody was fightin'! It was like the place exploded. So the sheriff's deputies came and got us and took us to a room backstage and shot off a bunch of tear-gas. It was wild!" Before they could continue to L.A., the Caps had to wire Dallas to get enough money to bail Gene out.

On March 25th they went into the Capitol Tower and started taping. Johnny Meeks was on lead guitar and Grady Owen played rhythm, though he's only audible on a couple of tracks. Bobby Jones played bass, and he and Grady used different channels of the same amplifier and shared a microphone. Clifton Simmons played Capitol's grand piano, with only one mike, and only one was used for Juvey's whole drum kit. As primitive as it sounds today, this remains the essence of the rock'n'roll sound.

Paul and Bubba did background vocals, which were taped live, and they were joined by Eddie Cochran, singing bass. He'd played with the Caps for a week in Philadelphia and been with them on the month-long tour of Australia. He lived in Los Angeles and had dropped by the session. Juvey remarks, "Eddie had a real happy

5. Finnis & Dunham.

From *Hot Rod Gang,* left to right: Johnny, Bubba, Gene, Paul
(courtesy of Steve Aynsley)

personality. He was refreshing to meet. Gene and Eddie were real close, just two good buddies." Bubba says, "Eddie was close to all of us. We always seemed to get booked together. He might have done that on purpose, because when the popularity of rock'n'roll started to die out, it was dyin' out for Eddie too. That was when Bobby Rydell and Frankie Avalon were so popular. So Eddie may have asked his manager Jerry Capehart to get him booked with us, 'cause we were doin' the same kind of music. Eddie had a lot of stage savvy."

Paul Peek remembers Eddie helping them construct a home-made sound-proof room in the middle of the huge Capitol studio: "It was like a little house made of baffles. We were trying to separate the sound. We might have worn headphones, but I'm not even sure about that. We just crawled up inside our little 'house' and all sang together."

Ken Nelson gave Gene a bunch of demos and let him have a relatively free hand in choosing his material. Says Juvey, "Gene would play the demos, then ask us, 'What do you think of that one?' He seemed to take our opinions seriously. . . . Ken Nelson was easy-going and jovial. He seemed to be real happy with Gene." Bubba comments: "Ken Nelson was a fair man, one of the fairest I've known. And he'd seen us live. He knew the potential we had!"

Their first song was *Dance in the Street*, and featured a piano intro. Clifton Simmons had adapted from country music to rock'n'roll, and at these sessions there was a piano solo on almost every song. *Dance in the Street* would be used in the forthcoming movie *Hot Rod Gang* and the lyrics fit perfectly:

> We're gunna find a street that's not in use,
> Park in a circle and kick off our shoes,
> Turn on the radios and leave 'em up loud,
> Grab a little chick and dance all night!

Eddie Cochran sang the bass part on the next song, *Git It,* and probably arranged it, or at least helped. The intro is a classic with Eddie singing, "Well oh well oh wop, whip whip whip!" Paul and Bubba come in on the next line, then Gene enters with a wordless falsetto improvisation, until:

left to right: Grady, Johnny, Bubba, Gene, Bobby, Paul, Clifton
(courtesy of Steve Aynsley)

Once there was a girl,
Oh oh, what a girl!
She looked at me,
She said, 'Where can it be?
Where's your Cadillac car?'...
Well, I don't have one now
But I can git it.... *Git it!*[6]

In the following four days they recorded fourteen more songs, most with Eddie Cochran on bass vocals. They did rockers such as *Teenager Partner* (by Gene), *Lovely Lovetta, Little Lover, Rocky Road Blues* (originally a Bill Monroe bluegrass tune), *Somebody Help Me, Five Feet of Lovin'*, and *Look What You Done To Me;* standards such as *Hey, Good Lookin'* and *I Can't Help It* (both by Hank Williams), as well as *The Wayward Wind* and Gershwin's *Summertime.*

On March 30th, Gene and the Caps went into the American-International film studio to appear in *Hot Rod Gang*, written and produced by Lou Rusoff and directed by Lou Landers. The songs for *Hot Rod Gang* were *Baby Blue, Dance in the Street, Lovely Loretta* and *Dance to the Bop.* Gene wore a black shirt and white pants and the Caps wore white jackets and black pants. Unlike *The Girl Can't Help It,* where Gene held a guitar and had no microphone, or the Ed Sullivan Show, where he had a mike hung around his neck, in *Hot Rod Gang* Gene was given his most important prop: a mike on a stand.

The film was released in the States on July 2nd. In Britain it was released under the title *Fury Unleashed,* but not until January of 1959. *Hot Rod Gang* was a B movie meant to capitalize on the sudden rock'n'roll craze, but it has become much sought after because it features Gene Vincent and the Blue Caps.

While they were in Los Angeles, Gene and the Caps stayed at a hotel in Hollywood. They'd have parties at night and other artists would show up. Juvey Gomez remembers Gene being visited by Johnny Cash, Ricky Nelson (who apparently idolized Gene and the

---

6. Nineteen years later a British rock'n'roller, Dave Edmunds, paid tribute to Gene, Eddie, and the Caps in an album called *Git It.*

Date **Sept 2** 19 **84**

M _____

No. _____

Reg. No.	Clerk	ACCOUNT FORWARDED		
1			9	95
2				
3				
4			7.	46
5				
6			6	2
7				
8				
9				
10				
11				
12				
13				
14			$	8 08
15				

013254 - 1

Caps), and, of course, Eddie Cochran. Bubba remembers one night when a party was going on and a bottle was thrown out a window. Soon afterwards the hotel detective showed up and he and Gene argued. The next day they moved to another place and rented an entire floor. (As much as Gene liked to party at night, at the sessions it was a different story. According to Juvey, "Gene never drank in the studio. And he seemed to take the recording very seriously.") Though he only played with Paul and Bubba briefly, Juvey Gomez remembers them well. "Bubba was a pretty boy. And he thought *he* was the star! He'd try to up-stage Gene and Gene would look over his shoulder and look at him as if to say, 'Back, man! Back!' And Paul Peek, he was always combing his hair. One time we walked down Hollywood Boulevard and Paul combed his hair solid for five blocks! Then the wind would just blow it back! Paul and Bubba did good harmonies, but they were highly visual too. And always trying to upstage Gene! But at least Gene saw the humour of it."

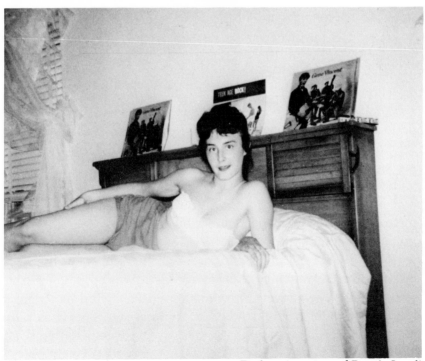

Darlene (courtesy of Bonnie Lund)

95

Darlene came out while Gene was in LA, and together they went up to Hazel Dell, outside of Portland, to see her parents and tell them of their marriage plans. Darlene's father was a truck driver, and both he and his wife were members of the Assembly of God. Says Darlene, "It was a very religious home. They thought rock'n'roll was pretty wild." Gene and Mr. Hicks went out into the garden and talked while Darlene waited nervously. "I was shaking!" She was only nineteen years old and her daughter Debbie had just turned two. Gene and Darlene had only been going together for six months. Gene promised Mr. Hicks that he would take care of her and Debbie, and Mr. Hicks reluctantly gave them his blessing. According to Darlene, "He wasn't really too hep about it." They returned to Dallas and Darlene says they were married on the first of May, the same month that Capitol released Gene's new single, *Baby Blue* b/w *True To You*.

Baby Blue is one of Gene's best recordings and was one of his personal favourites. Ken Nelson certainly knew what he was doing, and he was, along with Sam Phillips of Sun Records, one of the great producers of the fifties. The secret of his success was that he just let Gene and his band play the way they wanted and tried to capture them live in the studio. In spite of this, *Baby Blue* never made the charts.[7]

Gene's lack of chart success with his first two singles of 1958 had a profound influence on his moods and behaviour. Paul Peek noticed that Gene changed considerably: "Gene's drinking got a little heavier and he was taking a lot of medication for the pain in his leg. He got to be more of a recluse and he didn't want to sign autographs or do interviews. He'd stay in his hotel room and brood, and he got to thinking that the world was down on him. Gene had a huge hit with *Be-Bop-A-Lula* and a big hit with *Lotta Lovin'*. Then the others weren't hits. And it hurt Gene pretty hard. Every week we'd get the *Cashbox* and *Billboard* magazines and check them out, but they weren't making the charts. So Gene was brooding. He was always really moody, even in the happy times. He'd be laughing, then he'd suddenly withdraw. You could see it in his eyes. Gene had a lot of problems. It was in the way he was made up. Gene

---

7. It would become the title song of Gene's American Fan Club.

wasn't made to take a lot of disappointment."

Dickie Harrell adds, "Gene had a lot of trouble with that leg, more than most people realize. The pain was just so bad, you'd wonder how he'd go on stage. But he'd go out there and sing and do the show. That was his thing. And he put a lot more into it than most people realize."

The spring of '58 was perhaps the high point of original rock'n'roll, but it wasn't to last much longer. In March, pop arranger Mitch Miller made a widely-reported speech criticizing radio programming. He said that it pandered to "eight to fourteen year olds." Alan Freed replied, "It sounds like sour grapes to me."And he was right. But Freed was on the eve of his own downfall. Two months later he was charged with 'inciting a riot and anarchy' after a rock'n'roll show in Boston, and within two years he would be hounded out of the music industry, his position as top American deejay usurped by Dick Clark.

During that same spring, at a hearing of the Senate Sub-Committee on Communications, a group of pop song-writers reiterated charges about how the interlocking interests of BMI and broadcaster-owned stations stifled ASCAP songs. Vance Packard claimed that, "Conniving disc jockeys and BMI" foisted "cheap music" on passive teenagers.[8]

In May of 1958, Elvis Presley was in an army training camp in Texas; Little Richard was in a Bible college in Alabama; and Jerry Lee Lewis had caused a scandal and seriously damaged his career by marrying his bass player's thirteen year old daughter. Rock'n'roll was in serious trouble, but Gene had just recorded his fourth album and he wasn't about to give up. McLemore's agency put another tour together, and Gene and the Caps went back out on the road. This time the band was quite different. Not only were the Clapper Boys gone, but both Johnny Meeks and Bobby Jones had gone back to Greenville. Meeks comments, "I was just getting tired. I probably just said, 'I don't wanna go out there! I wanna go home!'" Bobby Jones says, "I was married and tired of the road.

---

8. Arnold Shaw, *The Rockin' 50's* (New York: Dutton, 1974).

There were no problems with Gene or the group."

Gene hired Howard Reed, from Dallas, to play lead guitar. Grady Owen switched over to bass, and Gene re-hired Max Lipscomb to play rhythm. Juvey Gomez was still in school, so Dude Kahn came back to play drums. Clifton Simmons remained on piano and took over leadership of the band from Johnny Meeks. They played in Dallas at the Yellow Belly Drag Strip, then they went up to Arkansas, heading for Canada.

It wasn't long before Kahn quit. After Elvis was drafted, his drummer, D.J. Fontana, returned to his home town of Shreveport, where he played on the Louisiana Hayride. Fontana got a call from Fargo, North Dakota, asking him to come up right away. He flew up that night and played his first gig the following evening. Says D.J., "We rehearsed maybe for an hour. I'd heard most of his stuff already." They played a few more dates in the States, then crossed over into Canada and did a string of one-nighters. D.J. comments: "Gene had a good act. He had that bad leg, but he still got around good. He was a good entertainer. I enjoyed working with him. He got a heck of a crowd. Elvis and Gene were basically in the same category. There were kids screaming. . . . Gene had a lot of hits. He was pretty hot, a hot artist." Darlene was on this tour and she recalls D.J. fondly. "He was a funny guy. If we were in a restaurant with a juke box he'd get up and play an Elvis Presley song. Then he'd come over and grin and say, 'Hey, listen. Listen to them drums!'"

Halfway through this tour, Gene decided that he needed some new Clapper Boys, so he re-hired Bill Mack (who'd played the Rockabilly Spectacular tour in 1956), and got Grady and Max to do background vocals and dance routines.

By now Gene probably wasn't making as much money as in '56 or '57, but he was still squandering it despite Thacker's attempts to keep him on an allowance. Darlene remembers that Gene had no money sense: "He'd buy clothes and booze and just junk. He'd grown up poor and he wanted things. One time we walked past this store and Gene saw some shoes and wanted to get them for Debbie. They were pink and white patent leather. So he made *me* go ask Thacker for some money!"

Gene's leg was still bothering him. He took a lot of drugs and his drinking escalated: "He'd take uppers during the day. And sleeping pills at night. He wouldn't get out of bed in the morning unless I brought him a tumbler full of whiskey. And that leg was bad. He usually had a bandage over it, but it was kinda gooey-looking. Sometimes before the show he'd get one of the guys to drive him to a doctor and get an injection of local anesthetic before he could go on stage."[9]

The Caps played Winnipeg, then moved west. Says Max Lipscomb, "Cliff Simmons got hit up in Calgary by the Mounties because he was with this under-age chick. As a matter of fact, I was in the bathroom just as the Mounties broke into the room. And they got him and beat him up and I was hiding in the shower!"[10]

It was also in Canada that Max Lipscomb drove Gene's car off a cliff: "Some kids were throwing rocks at wild horses and in my efforts to scare them I kinda lost control of the car and it left the road. It got wrecked and they bought a new one."[11] As much as Gene liked to squander money, he could hardly have been happy about this, especially since he hadn't yet had a hit that year.

The Caps left Canada and worked their way down South. They played some dates around Pontchartrain, Louisiana, then D. J. Fontana left. "I quit just because I didn't want to travel. The money was pretty good. Better than most."

About this time, Gene decided to get rid of the 'new' Clapper Boys, and Max and Grady both lost their jobs. Max says, "Gene was kinda mad at me." Grady adds, "They decided to get rid of the dancers about the same time they bought the new car. One guy had to go and it was me. It pissed me off."[12]

Years later, Max and Grady intimated that Gene had ripped them off for some of their wages, and this story has been repeated in a booklet, *Gene Vincent and the Blue Caps,* and in the liner notes of the album *Rock'n'Roll Heroes.* However, Johnny Meeks, Pat Mason and Darlene all deny this story. It's also been said that because of this alleged rip-off, Gene was kicked out of the musicians union, and this is why he later moved to England. This story is obviously false

---

9. Darlene.
10. Finnis and Dunham.
11. Ibid.
12. Ibid.

because the Norfolk, Dallas and Los Angeles musicians unions all say that Gene was never a member. He was a singer and a band leader, and according to the Dallas union, singers couldn't even join their local. The difficulties with Max and Grady were very probably personal, and conflicts with Gene were usually the result of his drinking and his violent temper.

When Gene got back to Dallas, Juvey Gomez was out of school, so he was hired as drummer and the band headed out west to do some dates in California. Howard Reed was still on lead guitar, but Gene wasn't too happy with his playing. Juvey explains: "It wasn't that Howard was bad. Gene just wanted Johnny back. Howard was let down, but by that time he'd probably had enough. He was a good clean picker. But that was probably the problem: he was too clean." Gene phoned Johnny Meeks and Meeks flew to Oregon to re-join the Caps.

From Oregon they went up to Washington then swung down through Idaho, Wyoming, Utah, Arizona and New Mexico, then back into Texas. A fellow named Ed Watt at McLemore's agency planned their tours and they'd have to phone Dallas occasionally to find out where their next gig would be. Says Meeks, "Ed Watt was a nice guy, a business man. He didn't want a whole lot of B.S." Juvey characterizes him a little differently: "Watt was the slave driver. We'd phone him to ask where the next gig was and he'd say, 'Just down the road.' Yeah, just seven hundred miles down the road!" And according to Juvey, the road manager, Larry Thacker, "was grouchy, but kind of funny. He had a strange sense of humour and he drank quite a bit. He made people mad sometimes, but he got the work done. He'd try to hurry us up to the next gig. He'd say, 'We're in a hurry! We gotta hook 'em!' But Gene didn't like him. He wanted to do things his own way, so they were always bickering. Gene was moody. And he drank a lot because of his leg. He was in constant pain. He acted weird sometimes, but a good part was the alcohol. He carried a gun and pulled it on Thacker one time. I walked in the motel room and saw this big scene. Then I walked right back out! But I felt kinda sorry for Gene 'cause of all the pressure, all that driving. Gene was pretty sad most of the time.... Sometimes he'd be so stoned that you couldn't tell what it was from. Then, other times, he'd be so restless, like a cat in a small cage, walking back and forth. He hardly slept. All he cared about was, 'Damn it, where is the next job? How far to the next town?' He used to make us pee in pop bottles and throw them out the window. He'd say to us, 'Man, we ain't got time to stop!'"

One time the band let Juvey drive, though he'd only just turned seventeen. They were cruising along and approached a narrow bridge at the same time as an on-coming diesel truck. It was too late to stop so Juvey just kept going. "The mood was kinda tense. I could hear the other guys sucking in their breath." They just barely squeezed by the truck and when they got to the other side of the bridge Clifton turned to Juvey and said quietly, "Pull over, Juvey. I'll drive for while." As the truck had roared by, Gene had only glanced up for a second. Then he went back to sleep.

Juvey finished the tour, but the pace was a bit much for him and he gave Gene his notice. "I wasn't really that much into rock. And I didn't like the lifestyle, all that driving and eating hamburgers at five in the morning. Gene was really nice about it. He tried to talk me into staying and said that there'd be better gigs ahead. But I'd had enough."

In July, Capitol released another single, *Rocky Road Blues* b/w *Yes I Love You Baby*. Gene spent the rest of the summer touring with the Caps, but without a hit it's doubtful that they were making as much money as they had on previous tours. Johnny Meeks remained on lead, Clifton Simmons on piano, Bill Mack on bass and Butch White joined on drums.

In September, Capitol released Gene's fourth single of 1958, *Git It* b/w *Little Lover*. Like his last release, this was a classic combination of two wild rockers, songs which to many fans and critics remain as perfect examples of uncomprised rock'n'roll . *Git it*, like *Rocky Road Blues*, didn't even make the national charts. A glance at the Billboard magazines of September '58 is very revealing. The only rock'n'roll songs to make the top ten were *Bird Dog* by the Everly Brothers, *Rockin' Robin* by Bobby Day, and *Summertime Blues* by Eddie Cochran. The only hits Capitol had were Peggy Lee's *Fever* (number 12) and Johnny Otis' *Willie and the Hand Jive* (number 16). For most of the month the number one hit was Domenico

Modugno's *Volare*, certainly the most loathsome pop song of the entire decade. Things weren't looking too good for rock'n'roll.

In October the number one position was taken over by Tommy Edward's *It's All in the Game*, a pleasant but string-embellished ballad. It stayed in the number one spot all month, fending off even the Big Bopper's *Chantilly Lace*.

In the meantime, Butch White quit the band and Clyde Pennington replaced him as the Blue Caps' drummer. Clyde had grown up with Johnny Meeks back in Greenville and had already played bass briefly with the Caps in Portsmouth in the spring of '57 before Bobby Jones was hired. He flew out to Dallas and practised with the Caps for two days, then they went on the road. They worked their way up to St. Paul, Minnesota, where Gene was still very popular despite his lact of chart success. They stayed in the Hastings Hotel and for a joke the Caps locked a thirteen year-old fan in Gene's room. To further the joke, they tried to blame it on Bill Mack who was, according to Clyde Pennington, "a funny guy, a nut, but funny." However, Gene didn't quite get the humour of it all, probably because of the hassles he'd had with the police in Canada over under-age girls. At any rate, Gene and Bill got in a fight in the lobby of the hotel and Bill was soon replaced by Grady Owen.

They toured their way toward Los Angeles and the Caps continued with their practical jokes. According to Clyde Pennington, "Gene would get to drinking, so we'd do things like raise the key on *Be-Bop-a-Lula* without telling him. We'd drive him crazy... but he'd still reach it!"

On October 13th Gene and the Caps went into the Capitol Tower and in five days they recorded 23 songs. The biggest improvement in the over-all-sound came on ten of the songs on which Jackie Kelso, of the Johnny Otis Show, added tenor saxophone. These R&B-influenced takes were some of Gene's best and included *High Blood Pressure, Say Mama, Be Bop Boogie Boy, Who's Been Pushin' Your Swing, Anna Annabella* and *Gone, Gone, Gone*. Perhaps the best song is *High Blood Pressure*, written by Huey 'Piano' Smith. In the original version the singer has high blood pressure because his girl is so fine, but in Gene's version, true to character, he gets high blood pressure because he's heard she's fooling around. Gene and the Caps speeded up the song and *High Blood Pressure* is a prime

Bill Mack and Johnny Meeks (courtesy of DiAnne Kaslow)

example of how Gene's style had gone from country-influenced rockabilly to R&B-influenced rock'n'roll.[13]

In November, Gene's fourth album, *A Gene Vincent Record Date*, was released. All the songs were from the spring '58 sessions with Eddie Cochran. About the same time, Capitol released Gene's new single, *Say Mama* b/w *Be Bop Boogie Boy*, but, like all his 1958 releases, it did very poorly. Looking back, it seems almost impossible that it wasn't a colossal hit. Both songs are classics and *Say Mama* was featured in Gene's stage act right until the very end. Clyde Pennington says, "I loved Gene's stuff. He had a great voice. And I really thought that *Say Mama* would be the song that would make it for him again." It didn't.

Perhaps this was because of the general state of rock'n'roll. It must be remembered that many of the greatest rock'n'rollers such as Sonny Burgess, Warren Smith and Billy Lee Riley, all of whom recorded for Sun, *never* had anything but small local hits, even though they recorded some of the hottest cuts of the fifties.

A month before, in October '58, the Smathers Committee had published a 1237 page document detailing the Senate SubCommittee hearings on bill S2834. The intent of the bill was to prohibit broadcasters from owning music publishing or recording interests. Although the chairman of the Committee said that there was "no clear proof of violation of public interest, as charged against broadcasters by ASCAP songwriters," the whole music industry was about to be engulfed in the payola scandal, still smouldering just below the surface. And Capitol didn't pay payola.

The Caps stayed together only briefly after the release of *Say Mama*. In mid-November they did a Los Angeles TV program called the Country America Show, then they broke up. They had tried hard, toured from coast to coast, and had made some of the greatest rock'n'roll singles of all time, but it seemed they were now part of a passing phenomenon. Johnny Meeks got a job with a band in LA, and Grady Owen went back to Dallas. Clifton Simmons returned to Greenville. Clyde Pennington stayed with Gene, and for a couple of months they toured up the West Coast, using local bands for

---

13. This track was never released in America in Gene's lifetime. It came out on an album in France in 1963.

back-up.

Darlene comments on the break-up: "Gene couldn't keep a band together because he was so hot-headed and the guys just wouldn't take it. If I even looked at somebody the wrong way, he'd fly off the handle." Three years of constant touring, four years of pain from his leg, and a fair bit of drinking had taken their toll on Gene's personality. He was no longer the shy Southern boy "just glad to be on a record." Certainly, Gene had his reasons for being angry and frustrated, but it didn't help either his career or his personal relationships. As Clyde Pennington says, "Gene didn't get along with anybody!"

All through 1958 Gene had put out hot singles, but none of them had gone anywhere. He'd toured with the hottest band in the world, but that hadn't helped either.

Jerry and Gene, Japan, 1959 (courtesy of Jerry Merritt)

6

The Screaming End

Gene wanted to have class, but he didn't have a business head. He was too good-hearted. He trusted everybody.
— Jerry Merritt

One of the reasons Gene was so angry and frustrated was because he had recently lost his house in Dallas to the federal government. Gene had assumed that McLemore's agency would pay the taxes, but they didn't. According to Bonnie Lund, "Gene and Darlene didn't get anything out of that place. It was worth about $80,000 and had a swimming pool and a big backyard, but the government took it over 'cause the Big D people weren't paying the taxes. They lost the furniture and everything. It was a disaster." Pat Mason says that Gene owed about $60,000 in taxes. Darlene comments: "We didn't know we were going to lose that house. Gene just couldn't understand it. He was on the road all the time and he didn't get a lawyer or anything. Gene wasn't like that. He just sort of shrugged it off."

Gene broke with McLemore, went up to the Northwest and asked Pat to become his manager. Gene and Darlene stayed in Vancouver, Washington, with Bonnie and Milo Lund. They had taken Darlene in as a housekeeper when she'd broken up with her first husband. "Darlene was just like a daughter to us," says Bonnie. "And Gene was a pretty favourite person around here too. And pretty upsetting sometimes! But that was all right. I remember the first time I met Gene. He had probably just taken some time off and come up on his own. He was a very quiet shy young man, hardly the man we got to know later. Gene was always doing something, having fun. He and my son used to go out into the backyard with their guns and practise fast-draws. Gene even said in an interview once that it was his favourite hobby. But Gene was in a lot of pain. I used to take him to the hospital to get pain pills when his leg was bothering him. And Gene was very good to me."

Gene and Darlene stayed with Bonnie and Milo over Christmas, then rented a house in Seaside, Oregon. Pat Mason lived there and owned a club called the Bungalow where Gene often used to play. According to Bonnie, Gene and Darlene quarrelled quite a bit, but never over anything important: "Usually it was just petty jealousy. Sometimes Darlene's old friends would be where Gene was playing and he'd get mad if she talked with them. But more than anything it was the drinking that did it. And Gene could be pretty ornery when he was drinking!"

One time, Darlene phoned Bonnie from Seaside, and said that Gene wouldn't let her out of the house. She asked Bonnie and Milo to come and pick her up. They drove to Seaside and found that the police had already been called: "Gene had been drinking and they were arguing. So we took Darlene home with us. But by the time we got there, Gene's car was already parked in the driveway! He'd beaten us back! I think we'd stopped for a coffee somewheres. So Gene asked if he could come in and I said, 'Sure, as long as you're not going to be fighting or arguing.' And he said, 'Okay, Mom.' So Darlene went to her room and Gene slept on the couch. Then the next day, when I got back from work, they were both gone. They'd already made up and gone back to Seaside!"

Bonnie also remembers that Gene really loved Darlene's daughter Debbie and didn't mind that he wasn't the natural father: "Gene used to take Debbie on stage and introduce her as his daughter. He was very proud of her. And even later, after Melody and Baby Gene were born, Debbie still held her spot in his heart."

Bonnie noticed that performing was beginning to take its toll on Gene: "I've seen him on stage many times and he put on such a show that afterwards he'd just collapse from exhaustion. Basically, Gene was a very strong person. But he still couldn't keep up the pace, all that travelling and playing at a different place every night. He just got exhausted. And he wouldn't go on stage unless he knew he could put on a really good show, so sometimes he'd cancel or just not show up. I've known him to do that many times."

On January 5th, 1959, Gene resumed gigging and played at the

Prom Ballroom in St. Paul with the Big Beats. At the end of the month he played the Division Street Corral in Portland with Clayton Watson and the Silhouettes. That January, Capitol released *Over the Rainbow* b/w *Who's Been Pushing Your Swing?* It was a strange combination, a slow standard for the A side and a risqué rocker for the B side. It didn't go anywhere.

On February 3rd, near Clear Lake, Iowa, three young singing stars, Buddy Holly, Ritchie Valens and the Big Bopper, died in a plane crash. Gene had played with the Big Bopper in Texas and had met Holly when the Caps were playing in New Mexico. Darlene says Gene was shocked and depressed when he heard the news. Kids all over the world were stunned by the loss of their heroes, but they should have mourned for the music as well. This tragic event, rightly or wrongly, marked the decline of rock'n'roll's primitive purity.

That week, the number one song was *Smoke Gets in Your Eyes* by the Platters. The best songs in the top ten were Lloyd Price's *Staggerlee,* Jackie Wilson's *Lonely Teardrops,* and Clyde McPhatter's *It's a Lover's Question,* all of them much closer to R&B than rock'n'roll. But even rhythm'n'blues was going 'pop' as groups like the Drifters started adding string sections and doing bland songs with blander arrangements. This approach, master-minded by producers and A&R men, had only a softening effect on R&B, but it devastated rock'n'roll. At first, pop producers had been amazed by this strange Southern hybrid and had pretty well let the musicians have their own way. Expecting rock'n'roll to go the way of other fads like Davy Crockett hats and hulahoops, they hadn't bothered trying to change it. But by '58 and '59 it dawned on the opportunists that the new music was still around and making big money, so they tried to cash in on it by 'producing' pop stars who sang in what *might* be called the rock'n'roll genre. In other words, they took from rock'n'roll what could be safely assimilated and abandoned its important part, its primitive essence. Thus began the era of the 'teen idols', harmless good-looking boys with an air of conformity and innocence. There was nothing rebellious about Frankie Avalon, Bobby Rydell, Fabian or Paul Anka, but they were just right for what had become the arbiter of teenage taste – American Bandstand.

Philadelphia was the home of Clark's show, and it was also the home of three labels, Cameo-Parkway, Swan, and Chancellor, all of them associated with or partly owned by Clark. They concentrated on 'teen idol' records. In an article in *The Rolling Stone Illustrated History of Rock & Roll*, journalist Gregg Shaw writes:

> Money was indeed a lot of it. The machinery was so well constructed that a good-looking teenager would be spotted on the street (as was Fabian, according to legend), cut a record, and, aided by few bribed DJ's, within a few weeks have a hit on the national charts—no uncertainties, no risks. It was such a blatant racket that in 1960 it came crashing down under government pressure. But while it flourished, the influence of Philadelphia on the musical tastes of young America was staggering, especially when compared with the actual musical value of the records being promoted.... The songs were aimed primarily at teenage girls, the ones in the suburbs who wanted big fluffy candy-coloured images of male niceness on which to focus their pubescent dreams. Charming, wholesome dreamboats, the singers were safe and well-mannered.... [1]

That pretty well sums up the horror of the teen idol fad. In the meantime, for people who cared, there was still 'The Screaming End.'

In the spring of '59, Gene and Darlene were still living in Seaside, Oregon. Gene kept playing around the Northwest with local bands, booked by Pat Mason. For Gene, it might have actually been a relief to not have his own band anymore and to not have to hassle with Thacker, Watt or McLemore. Darlene was pregnant and Gene was probably glad to have more time at home. Although the Blue Caps had broken up, and their records weren't selling very well, Gene was probably making almost as much money as before. He still had a reputation and he no longer had the expense of a seven-man band, a road manager, a chauffeur, a road agent, or a manager

---

1. "The Teen Idols," by Gregg Shaw, pp. 96–100 in *The Rolling Stone Illustrated History of Rock & Roll*, edited by Jim Miller (Random House/Rolling Stone Press, 1980).

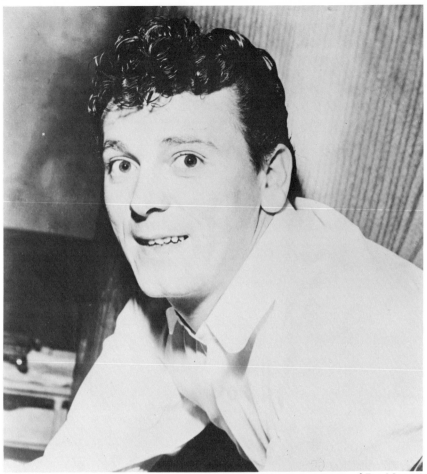

Gene, 1959 (courtesy of Pat Mason)

and agent at home. Now Gene could just drive to a local gig, have a quick rehearsal with a local band already familiar with his material, let them open the show, then come out for one or two sets and make himself several hundred dollars.

In April, Gene flew to Anchorage, Alaska, for a nightclub gig arranged by his friend Whitey Pullen, who was also a singer. Ten days later, Gene phoned Darlene and told her to come up immediately or else he'd cancel his booking. Darlene was almost ready to have their baby, but she went up and stayed with Gene and Whitey and his wife. On April 27th, Darlene went into the hospital in

Anchorage and gave birth to Melody Jean, Gene's first child. Gene was twenty-four years old.

left to right: Melody, Gene, Darlene, Debbie (courtesy of Bonnie Lund)

In the first week of May, the Craddocks and the Pullens flew down to Los Angeles where they rented apartments in the same building in West Covena, a suburb of L.A.

Throughout the spring Gene had been playing with a guitarist, Jerry Merritt, whom he'd met through Clayton Watson. Jerry was a real fan of Gene's and together they put on a great show, often performing as a duo and using only the rhythm section and the sax player from whatever local band was backing them up. "Gene was tired of them long tours," says Jerry. "He didn't want to stay on the road for months at a time anymore."

Darlene says that "Gene really liked Jerry. He respected him. Mostly 'cause he wouldn't take that crap [from Gene] like some of the other guys." Jerry apparently had a strong personality and just shrugged it off.

Jerry describes their stage act at that time: "They'd announce Gene and I'd hit the lick for *Roll Over Beethoven*. We'd be at separate ends of the stage. And when I finished the lick we'd run out toward the microphone and sort of bump into each other. Gene would actually skid across the stage. I don't know how he did it with his bad leg an' all, but he did it!" Their act included *Crazy Arms, Over the Rainbow, Lotta Lovin', Blue Eyes Crying in the Rain, Blue Jean Bop, Pretty Pearly, 'Lula, Chain Gang, Baby Blue, All I Have To Do Is Dream*, and usually ended with *Rocky Road Blues*. Jerry also remembers that Gene took a lot of aspirin – "Two bottles a day, washed 'em down with beer.... That's what killed him" – and concedes that Gene drank a lot of whiskey.

In June, Capitol released *Right Now* b/w *The Night is So Lonely* and Gene's fifth LP, *Sounds Like Gene Vincent,* which used material from the sessions of October '58. The album featured Gene's *In Love Again* and Johnny Burnette's *My Heart,* but some of the best and toughest songs Gene had ever done, like *High Blood Pressure* and *Gone, Gone, Gone,* were *still* left unreleased.

Though 1959 in America was a year of teen idols, in other countries there was still a demand for genuine rock'n'roll. Fans overseas were clamouring for the real thing, so Pat Mason, together with Capitol Records and their Japanese counterpart Toshiba, arranged for Gene to tour for three weeks in Japan.

Gene and Jerry arrived at Tokyo International Airport and were met by 10,000 excited rock'n'roll fans eager to see the first American rocker to tour the Orient. They were taken into downtown Tokyo (about ten miles away) with a huge parade that featured "top officials and famous movie stars, and models."[2] They stayed in the presidential suite of the Nakatsu Hotel and had to be protected from eager fans by twenty policemen, who stayed on guard in the hallways. They travelled to their engagement at the Nichigeki

2. Jerry Merritt.

Jerry and Gene, Japan, 1959 (courtesy of Jerry Merritt)

Jerry and Gene, Japan (courtesy of Jerry Merritt)

Theatre in a convoy of limousines, accompanied by bodyguards. Backed by a Japanese band, they played three shows a day, and each time they were seen by about 20,000 fans. In five days, 286,000 people paid to get in. Japanese currency was worth very little compared to the American dollar and people paid a relatively low price for tickets. Still, Gene was making close to $2,000 a day, and the surviving photographs indicate that Gene and Jerry put on their usual histrionic show in front of a wildly appreciative audience.[3]

After Tokyo they played Yokohama, Yakuska and Osaka, where they played for 45,000 fans. Gene and Jerry also did a couple of TV shows and a lot of interviews for magazines – "About forty a day". According to Jerry, they were continually visited by models and movie starlets and this was the first time he'd ever noticed Gene with anybody but Darlene. Pat Mason remembers that when he first met Gene, "He couldn't tell you on Tuesday who he slept with

---

3. Today, Jerry is still astonished when he thinks about the Japanese Tour. "It was the biggest thing Gene ever done. And nobody even knows about it."

on Sunday." Yet most people say that once Gene was with Darlene he lost interest in other women, though Darlene has intimated that Gene went with other women when she wasn't around. Gene had always enjoyed and always been surrounded by adoring young ladies, but at the same time he seemed to want marriage and children. This he had with Darlene. Gene loved her and was happy to be a father, but he was easily tempted. And in Japan in particular, he was a big star.

Movie starlets or not, Gene missed his wife and kids. He was a nervous fidgety person and he'd already made about $20,000. Jerry says that Gene called Darlene every day. Gene's first child was only two months old and he wanted to go home, but he was cooped up in his hotel room, unable even to go for a walk outside because of the cops in the hallway and the fans in the streets below. So one day he just sneaked off and left. Pat Mason got a call from a Japanese promoter saying that Gene had disappeared. As it turned out, Gene had flown home to see Darlene. Mason told the promoter, "That's okay. Use Jerry. He looks like Gene. He knows all the songs. . . . No one'll know the difference." So Jerry Merritt impersonated Gene for the last four days. And indeed, no one noticed!

Afterwards, Jerry flew to L.A., met Gene, and together they played a few local gigs. It was around this time that Gene wrote *Darlene,* a blues song with jocular but nasty lyrics that start, "Darlene, Darlene, how come you treat your daddy so mean?" Jerry explains that this was written after he had kidded Gene about having to do his own shopping. He feels that Gene was just joking. However, Darlene didn't think it was too funny. No matter how much they cared for each other, Gene and Darlene quarrelled frequently. Clayton Watson remembers being on the road with Gene and hearing him argue with Darlene on the phone: "Gene was a real moody type of guy and he got offended easily. He'd be on the phone with Darlene and hang up on her. Then he'd take it out on himself. He'd withdraw. And that's when he'd start drinkin' a bit more than was good for him."

On the third of August, Gene and Jerry went into the Capitol Tower for a four-day series of sessions. The other musicians were supplied by Capitol: Red Callendar on bass, Sandy Nelson on drums, Jimmy Johnson on piano, Jackie Kelso on tenor sax, and the

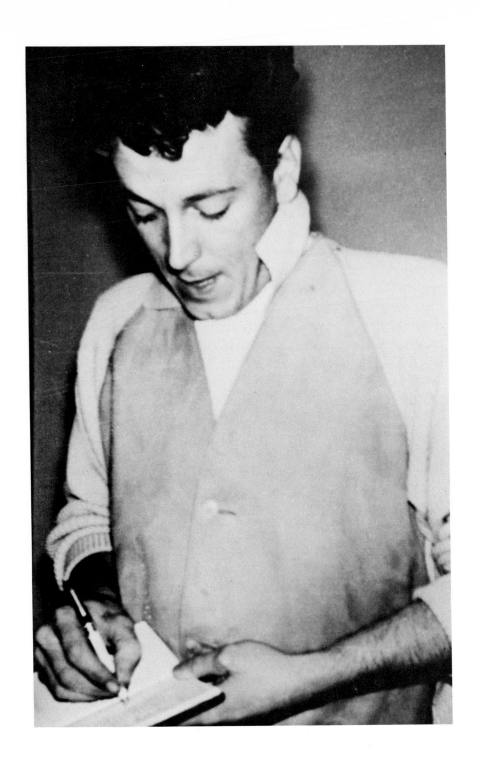

Elligibles, a three-man chorus. On the whole, Gene's sessions with the Blue Caps were generally superior to his recordings with a studio band, but these sessions produced at least four classics, Gene's *Pretty Pearly*, Jerry's *She She Little Sheila*, plus *Wild Cat* and *Right Here on Earth*.

Gene and Darlene had moved to a house in West Covena and Jerry stayed with them for a while. He remembers Gene, Darlene, Debbie and Melody all going to the amusement park at Long Beach and Gene riding the roller-coaster five times in a row. Another time, Gene took Jerry to Johnny Cash's big house and introduced him, then took him around the place. Afterwards, Gene got Cash's pistol and holster and practised quick-draws in front of a big mirror while giving advice to Jerry about the fastest way to draw. Darlene remembers Gene's pistol fetish, but not so fondly: "Gene had about three guns. He usually carried one in a shoulder holster. One time he fired it off in the house and it was just after Debbie had walked by. I was scared to death, as white as a ghost. And Gene had been foolin' around and puttin' it up to his head and stuff. Then when it went off, he wouldn't even apologize!"

For the rest of 1959, Gene lived in Los Angeles and continued touring through California, Oregon and Washington, either with Jerry and a local group, or with Clayton Watson and the Silhouettes. He also played a lot of gigs in Freemont, near San Francisco, at a club called the Garden of Allah which was owned by a couple, Chuck and Johnny Wayne, who became good friends with Gene. Chuck's band, the Heartbeats, would back Gene up. Usually, Friday night featured country music and Saturday featured rock'n'roll, but Gene played both nights since he could appeal to both crowds. Chuck's wife, Johnny, says, "Gene's music was always loud, but I learned to like it. Gene was his own individual. I can still remember him sitting around the kitchen table, playing his guitar and singing."

In November, while Gene was touring the Midwest, the ongoing practice of payola was finally brought to the public's attention. It started with the investigation of NBC's Twenty-One quiz show. The loser had already confessed to taking a bribe, and the $129,000 winner, Professor C. L. Van Doren, admitted that he'd been provided with the correct answers. NBC immediately cancelled this and two other similar shows and CBS eliminated all its quiz shows. Government investigators soon switched to the music industry when it was revealed that some of the quiz show producers had been getting kickbacks from music publishers for playing the publishers' songs on their shows.

On November 19th, the New York District Attorney's office got into the act and served subpoenas on a string of record companies, demanding their books. Sleuths from the Senate Subcommittee were investigating in six cities. Alan Freed was dismissed from WABC on November 21st after he refused on principle to sign a statement denying that he'd received payola. Freed was also fired from his TV show on WNEW. Several months later when he was subpoenaed before a grand jury in New York, Freed refused to testify, though he was offered immunity. Three deejays in Boston were fired, two in Cleveland and one in Philadelphia, but it was Freed they were really after and it was Freed who took the fall. In December, 1962, he pleaded guilty to two charges of commercial bribery and was fined $300. Then, fifteen months later, he was charged with tax evasion on over $50,000 in payola which he'd allegedly received between 1957 and 1959.[4]

Dick Clark appeared before the same investigators and admitted that he had an interest in 27% of his 'spins', but said that he'd already given up whole or part interest in thirty-three music firms. It was generally felt by people in the trade that the amount of payola Freed received was only a small percentage of what Clark derived from the sale of all his music-related firms.[5] Prior to his trial for tax evasion, Alan Freed died of alcoholism at age 43. Clark admitted to owning rights to 160 songs, but claimed that all but forty-three were given to him. He denied ever receiving payola, was never indicted, and went on to an even more successful career.[6]

---

4. Arnold Shaw, *The Rockin' 50's* (New York: Dutton, 1974).
5. Ibid.
6. "The Payola Scandal," by John Morthland, pp. 101–103 in *The Rolling Stone Illustrated History of Rock & Roll*, edited by Jim Miller (Random House/Rolling Stone Press, 1980).

President Eisenhower urged the Federal Trade Commission to clean up "the whole mess", and the immediate result was that three record companies and six distributors were charged with receiving bribes. Hysteria engulfed the music industry. One station, KDAY in California, forced its employees to take lie-detector tests that were filmed and broadcast by a local television station! The overall result was that most stations were more reluctant than ever to play rock'n'roll records lest they be suspected of being bribed to do so.

Ever since the advent of rock'n'roll, parents, politicians, journalists and clergymen had agitated against it, the most common argument being that it encouraged promiscuity, moral turpitude, and the mixing of races. By their standards, it probably did.

The fifties was a decade of immense social change, and this is perhaps best represented by the desegregation movement. Desegregation was touted as proof that American society was not racist, and the well-publicized American Dream suppressed any admission of the hypocrisy of this view. But the attack on rock'n'roll, because it led to the 'mixing of races', made the hypocrisy obvious. Rock'n'roll music's main strength, which to the conservatives was its main fault, was its honesty, whether in its unashamed sexuality or its open admiration for black culture.

Payola was shallow aggressive materialism at its worst, the result of which was the destruction of early rock'n'roll in America. But the conservative elements in American society had recognized that rock'n'roll was anti-authoritarian, and successfully so. Now they used the payola *scandal* to try to destroy the music.

For Gene it no longer mattered. At the beginning of December he was leaving the country. Gene had recently become involved with a new manager, Norm Riley, a middle-aged businessman, and Riley did the best possible thing for Gene at the best possible time. He arranged for Gene to tour Britain, where he was to find his largest and most faithful audience.

London, 1960 (courtesy of Adrian Owlett)

7

Black Leather Rebel

Gene was extremely strange. He had a very strong death wish. He was always buying guns and knives.... He was sort of a natural lunatic. He never shot anybody with those guns he had, but he sure frightened a lot of people.
— Joe Brown

The day before Gene arrived in London, the *New Musical Express* published an article called 'Break of Dawn Greeting for "The Screaming End" – Gene Vincent.' The article mentioned that Gene hadn't had a hit in Britain for three years, but that he had a loyal following and, along with Frank Sinatra, was one of Capitol's biggest sellers. Saturday the 5th of December, 1959, Gene arrived at Heathrow airport at six in the morning and was probably surprised by the greeting he received. On hand were reporters, television and record company executives, celebrities, and fans, plus a band led by Joe Brown playing *Be-Bop-A-Lula*. Afterwards, Gene went straight to a reception at a downtown restaurant, where he did a radio interview, then had a brief rehearsal with Marty Wilde's Wildcats.

The next day he made a guest appearance on the Marty Wilde Show at the Tooting theater in Granada, on the outskirts of London. The warm-up acts were Terry Dene, Vince Eager, Dickie Pride and Johnny Gentle. After Marty Wilde's set, Gene limped on stage in a red and black sweater and black pants, and before the applause died down, he grabbed the mike, swung his left leg over the stand, turned a full circle and tore into *Be-Bop-A-Lula*. The audience, mostly teenage girls, went wild, and after Gene's short set they kept yelling out, "We want Gene! We want Gene!" Joe Brown played lead guitar on this date and he remembers it well: "To me, being on stage with Gene Vincent was very exciting. I was nervous, of course. We'd had hardly any rehearsal. Gene's voice was great and much louder than the band. There were lots of screaming girls, and as a musician I couldn't understand why they didn't just listen to the music."

On the following Thursday, Gene went up to Manchester with Joe Brown to tape some songs for Jack Good's TV program, Boy Meets Girl. The house band consisted mostly of players from Ted Heath's band. In all, they had four saxophones and three guitars, but Gene just used one sax player and the rhythm section, plus the Vernon Girls, a three-woman singing group. Altogether they taped eleven songs: *Be-Bop-A-Lula, Summertime, Baby Blue, Frankie and Johnny, Blue Jean Bop, Say Mama, Five Days, I Got A Baby, Rocky Road Blues, Right Here On Earth* and *Wild Cat*, but the show was divided into three segments and broadcast on three different occasions. The first was on December 12th and there was no verbal intro. The screen grew dark and only Joe Brown's guitar could be seen. Then, as the words 'Gene Vincent' appeared on the screen, Gene could be seen bent over the mike in the background. The camera closed in as Joe Brown and the band started *Baby Blue*, and pulled back when Gene began singing. Gene picked up the mikestand and walked toward the camera until his face filled the screen. Up in Newcastle, a young rock'n'roll fan named Steve Aynsley was watching the program: "I'd never seen anything like it in my life. And I realized that nobody could ever make such an impression on me again. He wore black leather and the light faded as he moved around. He looked like a demon!"[1]

On Monday, December 15th, Gene flew to Paris and appeared at the Olympia theatre for a TV show in front of a live audience.[2] The fans went wild and rushed the stage. Gene's new black suede jacket was ripped off his back and he had to buy another one for his second show later in the evening. A young Cockney ex-prize fighter named Henry Henroid had accompanied Gene as road manager and he remembers that after the show the Olympia's owner, Bruno Coquatrix, ran up and said excitedly, "I've never seen such an

1. Steve Aynsley is now President of the Gene Vincent Fan Club in Britain.
2. See cover photo.

124

audience reaction in my life! I want to book this guy!"

His popularity in Britain and France was confirmed, and Gene spent the rest of December touring Germany, mostly playing American army bases.

London, 1960 (courtesy of Adrian Owlett)

On the sixth of January, 1960, Gene began a twelve-day tour of Britain starting at the Granada theatre in Maidstone. His back-up group was the Rockets and the warm-up acts were the Bachelors, Reith Keller, Al Saxon and Wee Willie Harris. The 'compère' was Don Arden, who later became Gene's manager. On the 11th of January he played the Granada in Kingston and a young rock'n'roll fan named Adrian Owlett witnessed a spectacle that changed his life:[3] "That show totally did it for me. The whole audience had never seen anything like Gene Vincent before. You could feel the suppressed tension in the air. . . . Gene was given an amazing build-up by Don Arden. All the house lights went out. We could hear the curtains being pulled back and then this beautiful high intro, 'Weeelll. . . . ' A pin spot went around the stage illuminating every-one in turn, then it opened up and hit Gene crouched beside the drummer. He wore a bright green outfit with a monogram, black shoes, white socks, hair way over his forehead. . . . The beat went mad, and, to the continuing strains of *Rocky Road Blues*, so did the audience.

---

3. Adrian Owlett would become Gene's U.K. manager, and a rock'n'roll producer. He is now owner of Magnum Force Records.

"Without saying a word he broke into *Say Mama*.... He went down to his knees, the mike was outstretched, then it was up high in the air with Gene singing up to the ceiling, still on his knees. Up he got, and shook, stomped, and rocked about the stage. He clambered onto the piano and jumped back to the floor and still the beat continued. The audience went wild.... He explained the story behind *Frankie and Johnny* before singing it, and after that he told the audience that he had just toured the world and England had given him the best reception yet. Hardly finished speaking, he broke straight off into *Wild Cat* and the audience went berserk. In the sax break, he fell to his knees, put his hands on his hips and shook himself in time to the music. He then jumped up and stood in the so-familiar mike-out left-leg-back crouching position. Next, he slowed the pace and sang *Summertime* and sat on the edge of the stage. The lights turned blue and the audience was, for the first time, hushed.

"He then rocked straight back into *Baby Blue,* and stomped and bopped through *Dance to the Bop* and *Dance in the Streets.* Gene then said he'd like to sing us his favourite number and again the lights went out and he began *Important Words,* but no sooner had the song ended than he plunged into *Brand New Beat* and again the audience went wild. Several girls were crying whilst many, many fellas were jiving in the aisles. By now the crowd was frantic and Gene drawled something about how much he'd enjoyed the show. Then, without warning, he swung his left leg in a 360 degree circle over the mike and broke straight into *Be-Bop-A-Lula*!

"Afterwards Gene literally staggered to the wings, but the audience chanted, 'More! More! More!' and 'Gene! Gene! Gene!' Don Arden went offstage and brought Gene back. He looked shy and embarrassed, but was obviously very, very happy. He thanked everyone again, then he slid his leg backwards, pushing the mike forward, threw his head back and rocked into *Blue Jean Bop.* Then he did *Right Here On Earth* and this was followed by yet another *Be-Bop-A-Lula.* The curtain finally closed. The time now was 11:20, twenty minutes overrun. I might add that at midnight there were still young people, inside and out, screaming and shouting for 'The Screaming End'. It was unforgettable. After that there was no one else.... Presley: forget it! When he got out of the army we went to see *G.I. Blues* and it was just total disbelief watching Elvis turn into a wimp. It was pure schlock. When he did *Wooden Heart* I thought I'd puke. . . . But Gene never became a wimp. He set a yardstick by which performances can be judged and are judged."

Gene, Joe Brown, Billy Fury, Eddie Cochran

By the middle of January, *Wild Cat*, released at the beginning of December, had reached the number 21 position on the *New Musical Express* best seller chart. Eddie Cochran's *Hallelujah, I Love Her So* was at number 28 the following week. Darlene flew over with Debbie and Melody and stayed with Gene in his apartment near Picadilly Circus. It was a comfortable flat and every day two maids came in and cleaned up, but Darlene wasn't particularly impressed with London, or the tremendous response Gene was getting from his English fans. Darlene had always hated travelling in any event, and for good reason: "There was no way I could be a real mother, living out of a suitcase."

At the end of the month Eddie Cochran flew over to do a month-long tour of England, Scotland and Wales with Gene. Gene hired a nanny to look after the kids so that Darlene could come, and they took the train up to Glasgow to do a week at the Empire theatre. It was produced by Larry Parnes and billed as 'A Fast Moving Anglo-

American Beat Show'. The whole show played twice nightly, once at 6:15 and once at 8:30. The first half of the show featured the Tony Sheridan Trio, Joe Brown and Eddie Cochran, and the second half featured Georgie Fame, Billy Fury, Billy Raymond, and 'The Rock'n'Roll Idol of Millions,' Gene Vincent. This was the first *all* rock'n'roll show ever to tour Britain. Previously, when rockers such as Buddy Holly or Jerry Lee Lewis had come over, they had played on variety shows, as Gene had done in January with Al Saxon and Wee Willie Harris.

According to Joe Brown, Glasgow was a tough town to play: "It was the worst gig we ever did. The crowds there were extremely rough. They generally threw bottles at the performers whether they disliked them or not. Glasgow was known in the business as 'The Death Place'. If you could go down in the Glasgow Empire, you could go down anywhere. But it was generally the sex-image types that got physically attacked, the pretty-boy types. Pool ol' Billy Fury had a bad time. I was in the wings and I could hear the whiskey bottles flying past. The girls loved him up there, but the guys took umbrage. The band eventually deserted him and left him standing there! But Eddie Cochran went down good. And Gene did very well."

Under the title 'Vincent, Cochran Rock Glasgow!', a Glasgow paper reported that:

Gene Vincent and Eddie Cochran descended on Glasgow Empire on Monday with a frenzied swoop, evoking screams galore from the delighted fans. Judging by their reaction, the show will register strongly with admirers of Eddie Cochran's forceful singing act and Gene Vincent's leather-clad contortions-cum-singing. The pity was that both these artists' words could scarcely be heard against the instrumental backing and the audience shouting.

Through *Hallelujah,* Eddie built up to an earlier hit *C'mon Everybody* and soon had the customers in the beat mood. His only tactical error was in talking about being in "England", resulting in cries of "You're in Scotland!"

Gene Vincent, on the other hand, is a more flamboyant showman, almost cuddling his microphone, kneeling and crawling on the stage, and generally leaping about like some leather-clad spaceman from another planet. This rock'n'roller built up to a frantic finale, before all the artists joined on stage for a frenzied rock session.

Darlene and Gene (courtesy of Serge Schlawick)

The week in Glasgow was a great reunion for Gene, Darlene and Eddie. Darlene remembers that Gene and Eddie would stay up late playing guitars, singing and writing songs: "Eddie was a very bubbly person. He was high-spirited and easy going. He was a nice guy, and very good looking. But he knew it. Though he didn't let it go to his head. Him and Gene would stay up half the night, playing their guitars and acting crazy." While they were in Scotland, Gene went to a fabric shop and bought a bolt of cloth in the Craddock tartan, along with a tam-o'-shanter. Later he had the material made into a suit and wore it in his stage act.

In Glasgow, Darlene became pregnant again. She comments, "Gene thought it was great. He was happy and wanted to have a boy. But I wasn't so sure. We had a lot of problems. . . . Gene sort of had a split personality. One side was an angel. . . the other side was the devil." After she'd been in Britain for about a month, Darlene flew back to Portland and stayed with Bonnie Lund while Gene completed the tour.

Gene and Eddie did some taping for Jack Good's TV show Boy Meets Girl, and by now Gene had adopted his black leather outfit on a more or less permanent basis. Jack Good has taken credit for suggesting it to Gene after seeing a production of Hamlet where the lead role was played by some fellow dressed all in black. It's just as likely that Gene got the idea from Joe Brown who was a motorcycle enthusiast and often wore black leather suits on stage.

For the second series of Boy Meets Girl shows, both Gene and Joe wore black leather jackets and pants, though Joe also wore a white shirt and tie. Joe's jacket was cut like a sports jacket, but Gene's was a jerkin-style pullover worn over a black t-shirt. For the rest of his career Gene would be associated with black leather and all its connotations of greasy-haired punks and hoodlums, as if Gene could always be as hard and tough as his music. Years later, in the antipathy and conflict between the Mods and Rockers, Gene's biker image would be adopted by a whole cult of anti-social hoods who were violently hostile to the pop sound of the mod beat groups and the seemingly effete clothing fashions and lifestyle of their fans. In the mid-sixties, holiday rumbles between Mods and Rockers at seaside resorts such as Brighton made headlines all around the world, and later these conflicts were emulated by the working-class skinheads of the mid-seventies.

As the years passed, pop music became wimpier and the new British groups took on a cuddly cuteness that endeared them to parents as well as fans. The music and the mythology of the early rockers like Holly, Cochran, and Vincent, created an enormous rift between the leather-clad punks of the fifties and the consumer-mad, scooter-propelled mods of the mid-sixties. To the Mods, the Rockers were anachronisms living in the past. And though some of the new bands, like the Yardbirds, the Rolling Stones, and the Pretty Things, played music that was just as tough as that of the fifties, the Rockers were repelled by the apparently feminine shoulder-length hair and sartorial elegance of the new groups. The image being as important to them as the music, they stuck to their greasy ducktails, drapes and bluejeans and their indispensable black leather jackets and hated everything that the new music stood for. These were the fans that stuck by Gene to the bitter end.

Gene was on the cover of the British music magazine *Hit Parader*, and it also featured an interview with him. When asked what he most liked about Britain he replied, "I get the greatest kick out of the historical things – Madame Tussaud's, the Changing of the Guard, the Parliament Buildings. . . . I also like being able to smoke in the movies, which you can't do back home." He was asked what he liked *least* about Britain and said, "Without a doubt I'd say the weather. It's always so darned gloomy! Another thing I can't get used to is the prejudice against bright colours. If I go out in a light blue suit, everybody turns around and stares." What Gene missed most was "Late night television. I'm a great TV addict, but it's all over the by time I've finished my shows at night. Back home it goes on until four or five in the morning." He mentioned that his favourite shows were mainly westerns, especially Maverick. When asked about hobbies, he said, "I guess you could say speed was a hobby of mine, you know, automobiles and motorcycles. Back home I have a Pontiac saloon and a Triumph Thunderbird bike. But I haven't done any driving since I've been in Britain. I can't get used to driving on the wrong side of the road." Gene answered a question about his motorcycle accident this way: "I was waiting at a traffic light when a lorry came along and hit me. I was in the hospital for eighteen months." He mentioned that he still got his pension of $127 a month and added, "It keeps me in cigarettes, I guess." When asked what the most important thing an up-and-coming singer should have, he said, "Determination. . . because nobody else is ever gunna worry about you. I decided a long time ago that I wasn't good-looking, so I would have to get by on my ability to perform."

Gene also mentioned that his favourite song was *Important Words*, one of his most beautiful ballads, and it suggests the 'romance' that was at the heart of both Gene and the music of the 'fifties. While his fans admired him for the tough hard-rocking songs of his stage act like *Say Mama, Baby Blue,* and *Rocky Road Blues*, his own favourite was a tender ballad more expressive of a sentimental Southern Gentleman than a 'Wildcat'. The lyrics reveal a gentle, almost asexual courtesy that is totally lacking in Gene's rockers:

The days, the nights, those, those lovely hours
We, we spent makin' plans
Have made both of us feel, feel the same
Since we first held hands.
Important Words. That's all I got,
They say, say say say say, 'I love you.'

That February, Gene and Eddie, along with the rest of the show, played at the Empire in north-west London, the Gaumont in Cardiff, the Hippodrome in Manchester and the Empire in Leeds. Their road manager was Hal Carter, and Joe Brown remembers all the trials and tribulations that Carter endured: "Poor ol' Hal. He went through hell with those guys. The theatres were always surrounded with crazy teenagers and Hal had to try and get Gene and Eddie out secretly. But he always seemed to screw it up. One time in Leeds the kids chased the cab down the street and caught up to it at a traffic light. All I saw was a bunch of hands coming in the cab door, then it slammed shut and Gene said in that funny voice of his, 'Eddie.... They got my trousers, Eddie!'"

Gene and Eddie (courtesy of Serge Schlawick)

132

Eddie and Gene (courtesy of Serge Schlawick)

Joe remembers Gene always fooling around with weapons: "Gene was extremely strange. He had a very strong death wish. He was always buying guns and knives and he was in a lot of pain with that leg. . . . One time Gene had a big knife and cut Hal Carter's suit right off. He didn't touch Hal, but his suit was in threads! And this was just a lark! But you never really knew with Gene. He was sort of a natural lunatic. He never shot anybody with those guns he had, but he sure frightened a lot of people. Me and Eddie Cochran used to keep an eye on him, and if he got a little bit out of hand we'd go over and talk to him. Eddie was sort of an older brother to Gene and looked after him. Gene would be sitting there looking sort of maudlin and Eddie would ask, 'Are you okay, Gene?' And Gene would say, 'Eddie, tell Hal to get me a hamburger.' Or if someone was bothering him he'd say, 'Eddie, get this guy outa here! He's buggin' me!'

"Gene used to really gear himself up for the show. He was pretty moody and he drank an awful lot, partly because of his leg. But he was very depressed. He was such a nice guy, but he did have a problem, I think. I've known guys that drank more than Gene, but he used to get very upset sometimes and worry about his wife. But he was a great artist and when he was onstage he would pour his heart into the microphone. And one time I thought, 'Man, this guy lives for singing!' Sometimes he'd try to talk to the audience, but he'd end up starting to ramble like, 'Here's a song for Darlene. Darlene's my wife." And I could tell he was worried about her."

In March, Gene did two dates on the radio show, Saturday Club, one of them with Eddie Cochran where they did a duet on the country-rocker *White Lightning*.[4] The rest of the month was taken up with week-long dates as part of Larry Parnes' Fast Moving Anglo-American Beat Show. The back-up band was Marty Wilde's Wildcats, and they did a week each at the Hippodromes in Birmingham and Manchester, and the Empires in Liverpool and Newcastle. Steve Aynsley saw the show in Newcastle: "Eddie was suffering from eye-strain and wore dark glasses. He had his back to the audience when the curtain came up, then he turned and went into *Something Else* and the audience went wild, screaming and so on. He was a real showman. He did *Sweet Little Sixteen* and asked if there was anybody in the audience who was sixteen. A girl stood up and Eddie took off his glasses to look at her. . . .

"When Gene came on, at first the curtain was closed. Then they strummed the first chord and Gene went into the "Weeeellll. . . " of *Rocky Road Blues*. Then the curtains opened and Gene was at the very front of the stage with his leg stuck out on the spotlights. He lifted the whole mike-stand up over his head. Then he brought it down and used it as a prop. The audience screamed and went wild! At this point rock'n'roll had really gone soft. Cliff Richard and Adam Faith had gone pop. So this was really different. *Wild Cat* was Gene's latest release and he did that and *Right Here on Earth, Frankie and Johnny, Summertime, Say Mama, Baby Blue, Blue Jean Bop* and a version of Jack Scott's *What in the World's Come Over You*. Then he said, 'We want to do the song that started the whole thing off. . . .' He kicked his leg over the microphone and did *Be-Bop-A-Lula*. Gene got a standing ovation, then he brought out the whole

---

4. The tapes from the Saturday Club have recently been released under the title *Rock'n'Roll Heroes* on Rockstar Records.

cast and they all did *Whole Lotta Shakin'*. It was just great!"

London, 1960 (courtesy of Adrian Owlett)

On April 1st, after finishing their week in Manchester, Gene and Eddie were invited to judge a beauty contest in nearby Oldham, and some interesting photographs have survived of Gene presenting a sash to the winning beauty queen and of Gene and Eddie cuddling up to her. Both of them look jaded and lecherous while she smiles sweetly between them, Gene in his leathers and Eddie showing his hairy chest.

In January, Capitol had released Gene's new single (not released in the States), *My Heart* b/w *I've Got To Get To You Yet,* both written by Johnny Burnette, and on March 10th it broke into the charts, eventually reaching the number 16 position. That month Capitol also released Gene's fifth album, *Crazy Times,* recorded the previous August with Jerry Merritt. It wasn't as good as Gene's LP's with the Blue Caps, but it did well in Britain.

Gene and Eddie kept touring and on April 4th they started a week at the Empire in Finsbury Park, a district in North London. Adrian Owlett and a friend tried to get tickets for both shows that evening, but the earlier one was already sold out, although they'd arrived about noon. They stood outside listening to the band rehearsing, then saw Henry Henroid arrive with Gene's black leather suit. Apparently Hal Carter couldn't hack it, and Henry was now road manager. Adrian had heard about Gene's leathers and was eager to see them on him. He comments: "Even the green outfit he'd worn in January had been scandalous." At the Empire that night, Adrian finally got to see Gene in his black leathers: "It was just another unbelievable show. Gene was just staggeringly good. He consolidated his position as being head and shoulders above everyone else. It was just pure rock'n'roll. I left the show just drained, drained of everything except enthusiasm for what I'd just seen."

Gene and Eddie were sharing a flat at the Stratford Court Hotel in Oxford Street and Henry Henroid remembers some lunacy: "One time Gene and Eddie came in with some ladies and they were pretty loaded. They had a double room but they'd forgot their key, so they just booted the door down. I got a call from the irate hotel manager and had to go down and pay for the door. I went up to their room and there they were in bed with the door still hanging from the bottom hinges! They'd had to step over it to get inside!"

About this time Gene and Eddie were interviewed in their flat by journalist Keith Goodwin and his article featured a photo of Gene singing *My Heart* with Eddie accompanying him on the guitar. When Goodwin arrived, Gene and Eddie were listening to Brenda Lee's *Sweet Nuthins* played at full blast and they both raved about the record. Gene mentioned that he was always being asked for souvenirs and usually handed out American dimes, which the reporter explained were 'small silver coins.' When asked about travelling, Gene complained that he didn't like British trains and Eddie said he was looking forward to some home-cooking when he got home. Both Gene and Eddie were planning to go back to the States in ten days. Goodwin ended the article by saying, 'A nice couple of fellows - quiet, polite, unspoiled and as devoted to their fans as they are to them.'

On Sunday, April 17th, after a week at the Hippodrome in Bristol, they rented a car to take them to Heathrow airport for their flight back to America. Their next British gig wasn't until April 30th and they were looking forward to some time off. Eddie had his girlfriend Sharon Sheely with him, and Gene was eager to get back to Darlene and the kids in Portland. The driver and Pat Tomkins were in front, and Eddie, Sharon and Gene were in the back. Gene was asleep when the driver, hurtling at 70 m.p.h. through the small town of Chippenham in Wiltshire, lost control and skidded off the road into a lamp post. The car was completely destroyed. Eddie Cochran was thrown against the roof, then out the door. He died of head injuries later that day at St. Martin's Hospital in Bath, without ever regaining consciousness. Gene was in the same hospital with a broken collar-bone and broken ribs. His crippled leg was also injured and had to be put back in a cast. The driver was charged with dangerous driving and was fined and banned from driving for fifteen years.[5]

In rock'n'roll history, April 17th, 1960, stands in equal importance with February 3rd, 1959, the day Buddy Holly died. No other occasions have been so tragic for true rockers, and no other events have moved so quickly from history to mythology, reaffirming the idea that the good die young, and that artists, in doing so, retain their vitality and integrity forever.

For Gene, Eddie's death was a personal tragedy. He'd lost his best friend and he would never recover from it. Henry Henroid recalls that a couple of years later when he went to Gene's dressing room to call him on stage, "Gene looked up with a sad face and quietly and sincerely said, 'Tell Eddie I'll be right out.'"

According to Joe Brown, "Eddie's death really shook Gene up. As far as I could tell, they were best friends. Rumour has it Gene would also have been killed if he hadn't been so pissed. But he was so relaxed that he was just thrown around a little. I always sort of felt sorry for him. He seemed like a very emotional and sensitive guy. You never joked around with Gene. He was too serious. . . . But I learned a lot from those guys. They were very much an inspiration." Henry Henroid adds, "I think the 'schizophrenia' set in when Eddie Cochran died. Gene was lost. They were like brothers."

---

5. It's said that Rockers in Bristol *still* spend their weekends looking for 'the guy who killed Eddie Cochran.' Apparently he gets a regular thrashing every time they find him.

(courtesy of Serge Schlawick)

Gene was only in the hospital for three days, and afterwards he flew back to the States to see Darlene. Photos of Gene walking out to the plane show a broken man, his left arm in a sling, a heavy overcoat draped over his shoulders, his left leg in a cast, his face a mask of sorrow.

Darlene says, "Gene was really shook up. He and Eddie were very close. He talked a lot about Eddie and sent flowers to the funeral. But he didn't go because he didn't think he'd be able to handle it."

Strangely enough, Gene didn't cancel the rest of his gigs and continue his convalescence, but flew back to England and played at the Gaumont theater in Hanley on the 30th. The next day he played at Lewisham and the gig was written up in the *New Musical Express* with the headline 'Gene Vincent Sings Eddie's Favourites':

Gene Vincent paid tribute to his close buddy, the late Eddie Cochran, when he resumed his long tour of Britain at the Lewisham Gaumont on Sunday, following his brief holiday in the States. "I want to sing a song for you now," he announced, rubbing his left shoulder softly, the collarbone of which was injured during the fatal car crash recently, "Eddie's favourite song." He then broke into a sad falsetto-voiced version of *Over the Rainbow*. Girls in the audience cried and moaned during it. But that over, Gene, in a new tartan outfit, was on the rock-a-beat trail again with *Be-Bop-A-Lula*. Despite a crooked leg and shoulder, he displayed more life and action than his able-bodied co-artists, and he gets more from his instrumental group (Colin Green and the Beat Boys) by being one of them. No standing in front of them to sing. He mingles right in among them and gives them generous solos, egging them on to greater heights of abandon. Yes, Gene is a great performer who makes others work for him – including the audience.

Obviously, Gene didn't only make the band and the audience work for him, but the memory of Eddie as well. Crippled physically and psychologically, for the rest of his life Gene would use his physical infirmities, his personal problems and his mythological associations to gain sympathy.

That May he continued doing one-nighters in Cheltenham, Salisbury, Guildford and Hull. On the 11th of May Gene went into the EMI studio in St. John's Wood in London and recorded two songs, *Pistol Packin' Mama,* a 1940's country standard by Al Dexter, and *Weeping Willow,* a slow ballad which featured the Norrie Paramor Orchestra, the first time Gene had ever featured strings in any of his songs. While Gene did a great version of *Weeping Willow,* the orchestra was certainly superfluous. However, the version of *Pistol Packin' Mama,* recorded with the Beat Boys, was in a no-nonsense rockin' style using an arrangement by Eddie Cochran, and when the song was later released, Cochran was given credit for it on the label.[6] The rest of May was taken up with one-nighters in Halifax, Chester, Wolverhampton, Romford, Brighton and Wembley, and at the end of the month Gene went to Italy and did a TV show where he performed *Blue Jean Bop* and *Baby Blue.*

In June, Capitol released *Pistol Packin' Mama* b/w *Weeping Willow* and by the middle of the month it was at the number sixteen position in England. Eddie Cochran was then at number three with his posthumous release. It had the sad but ironic title *Three Steps to Heaven.*

For the first three weeks of June, Gene continued doing one-nighters in Rochester, Norwich, Ipswich, York, Glasgow, Southampton, Plymouth, London, Nottingham, Carlisle and Sunderland. Alan Vince, who was the head of the Gene Vincent fan club, saw Gene in Rochester at the beginning of the month. He got there early to watch Gene rehearse with the Beat Boys, saw Gene come in with a newspaper and heard him shout out, "Eddie's at number four!" Gene was happy with Eddie's belated success, but while he waited to go onstage he stood in his dressing room throwing a knife into the door. Alan Vince writes: 'Gene was a different person on stage, completely and utterly lost in the world of whining guitars, pounding drums and screaming fans. One moment he was

---

6. The Beat Boys featured Colin Greene on lead guitar and Georgie Fame on keyboards. The rhythm section has never been acknowledged, but it is thought to be the same as the Wildcats': Brian Locking on bass and Brian Bennett on drums.

still as a statue with his left leg straight out behind him. Then suddenly he would spring up, hold the heavy mike above his head, then fall to the floor, his whole body beating time to the music. He would mingle in with the backing group, becoming one of them. Gene rarely looked at the audience. His head would always be turned towards the wings or facing the group. Sometimes he seemed to be staring at a 'vision' high above the sea of faces in the theater.... No group *backed* Gene: they worked with, and for, him.... A theater manager observed as he watched Gene one night, "The way that fellow's going, he'll fall apart any moment!"'[7]

As it turned out, Gene did fall apart. Afterwards he claimed he didn't even remember what happened, but on the 18th of June at the Royal Theater in Nottingham Gene announced to a spellbound and sympathetic audience that he had just received a telegram saying that his eighteen-month-old daughter Melody had died of pneumonia. He said he was cancelling the rest of the tour so he could fly back to see his wife Darlene.

Months later, Gene told reporters that he was the victim of a hoax and never found out who sent the telegram, but Darlene is convinced that Gene just made up the whole story so he could get out of his contract. At any rate, Gene put on a convincing act, crying on stage about his baby daughter, and the next day he flew back to Portland, cancelling his forthcoming dates in Liverpool, Birmingham, Cardiff and Blackpool. This was the first time that Gene had mixed his personal life so closely with his career and from now until his decline, they became increasingly confused and intermingled.

Gene took the summer off and spent it with Darlene and the kids. He told Darlene that he was seriously thinking of giving up performing and becoming a deejay. Darlene thought this was a great idea, although she says that Gene's claims of owning shares in radio stations were either lies or fantasies. Previously he had told several reporters that he was thinking of giving up show business to become a farmer. The truth is that Gene couldn't have given up performing even if his life depended on it, and his life did depend on it.

---

7. Alan Vince, *I Remember Gene Vincent* (Prescott: Vintage Rock'n'Roll Appreciation Society, 1977).

If he didn't keep performing, he'd go crazy from frustration. But if he continued to tour, he'd burn out.

On October 13th, 1960, Darlene gave birth to a baby boy. He was called Gene Junior and affectionately called Baby Gene by family and friends. A local paper published this announcement in their births column: 'Craddock – to Mr. and Mrs. Vincent Gene Craddock, 1515 N. Buffalo, Portland, a baby boy born Oct. 13th at Vancouver Memorial hospital. Weight 8 pounds 2½ ounces.' Gene and Darlene were very pleased.

In September, Capitol Records had released *Anna Annabelle* b/w *Pistol Packin' Mama* in the States. In November, in Britain, they released *Anna Annabelle* b/w *Accentuate the Positive*. Neither made the charts.

In November, Gene played at the Prom Ballroom in St. Paul with Wanda Jackson, another Capitol artist, and in December he played there again with the Fendermen. A young woman named DiAnne Kaslow saw both these shows and Gene was amazingly fit, obviously recovered from the ordeal of the previous spring, and put on a fantastic performance.

On the 10th of January, 1961, Gene went down to Hollywood and recorded four tunes with the Jimmy Haskell Orchestra: *Crazy Beat, I'm Gonna Catch Me a Rat, It's Been Nice* and *That's the Trouble With Love*. The next day he returned and did *Good Lovin', Mister Loneliness, Teardrops* and *If You Want My Lovin'*. Most of the material was fairly good, and the instrumental accompaniment was adequate, but afterwards Capitol added strings and a female chorus to almost every song. This was Gene's first experiment with pop music, and though it's certainly at least as good as what other contemporary singers such as Bobby Rydell, Bobby Vee, and Neil Sedaka were doing, it was a long way from the Blue Caps.

In America at this time, Elvis Presley was at number one with a soppy ballad called *Are You Lonesome Tonight* and there wasn't a single rock'n'roll song in the top ten. The only good songs making the *Billboard* Top 100 were R&B tunes such as *New Orleans* by Gary U.S. Bonds (who also came from Norfolk), and *Let's Go, Let's Go, Let's Go* by Hank Ballard and the Midnighters. In Britain, Johnny Tillotson was at number one with an idiotic tune, *Poetry in Motion*, and there weren't any rock'n'roll songs in the top twenty. Elvis

St. Paul, 1960 (courtesy of Di Anne Kaslow)

St. Paul, 1960 (courtesy of DiAnne Kaslow)

Presley was at number four with his own personal favourite, *It's Now or Never*, a wretched song more suitable to Presley's idol, Dean Martin.

Shortly after the Hollywood sessions, Gene flew back to London. Before he left he asked Darlene to rent a house in the Bay Area of California: "Gene hated the rain in the Northwest. He said it bothered his leg. He sent me some money from England and I rented a big house in Niles, not far from where our friends Chuck and Johnny lived. Gene used to phone and he asked me to go over to England and bring the kids with me. He thought that life on the road was normal. But I didn't want to go. I didn't want Gene to go either, but England was the only place Gene was selling records and he knew it."

Don Arden, Gene's English manager, Henry Henroid, his road manager, and Alan Vince, the head of his U.K. fan club, met him at the London airport. Gene wore a white leather jacket and a checked shirt and Alan Vince recalls: "He looked much better than I'd ever seen him. The long rest had worked wonders."[8] A few days later a newspaper article called 'Now Gene Must Face the Music' quoted Gene as saying, 'I should have stayed in hospital longer after the accident. Instead all I wanted to do was to get out.' The journalist commented, 'The price he paid was a complete breakdown.... A long spell in hospital and taking life easy since then have made him a changed man.... Now he really looks fit... and he's much happier.' The article also mentioned that, 'He has a great disc out.' The reference was to Gene's new single *Jezebel* b/w *Maybe*, a strange combination, especially in 1961, since *Jezebel* was recorded in '56 and *Maybe* in '58. Neither was a hit, and Gene, who didn't feature them in his stage act, was quite disappointed, especially as he wasn't consulted about the release. A while later, Capitol released *Brand New Beat* b/w *Unchained Melody*, another strange combination. *Brand New Beat* was recorded in '57 and *Unchained Melody* in '56 and again, Gene wasn't performing either of these on stage.

The same day he arrived, Gene began rehearsing with his new back-up band, the Echoes, and they did a series of dates in Feb-

---

8. *I Remember Gene Vincent.*

ruary with Johnny Kidd and the Pirates and Johnny Duncan and his Blue Grass Boys. Alan Vince saw them at the Granada in Maidstone: "Gene's act was as dynamic and popular as ever. He crawled, ran and jumped about the stage with the Echoes' guitarist following his every movement. Numbers like *Long Tall Sally* and *Say Mama* had the audience shouting for more and more. During one number, Gene ran over to the piano and launched himself over the top of it! As the pianist stood up, Jerry Lee style, staring back at Gene, Gene began to lift and bang the lid of the instrument. The audience was going wild! They had never seen the like of Gene Vincent. Each time the curtain came down, the cheering, shouting fans refused to let Gene go."[9]

Later, Alan Vince saw Gene at the Granada in Woolwich and went backstage to give him fan letters from the United States, South Africa, Holland, France, Germany, Australia and Ghana. "Then came Gene. The Echoes built up a tremendous beat as the curtains drew back and the audience caught sight of him gripping the mike. Only a short time before, Gene had been presenting a gift to a blind girl in his dressing room....Now he was a wild uninhibited rock star... a true Jekyll and Hyde!"[10]

The next Capitol release was two of the pop songs that Gene had recorded in Hollywood in January: *Mr. Loneliness* b/w *If You Want My Lovin'* and Gene performed *Mr. Loneliness* on the BBC's Saturday Club with the Echoes. Apparently the live version, without the horrible strings and chorus, was quite good.

In the middle of April, Gene was in the papers again in an article called 'The Nightmare Gene Can Never Forget'.

He rips out a number wild as they come, legs skidding, bending as he clutches the mike. The fans think him the zizziest guy alive. But they're wrong. For, off stage he is quiet, withdrawn, rarely raises his voice above a whisper, keeps himself to himself on tour and just lives for his wife, Darlene, and their three children. That's Gene Vincent, who won the title 'The Screaming Kid' with discs like *Be-Bop-A-Lula*, *Wild Cat*, and *Anna*

---

9. *I Remember Gene Vincent.*
10. Ibid.

Annabelle. But *why* is Gene so quiet? Away from the mike, why does the lean-faced fiery hepster fall silent? There could be a tragic reason.

The writer went on to describe Gene's motorcycle accident and the car crash with Eddie Cochran. He quoted Gene as saying this about waking up in the hospital after the accident with Cochran: "I suppose I was in a daze, but I kept thinking the guy in the bed opposite mine was Eddie. Seeing him there gave me comfort. It wasn't until I asked a visitor one day, 'Why don't you go over and see how Eddie's getting on?' that I learned the truth." The article ended with 'Today, exactly a year later, Gene-at-the-mike is still a different person from the offstage Gene. When other stars in his shows get together for laughs, Gene sits alone. . . . In five years time, Gene will be an even bigger star. We hope, too, that his nightmare memories will dim and he'll no longer be the quiet one.'

However, the nightmares were only just beginning. That April Gene flew back to the States to do some filming for a movie called State Fair, which starred Pat Boone and Connie Francis, but Gene's part was apparently deleted from the final version. This was nothing compared to the shock he received when he got back to his home in Niles: the house was empty. Darlene had taken the children and left. She explains: "I'd just had enough. I wanted a real marriage. I wanted to settle down. I just hated life on the road. I though that it was just nuts. But Gene thought that *I* was nuts! I wanted to break off with him, but I was scared. He still had all those pistols and knives. So I just rented an apartment and left. Then Johnny and Chuck phoned and said Gene was back. So I took the kids with me and went over to see him. We talked and he said that things would be different in the future. But he still had gigs to do over in England. So it was the same old story. We talked for a couple of hours, but my mind was made up. Then a neighbour came over, so I took the opportunity to grab the kids and leave. I saw him a couple of times after that. One time we sat in a restaurant and talked. But we didn't argue, 'cause he could tell my mind was made up. But he was upset all right. There was a lot of hurt there, that's for sure. He phoned a couple of times later, once from New York, and he wanted me to fly out 'cause he wanted to see the kids, but I said, 'No way!' I really didn't trust him. He'd get to drinking and get crazy and I didn't want no part of it."

Now Gene had nothing to come home to. There could be no turning back, no fantasies of settling down and becoming a deejay or a record producer. Now there was only the road.

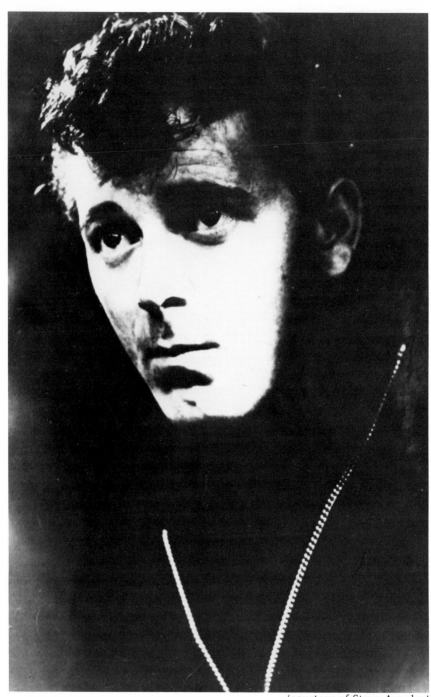

(courtesy of Steve Aynsley)

8

Rock'n'Roll Lunacy

We had to get him good bands. They had to be rockers themselves. When Gene came out the atmosphere was tense, like the entrance of the gladiators: 'Open the cage and let him out!'

– Henry Henroid

Gene returned to England and Henry Henroid booked a new band called Sounds Incorporated to back him on his next tour. They were an excellent group featuring Alan Holmes on sax and flute, Dick Thomas on bass, Barrie 'Baz' Elmes on sax and keyboards, John St. John on guitar, Dick 'the mad Major' Glyde on sax and Tony Newman on drums. According to Dick Thomas, "Henry came out to Leyton and booked us. He asked if we wanted to back Vincent for a two-week tour and we practically fell on the floor. We couldn't believe it. I mean, when we went to school, it was Elvis Presley and Gene Vincent. That was it, wasn't it! I mean, I had all his records! At the rehearsal, Gene was very quiet, a very nice guy. Then off we went to play Bradford, which was a pretty big place for us. . . then on came this lunatic! This maniac in black leather! I remember being really scared."

Barrie Elmes says, "He leapt on the piano. I remember that because I recalled that he *hadn't* done it at the rehearsal! And his medallion ground a big trough in the piano lid. The management wanted to know who was going to pay for the damage. . . . And the burst mikes! They looked like wilted tulips!"

Alan Holmes adds, "Gene Vincent was very much a Jekyll and Hyde character: quiet offstage, then he became a lunatic on stage with a maniac gleam in his eye! We were actually quite frightened. It was such an enormous character change. . . . We used to spend

151

half the night on our knees trying to duck the mike-stand!" Dick Thomas agrees: "Gene was a bit of a schizo. He had an on-stage personality and an offstage personality. It was like he was waiting in the wings sniffing Jekyll-and-Hyde powder. He sort of went from a mild-mannered Clark Kent to Superman-in-a-black-leather-jacket! The audience was ecstatic! He always appealed to the lower echelons of society, the hard men and would-be bruisers. But there were also the screaming girls!"

In May, Gene and Sounds Incorporated did a spot on the TV program Thank Your Lucky Stars and Adrian Owlett and a couple of his friends showed up at the studio. They were lucky enough to bump into Gene and Henry Henroid, and Gene invited them for lunch. They went to a local pub, and when Adrian asked Gene about the Blue Caps and why they weren't on the tour, Gene said "Well... things change." Gene then asked Henry to get him a small bottle of Scotch and handed him a ten pound note. Henry got the whiskey, but kept the change, which was about £8.50. Gene said, "Man, things are expensive here." Henry looked at Adrian and winked. Adrian thinks that Gene knew but didn't care, since he was making big money. Years later, when Gene used to stay at Adrian's place, five pound notes would fall out of Gene's pockets, but he wouldn't bother to pick them up.

At the end of the month Gene flew to South Africa for a short tour. While there, he had a hit with *Mitchiko From Tokyo*, which had been recorded two years earlier and wasn't released as a single in any other country. Gene played in Johannesburg, Capetown, Durban, Port Elizabeth, and East London. His back-up band was Mickey Most and his Playboys, and it was probably through Most that Gene met Jackie Frisco, Most's sister-in-law, a young singer who'd already had a couple of hits in South Africa. Rumour has it that Gene and Jackie liked each other right away, but that Gene told her, "Come and look me up when you're a little older." Jackie Frisco was only about sixteen at the time.

A young guitar player named Ray Loppnow was playing with the Blue Beats at an East London night club, the Windsor Bowl, and was delighted to find that his idol Gene Vincent was booked into the same club: "Mickey Most announced the star of the evening. The crowd went wild as the spotlight picked up a figure in black limping onto the stage. Crouching over the mike, Gene let rip into *What'd I Say.* The hits just flowed. *Rocky Road Blues* and *Wild Cat* and Gene swung his left leg over the bent-over mike-stand, which made the fans cheer with delight. During *Whole Lotta Shakin' Goin' On,* he picked the mike-stand up and pointed its base toward the ceiling. Then came the classic *Be-Bop-A-Lula,* which concluded his act. He left the stage to the sound of 'More! More!... We want Gene!'"

Gene returned to Britain to find that he had another hit: *She She Little Sheila* b/w *Hot Dollar* had entered the charts on the first of June, stayed there for eleven weeks and reached the number 22 position.

Gene continued touring with Sounds Incorporated, but he was depressed about the breakup of his marriage and he often phoned Darlene and tried to patch things up. "Gene obviously wanted to go home," says Dick Thomas. "He was with us friends... but really he was all on his own. He took to travelling with us in the bus... probably so Henry couldn't see him drinking." Alan Holmes adds, "Gene had this thing about stopping for Cokes. He could be quite funny and telling jokes. We were quite green: we really thought he wanted a Coke. But actually it was Scotch!" Barrie Elmes says, "When Gene was sober, as a person he was a really nice guy. He would always just buy half a bottle. Just to go to sleep. And he had sleeping tablets with him as well."

Gene's behavior began to be more erratic. Dick Thomas describes an incident in Gloucestershire: "Gene did another 'die' on us on the pavement outside the Village Hall. He just lay there with his eyes and mouth open. We got worried about it. We were freaking out. We all thought he'd really gone over the top. He was lying there on his back in his black leather suit... then he suddenly smirked. So we just picked him up, threw him in the back of the van and ' ¬aded for the next gig!"

Henry Henroid agrees that Gene was acting strangely: "I'd say Gene was a schizophrenic. He could be so kind and yet so hateful. You had to be very strong with Gene. There was no other way. You loved him one minute and hated him the next.... But on-stage he was an athlete. He'd kick his leg over the mike, then lift the whole stand over his head.... Rod Stewart based his whole act on Gene

Vincent. But he never did it half so good. . . . Gene would never do the same thing twice. He might jump right over the piano or smash in the drums with the mike-stand. He verged on actual lunacy! But he didn't care! When it was time for Gene to go on, I'd go to his dressing room to get him. That might take one minute or it might take ten. Sometimes he'd lock himself in and I'd have to kick the door down. I did that several times. . . . We had to get him good bands. They had to be rockers themselves. When Gene came out the atmosphere was tense, like the entrance of the gladiators: 'Open the cage and let him out!'"

For a while Barrie Elmes was Gene's personal secretary. Barrie tells this story: "I was writing letters for him and looking after him, sharing a room with him. I got a bit extra for that. Gene was always in dispute with people. His car was always being confiscated because he hadn't made the payments on it. He'd tell me, in his drunken Southern drawl, 'Baz, take a letter to the Chrysler Corporation. . . .' He'd also get me to write letters to his ex-manager, Norm Riley, and to Capitol Records. . . demented demands that never really got posted!"

One time in Glasgow, Gene woke up Barrie in the middle of the night and showed him an empty pill bottle. Barrie asked, "Have you eaten all those?" Gene replied, drunkenly, "Yes." Henry was in bed with some woman and Barrie woke him up with the news that Gene had taken an overdose. Henry yelled through the door, "I hope the bastard dies!" Gene was taken to the hospital and had his stomach pumped out.

At the end of June, Gene and Henry flew back to the States so that Gene could get his passport renewed. They were supposed to fly to San Francisco, but Gene had been drinking and when they got to Portland he refused to go any farther. He knew Darlene was there, so he dragged Henry with him and phoned her about wanting to see his kids. However, Darlene didn't want to see Gene. It was about one in the morning and they jumped into a taxi. "Take me to the police station!" said Gene. When they got there, he went up to the officer behind the desk and said, "I want to see my wife and kids!" The cop asked, "Do you know their address?" Gene replied, "Yeah, but she won't see me!" The cop tried to tell Gene that there was nothing he could do, but Gene pounded his fist on the counter and

(courtesy of Steve Aynsley)

yelled, "Don't try to tell me the state laws of California!" They were, of course, in Oregon, and the cop turned to Henry and said, "Get your friend out of here before I lock him up!" Henry dragged Gene outside and they caught a cab to a motel. Gene phoned Darlene again, and eventually she showed up, with the kids. But there was no reconciliation.

Gene and Henry flew back to London and kept on touring with Sounds Incorporated. Henry comments about life on the road with Gene: "It was like a living lunatic asylum. When we arrived at a venue we had to go out of our way to keep Gene away from the press. We had to hide the things that he did. Gene was the original punker. Gene made Johnny Rotten of the Sex Pistols look like a schoolboy. He couldn't even begin where Gene left off! ... Gene could get rid of money so fast! And you couldn't spend it all on booze. And he didn't have to spend it on women. In fact, Gene was the fastest getter-ridder of women I've ever met. When he'd screwed them enough, he'd ditch them. They would say, 'Gene, are we going now?' And he would look them right in the eye and say, 'What do you want, Madame? My autograph?' And that was my cue to give them cab fare."

At the end of July, Gene and Sounds Incorporated went into the EMI studios in Abbey Road in London and recorded two new songs, *I'm Goin' Home* and *Spaceship to Mars*. *I'm Goin' Home* is a classic, certainly one of the best songs Gene ever recorded. It's credited to Bob Bains, who was the compère on some of their tours, but the members of Sounds Incorporated doubt that Bains wrote it and think that it was probably penned by Gene. At any rate, it's a great song and Sounds Incorporated did a great version, the high points being the aggressive drumming of Tony Newman, the tight arrangement by Barrie Elmes and the great tenor solo by Dick Glyde. Alan Holmes makes this comment about Newman: "For his time he was absolutely out of this world. When we first met him, he had all his teeth knocked out after a two-hour fight in some car park. And he tried to combine that innate violence with the expertise of Buddy Rich, who was his big idol." It seems that Gene had found the perfect drummer and the near-perfect band. These sessions were produced by Norrie Paramor and two of the recordings featured his orchestra rather than Sounds. The songs were *Love of a Man* and *There I Go Again,* both tender ballads that showcased the other side of Gene's personality. *I'm Goin' Home* was picked for the A side of Gene's next single and it must have been released almost immediately because it broke into the charts at the end of August, but remained there for just four weeks, only going as high as the number 36 position.

Gene and Sounds Incorporated continued touring and Gene was referred to as 'The King of the Ballrooms' because he pulled in such large crowds. Steve Aynsley saw him in Newcastle: "Sounds Incorporated did their set, then they announced Gene. All the audience could see were Gene's hands sticking out past the curtain as he pulled on his black gloves and they all went wild. Sounds Incorporated came back on in single file and went into the riff for *Lucille.* Gene followed them on and did his usual numbers, including a real slow version of *Be-Bop-A-Lula.* He threw his leg over the mike-stand and twisted his body around it. It was a great gig. Brilliant. And he went down fantastic!"

However, Gene wasn't always fantastic. Henry recalls: "I only knew Gene to foul up once. That was at the Princess Theater in Torquay. He got so drunk that he collapsed in a heap on stage and we had to let the curtain down and drag him out! We actually had to escape afterwards!" Dick Thomas says, "Gene was pissed that night. He blew it away. He couldn't remember the words or anything.... You just wanted to cry for him.... When we left, we had to take our gear out another door."

One time, rushing home after a gig in the Studebaker Commander, Gene made it clear that he didn't like going too fast. He leaned over and said, "Henry.... Slow down! The front tires are as bald as a baby's ass and I ain't plannin' on dyin' yet!" Dick Thomas confirms that Gene no longer liked careless driving: "We'd just played the Bristol Hippodrome where he'd played his last show with Eddie Cochran and it seemed to bother Gene quite a bit. Afterwards we rented a car to get back to London. I was driving and at one point I nearly lost control. And it was almost the same spot where he'd had the accident before! Vincent was in the back seat and he just dived for the floor. It was rather uncanny."

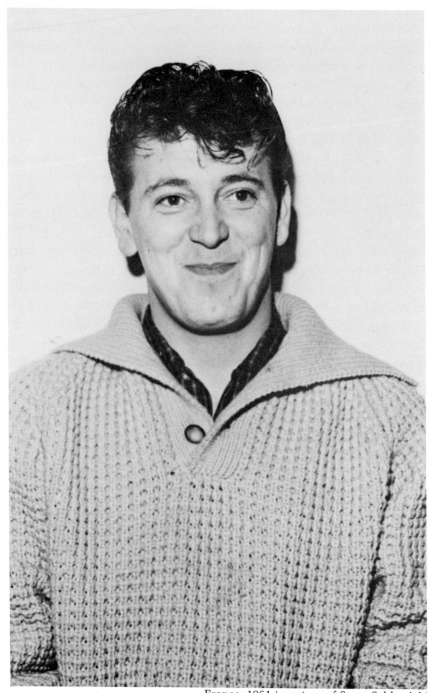

France, 1961 (courtesy of Serge Schlawick)

In the fall of '61 Gene went back to Hollywood, and on the 18th of October he did a session produced by Nick Venet. The band was led by Dave Burgess, who'd been the rhythm guitarist with the Champs when they toured with the Blue Caps in the fifties, and they did only two songs, *Baby Don't Believe Him* and *Lucky Star*. They were fairly good cuts, though not very rocky, but unfortunately strings were added on later.

1961 saw the real beginning of Gene's lunacy and it peaked in 1962. By now Gene had been touring constantly for six straight years, and for most of this time he'd been drinking heavily. In the spring of '62 he went back to Britain for his seventh tour, this time with Brenda Lee, and they were billed as The King and Queen of Rock. For this tour Gene had a new white leather outfit and his repertoire included *Lucille, What'd I Say, Corrina Corrina, Tutti Frutti, Over the Rainbow* and *Lucky Star* (his current release), as well as his usual numbers. Sounds Incorporated backed up both Gene and Brenda Lee and their performance at the London Palladium was broadcast on TV. *Disc* magazine did an article on the show and described Gene as 'a real gone rocker of the first order.' But the author didn't like Gene's new white outfit and said, "It doesn't suit his storming high-voltage style as well as the old all-black rig." Years later, Brenda Lee was interviewed in the British rock'n'roll magazine *Not Fade Away,* and when asked if she had any anecdotes about Gene she replied, "He was always a gentleman with me." About the same time as this tour with Brenda Lee, Gene and Sounds Incorporated did a spot in a film called *It's Trad, Dad.* Gene wore his white leathers and sang *Spaceship to Mars.*

It was also on the King and Queen of Rock tour that Gene began an affair with a cabaret dancer named Margaret Russell. Later, after Gene's death, in a series of tacky articles in an English tabloid, Margaret referred to Gene as a 'tempestuous rock singer and marathon drinker.' Margie Russell had gone to a gig at the Granada in Tooting in hopes that she would be invited to a party that was planned for afterwards. Henry Henroid had known Margie "for years." She'd hung around the 2 I's coffee house in Soho when Henry had been the manager, and had gone out with a rock singer named Terry Dene. Dick Thomas comments: "If she went out with Terry Dene, then she definitely had a death wish. He was the British Vincent!"

Margie was attractive and she *was* invited to the party. As soon as she arrived, Gene came over, pressed a drink into her hand and steered her into a corner. He was already drunk, and later Margie learned that this was nothing unusual: 'But that night, all I could think about was that I was the girl the others envied. Drunk though he was, Gene managed to play the perfect gentleman.'[1]

It's strange that at the same time as Gene was rapidly approaching the height of his lunacy, both Brenda Lee and Margie Russell received the initial impression that Gene was a "perfect gentlemen." And no doubt he acted that way. Unfortunately this act could seldom be maintained for long, and sooner or later Gene's erratic behaviour would prevail, as it did with Margie. Gene was about to begin the most tempestuous relationship of his life.

Gene had to go up to the North of England, but he phoned Margie every night. The last date of the tour was in Slough, just outside London, and Margie showed up and was let into Gene's dressing room. He embraced her and said, "This time I'm going to hang on to you." Gene was supposed to fly back to the States the following day, but he stayed another week so he could spend some time with Margie. They went for walks and took trips down the Thames 'like any other young lovers.' When Gene met her mother and father he made such an impression on them that Mr. Russell found it hard to believe the stories he heard about Gene. Every night Margie would take a taxi from work to Gene's hotel. There were always people in his room, talking and drinking. Margie 'would creep quietly into bed while Gene sat up with his friends – and a bottle.'

Gene had planned to stay in the States for six weeks, but four days after his arrival he wired Margie that he was coming back right away and asked her to meet him at the airport. He arrived with 'just one suitcase containing next to nothing.' Gene didn't yet have a current work permit for Britain, so Don Arden got him some bookings on the continent and Margie quit her job to go with him. In Germany, *Pistol Packin' Mama* was a big hit and Gene was the headliner at the Star Club in Hamburg, the first famous rocker to

---

1. Margaret Russell was not available for an interview. Her comments, and comments attributed to Gene, are from an unidentified English tabloid, c.1971.

play there. The Star Club was similar to its English counterpart, the Cavern Club in Liverpool, and was the centre of rock'n'roll in continental Europe. Margie stated he was getting £1,500 a week and drinking 'a bottle of Scotch a day, more when he was under stress.' But Margie didn't seem to mind: 'Gene was a great romantic and made a gigantic production out of buying me a beautiful platinum ring in the shape of a Maltese cross and set with nine diamonds. It was worth about £1,000.'[2]

Gene and Margie (courtesy of Evelyn Butler)

Margie was soon to see the other side of Gene's personality. One night Gene abandoned Margie in a night club and went home alone. Margie showed up later at the hotel room and Gene was waiting for her, 'drunk and vicious. He grabbed me, held both my wrists with one hand and slapped me around the face with the other.' In the morning Gene felt contrite. He put his arms around Margie and told her, "Never, never again! I'll never behave that way

2. Ibid.

161

again!"[3]

They made up and returned to England and Gene did a session at the EMI studio in St. John's Wood. It was produced by Bob Barratt and the band was led by Charles Blackwell. They did four songs: *King of Fools, You're Still in my Heart, Held For Questioning* and *Be-Bop-A-Lula '62*. This was to be Gene's last session for Capitol, and in retrospect it seems odd that Gene ended it with his first big hit. Unfortunately, this second version of *'Lula* doesn't compare to the original.

In the summer of '62 there were some interesting articles about Gene in the British press. *Hit Parade* featured a story called 'Gene Vincent – Citizen of Britain':

> Britain is to be the new home of Gene Vincent. The long and complicated procedure of being accepted as 'one of us' has been set in motion to allow one of the greates rock'n'rollers of all time to settle here. At present Gene has a flat in London, but his working permit only allows him to play restricted periods during each stay, so he has had to go out of the country in order to return and work. The news that Gene Vincent Craddock was applying for British citizenship came shortly after he made an unexpected dash back to Britain from his Niles (California) home only a few days after flying back there from yet another successful tour of this country.... Gene remains one of the few consistent box office draws to emerge from the early rock'n'roll era.... Those who have known Gene in the past will remember him as a riotous-living person who had little respect for conventional clothes or conventional living. Rarely did his suitcase contain a suit when he visited Britain despite his phenomenal earnings. Here he lived in the best hotels and travelled in a big American car.... His stage act has always been reminiscent of his way of living. He has never cared about himself or his property but always about the performance he is giving. Often he has come off stage in severe pain from throwing himself on the piano, often with his expensive leather suit damaged from the way in which he used to move

---

3. Ibid.

around on his knees. Many's the time he has smashed microphones too delicate for the way he pounds them when the rhythm gets strong. Only recently the manager of one theatre approached him after the show complaining, "Gene, you've wrecked three of our mikes." To which Gene replied, "Mister, you bought my act."

Another magazine featured an article–titled 'Gene Vincent – The Star Who Doesn't Need Hits':

The artist without a record. That's what they are beginning to call him. Gene Vincent has not had a hit record in over a year. And yet he is capable of pulling them in on one-nighters to a greater extent than some American artists who visit this country to cash in on a hit disc in the charts. Gene Vincent is different. He is still living off the records that are behind him. It is the name, he contends, and not the disc that counts. "I was in at the beginning of things," he says. "Then it was the artist who was sold to the public and not, as it is now, his latest record. I came in at a time when the name of the artist meant more, and the name I built up then has stood me in good stead. I don't believe that I have to rely on being as good as my last record. . . . It always helps, of course, to have a hit in the charts at the same time that you are touring. That much is obvious, but it is not necessary if you are a name artist, and a hit doesn't give you guaranteed drawing power. I'm not one to ignore the charts, but I think that it is stupid to rely on them as a reflection of your popularity off record. . . . When I set out to give a British audience a performance I remember this: first of all they want a show. They don't just want to hear that voice they've heard on records, on the radio. They don't just want a pretty uniform and a pretty face to go with it."

In July, Gene did a tour of Italy with Rory Blackwell and Sounds Incorporated. Margie Russell went along too, despite her ongoing feud with Gene. After one of the gigs, Henry Henroid was having his usual trouble getting payment from the Italian promoter. The promoter brought out "some heavy dudes," so Henry turned to the

163

band members who had been loading their equipment onto the roof of their bus.

"All right, unload the equipment," he ordered.

Tony Newman turned around with a pained expression. "Jesus, mate," he said. "I've already been up and down this ladder twenty bloody times!" Then Henry noticed that the promoter was looking in the bus, wide-eyed with amazement. There was Gene, "the star of the show," engaged in a knock-down battle with Margie. Henry's story is that he leapt into the bus and threw Margie towards the front, at the same time yelling at Dick Thomas, who is quite a hefty fellow, to grab Gene. Dick's story differs only slightly: "Henry was outside trying to get the money," he recalls. "Then Gene and Margie started their hourly fracas." Dick says he told Gene to cool it, but Gene took a drunken swing, so Dick stopped him with a shot in the mouth. Gene went flying. His crippled leg was caught in the seat and broken again, though no one knew it at the time.

Meanwhile, the promoter had become convinced that he was dealing with a busload of violent psychopaths, and paid up promptly.

The next gig was a night's drive away. Everyone slept, or passed out, while being driven through the Appenine Mountains by a "lunatic" Italian chauffeur named Bruno, whose idea of competent driving was to keep himself well lubricated with *grappo*. As Dick Thomas remarks, "Bruno was the Vincent of the bus world!"

Suddenly, in the middle of the night, Gene sat up and quietly drawled , "Henry. . . . He's broken my leg, Henry." Gene's left leg was so badly swollen that the seams of his pants were bursting. The interpreter was asleep, so Henry had to try to tell Bruno in English and bad Italian to turn around and go to the hospital. Bruno just kept on driving and sipping *grappo*. Finally Henry grabbed the hand brake and pulled it on. This jarred the roadie awake enough to communicate their demands to the stupefied driver.

Gene's leg had to be put in a cast, and the band couldn't wait for him. They drove on to the next gig, leaving Henry and the roadie behind to take care of him. Henry asked Gene if he wanted to cancel. "No, Henry. . . . I wanna do the show, Henry." The roadie couldn't believe that Gene wanted to continue, but he rented a car and they rushed off to catch up to the bus. An hour later Gene said

164

he had to pee, so they pulled in at an all-night restaurant. A few minutes later Gene hobbled out of the establishment on crutches, with a bottle of whiskey tucked under one arm and the proprietor running behind him screaming, *"Polizia! Polizia!"* Gene had stolen the booze and Henry had to pay off the restaurant owner. "Gene was very clever," says Henry. "I swear he could smell bars. In the middle of the night he could find them."

Henry Henroid (courtesy of Alan Holmes)

Continuing through the mountains at breakneck speed, with Gene sitting in the back drinking whiskey "like it was Coke," they caught up with the band at the next gig. There things went from bad to worse. While Henry was at the venue checking out the PA system, Margie suddenly ran in yelling, "Quick! Get back to the hotel!" Henry rushed back and found Gene in a hot bath trying to pry his new cast off with a coat-hanger. Henry grabbed it out of his hand and tried to pull him out of the bath. Gene got out rather sheepishly, after token resistance, but the cast soon began to shrink. Again Henry had to rush him to the hospital to have it replaced. That night Gene performed sitting on a stool, abandoning his flamboyant stage act for one of the few times in his career.

The next morning, in search of a little recreation after the bizarre events of the last two days, the whole band went down to the beach and rented pedal-boats. As Dick and some of the other guys were pedalling along, they met Gene and Margie in another boat. Gene gave them a dirty look and Dick thought, "Here's our chance. We can push him overboard. He'll never be able to swim with that thing on!"

One of the Italian gigs was at a resort on the Riviera, and Henry met a beautiful woman on the beach. They were walking hand in hand back to the hotel when Henry heard Gene yelling out, "Henry... Margie's a whore!" He looked up and saw Gene standing naked on the balcony: "I could feel the young lady's affection decidedly dampening." They went into the lobby and Margie came running up with a black eye and tears streaming down her face.

"I want a ticket! I want to go home!" she cried.

"Oh, wait till the morning," replied Henry. He tried to comfort Margie, but when he turned around he discovered that his beautiful 'bird' had vanished. Henry looked up and thought, "That bastard! I'll kill him!"

In Venice at a ritzy nightclub called the Lido, teenagers in bluejeans tried to get in but were turned away. According to Dick, "It was a millionaire's club, bloody up-market." Henry Henroid also remembers the Lido: "It was a ritzy Las Vegas-style club with a floor show and dancers. But it was the wrong type of club for Vincent. He went on and died a death. But he verbal-ed them." When confronted with hecklers, Gene would say things like, "I won't make a fool out of you. Your parents already beat me to it!" or, "I do a single act. When I want to do a double act, I'll come over and rattle your cage!"

After the Italian tour, Gene and Margie flew to Frankfurt, then to Hamburg, where Gene was headlining at the Star Club. Gene was so popular in Germany that a banner with his name on it was hung across the infamous Reeperbahn outside the club. Sounds Incorporated had taken the train from Italy, and didn't arrive in time for the opening night. Instead Gene was backed up by an unknown group called the Beatles. Actually, Gene had played with them in the summer of '61 at the Cavern Club in Liverpool, and a newly-issued rock magazine called *Mersey Beat* had featured a picture of Gene side-by-side with an article about the Beatles on the cover of its first issue. But Gene had played with so many bands in

166

Britain that he probably didn't remember them. Barrie Elmes recalls that when Sounds Incorporated got to Hamburg they asked Gene what the Star Club was like. He replied, "Oh, it's okay there. I had a nice band backing me up. They're called the Beatles." According to Margie, the Beatles considered Gene as 'something of a hero.' She sat backstage listening to them talking with Gene about music and 'how desperately they wanted to make records.'[4] Henry Henroid says, "John Lennon was a Gene Vincent freak! He adored Vincent!"

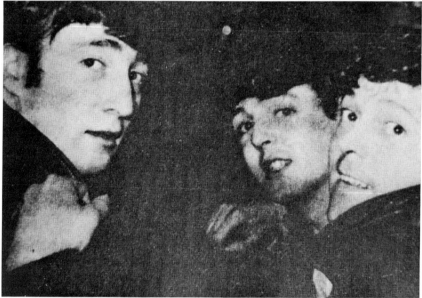

John Lennon, Paul McCartney and Gene (courtesy of Jerry Merritt)

Gene and his entourage were staying at the Hotel Metropole on the Reeperbahn, and one night Henry was woken up by Margie. He looked up and she was standing there with a pistol in her hand. "Gene's asleep," she said. "But earlier he came in with a gun in his hand saying, 'I'm gunna kill somebody!'" Margie had waited till he fell asleep, then taken the gun. Henry was convinced it was a toy, and to demonstrate he fired it at the ceiling. It turned out to be a gas gun and the whole room filled up with tear-gas. Within seconds

---

4. Ibid.

Paris, 1962 (courtesy of Serge Schlawick)

their eyes were blind with tears and they ran out into the hallway, Henry naked and Margie in her nightie. And at the end of the hall, limping toward them with his fists clenched, was an angry drunken Gene.

"Henry, you've been fuckin' Margie!"

Henry yelled at him, "You crazy bastard! My whole room's filled up with smoke 'cause of you!" Henry showed Gene the gas-filled room and Gene started laughing. The next day he got another gas gun and cleared the Star Club at two AM by firing it over the bar. About four or five hundred people were there and most of them ran out into the street while Gene stood there laughing. Alan Holmes remembers Gene picking up the gun and being told to leave it alone. Gene had replied in his inimitable Southern drawl, "Oh, don't worry... I know all about guns." A few seconds later people were running for the exits.

Gene played at the Star Club for two straight weeks. One time he pulled a gun on Tony Newman and said, "Tony.... You've been sleeping with Margie!" Newman ran for it. Gene was obviously paranoid about Margie's relationships with other men, but according to Henry this was not without justification as Margie had apparently had a very brief affair with Freddy Fascher, one of the waiters at the Star Club. This brief indiscretion apparently resulted in a pitched battle between Freddy and his brother Horst, who was a good friend of Gene's. But afterwards Gene and Freddy were seen at the bar drinking and talking like old friends. And this incident didn't seem to make any difference to Gene and Margie's relationship: when they got back to England the rented a three-bedroom house in Welling, Kent. Gene also bought a car, an Austin A40, and Margie started taking driving lessons.

Next, Gene went to Israel where they played an open-air concert in Jerusalem, then on to Haifa to play at the Caliph Club. Henry says, "The tour was supposed to last two weeks, but we only stayed about five days. Gene raised all hell and they chucked him out." One night Henry was at the club and got a phone call from the back-up band's piano player Roy Young, saying that Gene was dying and he'd called an ambulance. Henry had already gone through several of Gene's dying acts, so he hurried back to the hotel and said, "Oh, c'mon, Gene! Get out of bed, you bloody idiot!" The ambulance had already arrived and Gene was put on a stretcher and taken to hospital. Roy Young thought that Henry was being "a real bastard," but at the hospital Gene was examined and there was nothing wrong with him. Gene just kept repeating, "I'm dying. I'm dying." The police were called and the doctors threatened to charge Gene with misuse of an ambulance. According to Henry, Gene would do this just for attention and to get people excited and/or worried. At any rate, they packed up and returned to England, which is probably just what Gene wanted.

At the end of October, Gene played at the Theatre d'Etoile in Paris with a French group, Les Champions. Margie went along and they stayed at the Hotel Napoleon. About the third day, Henry came down with the flu, but the franc had been devalued that day and he had to go to the theater and argue with the promoter about their rate of pay. When he got back to the hotel he was "completely knackered." Gene was in the bar, as usual, and Henry told him that he was going straight to bed. About two in the morning, Henry was woken up by a phone call from Don Arden's wife, Paddy. She said that Gene had phoned her twice. The first time he'd told her Henry was dying and had to fly back to London because he didn't want to die in Paris. Ten minutes later Gene had phoned and said, "Paddy... Henry's fuckin' Margie!" As Paddy was telling this to Henry, Henry's door suddenly swung open and the concierge stepped into the dark room, holding Gene in a headlock. Henry hung up the phone and asked what was going on. In a thick French accent the concierge said, "Mr. Vincent, he say 'is wife is in your room." Henry looked at Gene: "He was leaning against the wall with a smirk on his face... a smirk he used to get whenever he had succeeded in creating havoc." The concierge let go of Gene so that he could search Henry's room and Gene took the opportunity to flee from Henry's wrath. Shortly after the concierge had left, Henry got a call from Margie, who said, "I've had enough! I've just had the concierge in my room accusing me of being in bed with you!" Henry calmed Margie down, hung up the phone, and immediately got a call from the concierge telling him to hurry down to the bar. He dressed, rushed downstairs and found Gene arguing with the bartender about getting another drink. Gene hit the bartender and knocked him down. ("Gene could punch. And he wasn't afraid to fight!"). The concierge hit *Henry*, so Henry grabbed him by the throat and was going to punch him, but out of the corner of his eye he saw Gene raising a bottle in preparation for bashing the concierge. Afraid that Gene might kill him, Henry pushed the Frenchman out of the way. Gene missed his target and hit a large aquarium filled with live fish for the fancy restaurant patrons. As fish and water flooded all over the dining room floor, a bunch of hotel staff rushed out of the kitchen. "Back against the wall, Gene!" said Henry. They both grabbed bottles and backed up to the nearest wall. Fortunately, Henry talked their way out of the fracas, insisting that the concierge had started the whole thing by coming into his room without knocking or asking permission. After a great deal of arguing, Henry got Gene into the lift and they headed up to their rooms on the seventh floor. When the lift operator opened the door, Margie charged in "like a raging bull!" She tried to punch Gene, but instead hit the lift operator and knocked him off his stool. Gene fell on top of him and Henry grabbed Margie until she calmed down. Henry put her in his room, then he and Gene went back to Gene's room, which had two double beds. The next morning Margie flew back to England, but she and Gene would soon make up. At this point Henry had begun to call her 'Rocky' because of her frequent black eyes.

Shortly before Christmas, 1962, Margie announced to Gene that she was pregnant. He was happy with the news and so was she. Margie hoped that Gene would straighten out if he had to face up to the responsibilities of being a parent. According to Margie, one lovable quality about Gene was his 'unpredictable childish charm' which made her forget his drinking problem. 'Gene was like a little boy' at Christmas, and invited Margie's entire family to Welling. He bought presents for them all, and gave Margie a gold watch with heart-shaped links in the bracelet, and a wedding ring in a heart-shaped box.[5]

But all did not go well. On the evening of Christmas Day they attended a party at Don Arden's home and Gene became jealous

---

5. Ibid.

when he saw Margie talking to another man. He demanded they leave. They had a heated argument on their way home, but still managed to put up a front for Margie's family.

At the end of December, Gene went into St. George's Hospital in London for an operation on his leg. But this didn't stop him from going out on the road again. In January, while Gene was away touring, Margie wondered if their relationship was going to work out. But when Gene returned he gave her a gorgeous white miniature poodle and insisted on marriage. They got a special license and on the 23rd of January, 1963, with Henry Henroid as witness, they were duly married at the registry office in Dartford, Kent. Margie was five months pregnant. Apparently, there was not quite enough celebration or ceremony to satisfy Margie: 'You would think that a girl marrying a star in the £50,000 a year bracket would have had the wedding breakfast of a lifetime, the best that money could lay on. Not me. I married Gene Vincent, rock'n'roll singer extraordinary, at the peak of his career. And afterwards? We simply popped to the nearest pub for a drink. Drink. That was what dominated our lives.'[6]

A few days later, Gene left England for France where he played Metz, in front of 2,000 people, then Nancy and Paris, where he played for 6,000 people at the Palais de Sport. The back-up bands were Les Champions, Les Dragons, les Chats Sauvages and les Chausettes Noirs. While they were in Paris, the French distributors of Gene's records, Pathé Marconi, invited Gene and Henry Henroid to dine with some top executives at a fancy restaurant. Gene showed up drunk and banged on the table, shouting, "Gimme my money! Gimme my money!" Gene's royalties, of course, weren't paid directly to him, but to Capitol Records. The executives were astounded.

In February there was an article in a British paper called 'The Wild Mr. Vincent Doesn't Change':

Gene still puts over basically the same act. He has remained a rock singer, and for him there has been no wearing a nice grey suit and trying to woo mums and dads with a neat line in

---

6. Ibid.

ballads. In the spotlight Gene is a violent performer.... He says, "I'm a rock singer and that's what I'll stay. I've never changed the act because the fans like the style and I stick to it. People don't pay money to see me look pretty. They pay me to see me work. And I work hard."

(courtesy of Steve Aynsley)

That same month, Gene and Margie returned to Hamburg where Gene was again headlining the Star Club. They had another fight and Gene slapped Margie's face again. The next day she flew back to England, and when Gene was finished in Hamburg he rushed home with flowers for her: 'The amazing Jekyll and Hyde character of my husband was showing again, and again I convinced myself that things would get better.'[7]

They didn't. One night they had a violent quarrel at home and Gene pitched all Margie's clothes out in the snow. She ran to get them and he locked her out. It was two in the morning. Margie went to a neighbour's and phoned the police, who informed Gene that he had to let Margie back in. He refused. Margie's mother, who'd been staying with them, went home in a taxi. The following day Margie became ill and had to go to the hospital. There was concern she might miscarry, but she didn't. Gene bombarded her with flowers and they made up again.

The members of Sounds Incorporated remember a similar incident where Gene kicked Margie out. They got a call from Don Arden saying that Gene had gone over the top again: "We went over there and calmed him down. We were sort of his pals. He related to us much more than the management. It was sort of Us versus Them. . . . And I think Don Arden wanted Gene to stay out in Welling. He thought it would keep him close to the boys and out of trouble."[8]

Keeping Gene Vincent out of trouble was becoming less and less possible, but for the next two months Gene and Margie got along all right: 'Gene became more like the young man I had met at a party just over a year ago, and both my mother and I accepted that his drinking was an illness and that we should work toward a cure.'[9]

Henry Henroid and Don Arden had come to the same conclusion, and shortly before a tour was to start they took Gene to a doctor in Harley Street and asked him to try to cure Gene of his alcoholism. The doctor said, "I'll give him something that will put him to sleep for a week, and when he wakes up he'll be sick as a dog

---

7. Ibid.
8. Dick Thomas.
9. Unidentified English tabloid, c.1971.

if he even smells alcohol!" Gene slept for four days and was fed intravenously. He'd been given a drug that was supposed to make his body reject booze, but the night after he woke up, Henry found him "drunk as a sack." Gene laughed and said, "I did it, Henry. I fucked them doctors. I ain't sick!" He went back on the road and kept drinking.

Gene couldn't keep up the pace forever, and at the end of April he was back in the hospital having his leg examined. The doctors ordered him to have a week's rest. Gene and Margie flew to Majorca, and shared a brief holiday. Then it was back to work for Gene. He and Margie flew to Paris and were greeted by thousands of teenagers, at the airport and outside the Hotel Napoleon. Margie was impressed: 'I was still star-struck enought to enjoy all the adulation. . . . Every night the top French rock stars came to our room to pay homage to Gene – and he loved it. He would sit in our suite, drinking steadily and soaking up their praise.'[10]

When they got back to England, things erupted again. One night Gene had a temper tantrum and threw his meal on the floor. When Margie's mother tried to break up the fight, Gene threw a cup of tea on her and phoned the police, telling them his mother-in-law was breaking up his marriage. The next day, Mrs. Russell left.

On May 29th, Margie had a baby girl named Sherri Ann, and Gene came down from Hull with flowers and champagne: 'Now he was playing the proud father and loving husband, bragging to nurses and hospital staff about the baby and making the most elaborate plans for her future. . . . For the umpteenth time I convinced myself that we would settle down.'[11] According to Margie, Gene's drinking and bad behaviour had alienated a lot of pop promoters and his wages began to drop: 'But the less he earned, the more he drank, and his agent gave orders that Gene was not to be allowed to drink before a show. With the ingenuity of a dedicated drinker, Gene got round this by getting hangers-on to slip out of stage doors to buy him a flat half bottle of whiskey which he could slip into a pocket. He gave his 'messengers' £5 a time and let them keep the

---

10. Ibid.
11. Ibid.

175

change. With tips like this there was no shortage of helpers!'[12] This story, with a slight variation, is corroborated by the publisher of *Mersey Beat*, Bill Harry, who often saw Gene at shows around Liverpool: "They confiscated all the booze and kept a 24 hour watch on Gene, but he still got progressively drunker all day. He

France, 1963 (courtesy of Serge Schlawick)

12. Ibid.

had bought some miniature bottles and stuffed them down his cast."

Gene should have been a happy man, but he wasn't. In 1959, when he'd first played in Britain, his career in America was almost at a standstill. In 1960 he'd had three hits in the UK: *Wild Cat, My Heart* and *Pistol Packin' Mama,* and in '61 he'd had two more, *She She Little Sheila* and *I'm Goin' Home.* But a new phenomenon had appeared in Britain and it was soon to conquer the world: Beatlemania. The Beatles first entered the British charts in December, '62, with *Love Me Do.* In early '63, *Please Please Me* got as high as the number 16 position. Then in May, just as Gene's daughter Sherri was born, the Beatles were at number one with *From Me To You,* which soon broke into the American charts as well. From 1959 to 1963, Gene Vincent had been, along with Jerry Lee Lewis, about the only true rocker on the music scene. Now the Mersey Sound was to take recycled American rock'n'roll right back up to the top of the charts. It's easy to understand the rise of the Beatles from obscurity in the working-class slums of Liverpool when one realizes that their counterparts in America were listening to the clean-living suburban sounds of the Beachboys and watching films like *Beach Blanket Bingo.* The American pop music industry served up bland mindless pap for its by now brainwashed audience and rock'n'roll had fallen straight into the hands of the British.

In 1963, Gene's contract with Capitol expired, probably an indication to Gene that they had lost confidence in his work. His subsequent signing with Columbia, another subsidiary of EMI, did little to counteract this. Gene was definitely going through a hard emotional time and it showed in his behaviour: he drank even more and acted more irrationally. In August, while Margie was away visiting a friend, Gene moved out and took all his possessions with him. Not long afterwards, he moved back in. In September he broke a contract in Ireland and came back home in rough shape: 'He was slumped in an armchair surrounded by empty whiskey bottles. And worse, blood was seeping from his mouth. Suddenly he rushed into the bedroom and returned waving a pistol. He screamed that he was going to kill me, the baby and then himself. Laughing like a madman, he showed me the bullets he had for the gun. With Sherri in my arms, I ran out the door and phoned the police.'[13]

Gene was charged with assault and possession of a handgun and a tabloid ran the story under the headline 'Jealous Rock Star Pulled Gun on Wife'. Gene said that the pistol, a Luger, was given to him by a fan. He added, "I pulled it just like any other jealous husband would have." The pistol was confiscated and Gene was fined twenty pounds and given a year's conditional discharge.

In October, Gene did a tour through France and Belgium called *Tournée Age Tendre*. He was backed up by Les Sunlights, and also on the bill were Les Aiglons, les Chats Sauvages, and Moustique. They played 25 cities in 28 days and Gene was no doubt exhausted when he got home.

In November, Gene went back to Harley Street, this time to see a psychiatrist. It didn't help. In mid-December, Margie moved out, but four days later Gene talked her into coming back. The peace didn't last. On Christmas Day, Don Arden came over, and Gene, already drunk, pulled a knife on him. When Arden finally talked Gene into putting it away, Gene grabbed one of his crutches and hit Margie over the head. Arden phoned the police, and Margie, Sherri and Mrs. Russell were all taken to the police station, presumably to escape from Gene and to lay charges against him. Gene was persuaded to go back and see the psychiatrist, but the doctor said that there was nothing he could do. Gene and Margie holidayed on the Isle of Wight, but the troubles continued and culminated when Gene threw a five pound note at Margie and stomped out of their hotel, saying, "This is the last cent you'll get out of me!"[14]

It could be that Gene's self-destructive behaviour was due in large part to his belief that Margie was only interested in his money and fame, and not giving him any genuine affection. Margie moved out of their new house in Streatham and got a flat in Bayswater. Gene offered to give her all their furnishings and twenty pounds a week if she'd drop the assault charge that was pending against him. She dropped it and three months later Gene stopped making the payments.

Gene had hit the zenith of his lunacy. At a gig in Cambridge,

---

13. Ibid.
14. Ibid.

Henry argued with Gene after he had refused to go on stage. Henry was in his hotel room shaving when, in the mirror, he saw Gene coming at him with a chair raised over his head. Henry spun around, punched Gene in the head and knocked him out. That was Henry's last gig with Gene.

Gene's partnership with Sounds Incorporated also came to an end, not because of personal difficulties, but because Sounds had their own recording contract with Columbia Records and would soon have albums and hits of their own. They continue to think of him fondly. "For us it was a great honour to be playing with Vincent. And afterwards when we played with the Beatles at Shea Stadium and all that, it was really because of Gene. He was the reason we all got going. He got us all to give up our day jobs and go out on the road. . . . And you can thank Gene Vincent for our taste in Scotch whiskey!"[15]

Barrie Elmes adds, "All I remember is, his feet smelled and he took all those sleeping tablets! . . . But in his magic days he was just one of the boys."

---

15. Dick Thomas.

Paris, 1962 (courtesy of Serge Schlawick)

9

Don't Knock the Rock

I think that Don Arden was starting to get heavy. Margie was also getting heavy. The world started shrinking in on Gene. His creditors and would-be creditors were beginning to pounce.

— Adrian Owlett

1963 had been a strange year for Gene. There had been all the turmoil with Margie, compounded by Gene's drinking problem, as well as the challenge of the Mersey bands both in the charts and on the ballroom circuit. Shortly after singing with Columbia, Gene did a number of sessions with the Bill Shepherd and the Ivor Raymonde orchestras. Regrettably, these were in the same pop style as his last Capitol sessions. For the second year in a row, Gene had failed to make the British charts, though fellow rockers Buddy Holly and Chuck Berry both broke into the top ten, Holly with two re-issues, *Brown-eyed Handsome Man* and *Bo Diddley* (both of them demo tapes recorded in 1956), and Chuck Berry with a re-issue of his 1958 hit, *Memphis*. Presley had hit Number One in August with *Devil in Disguise*, and at the end of '63 an even bigger challenge appeared: the Rolling Stones entered the charts with *I Wanna Be Your Man*.

In December '63, Columbia Records released *Where Have You Been All My Life* b/w *Temptation Baby*, and followed in the spring of '64 with *Humpity Dumpity* b/w *Love 'Em Leave 'Em Kind Of Guy*. Neither release made the charts. Gene sang *Temptation Baby* in a film called *Live It Up*, his fifth film so far, and it was screened in America as *Sing and Swing*. Gene is seen standing in front of a locomotive. He smiles and leers at a tall attractive woman walking by while he sings "Whoah, Temptation Baby."

1963 also saw the release, in France only, of Gene's last original Capitol LP, *The Crazy Beat of Gene Vincent*. It was a strange compilation of older tracks, including some great ones from the Blue Caps era *(High Blood Pressure* and *Gone, Gone, Gone)*, as well as some less inspired pop songs from the early sixties.

The Liverpool invasion continued into '64 and in January the Beatles had their third consecutive Number One hit with *I Want To Hold Your Hand*. In March the Rolling Stones had their first top ten hit with a Buddy Holly song *Not Fade Away*, and the following month the Beatles were again number one with *Can't Buy Me Love*. Other British bands with top ten hits around this time were the Dave Clarke Five, the Searchers, the Swinging Bluejeans, Gerry and the Pacemakers, Manfred Mann and Billy J. Kramer and the Dakotas.

Gene must have known that a come-back would be difficult, but he hired a Liverpool band called the Shouts and went back on the road. Steve Aynsley saw them in Newcastle at the Majestic Ballroom, and though he didn't like the Shouts, mostly because they featured a squeeky 'new wave'-style organ, he was still impressed by Gene's performance: "At this point Gene was making a sort of come-back. The Shouts did their own set of '60's R&B, and there might have been some dancers then, but when Gene came on they all rushed to the stage. Gene still had a reputation for a great show and there were shouts and applause and standing ovations. Gene appeared to be in good health and his voice was fine. He did *Lavender Blue* and handled the high ending perfectly."

Steve had tried to meet Gene backstage on previous occasions, only to be told that Gene had "collapsed." This time he got to meet him, but he was so excited that he could hardly speak: "I wasn't very articulate, 'cause I was in a state of shock. But Gene was certainly sober that night. I asked him to sign some photos for me and he got nervous 'cause the pen wouldn't write properly. He apologized and offered to sign the backs of the photos. Then I asked him about the new song he featured in his act. It was actually *La-Den-Da-Den-Da-Da*, but Gene thought I meant *You Are My Sunshine*. I said, 'I just love that new song,' and Gene thanked me, then he looked up enthusiastically and told me how great Ray Charles was. He was very soft-spoken and polite. But he raised his voice one time when the band members were making some noise in the background. He turned and said, 'All right, you guys!' His face changed and he looked real mean. His eyes stood out as he stared at them. They left immediately. Then he went back to being soft and nice."

Star Club, Hamburg, 1964 (courtesy of Serge Schlawick)

Another young fan who saw Gene with the Shouts in 1964 was Graham Fenton, who later became a star himself in the band Matchbox. Graham saw Gene at a big ballroom in London: "The Shouts were doing their set and there was a lot of people there. I was in the lobby waiting to get in, and suddenly these heavies appeared and ushered Gene through the crowd. He was wearing a suede coat and he had a mop of curly hair and I thought, 'It's him!' I was just astounded. We got inside and there was this big build-up, 'Now, ladies and gentlemen, from the USA, the one and only, the amazing, the fantastic, the man in black... Gene Vincent!' The crowd just went berserk! Gene started with *Say Mama*, threw his leg over the microphone, then held the whole stand over his head. When he did *Baby Blue* he jerked his body to the beat and pushed the mike-stand back and forth at the drummer during the guitar solo. At the end of the show he teased the audience by going off stage. They all screamed for him to come back, so he reappeared and did *Be-Bop-A-Lula* and the crowd went mad. They were all pushing and shoving and going crazy."

In early '64, Gene and the Shouts went into the studio, and for the first time since the fifties Gene recorded a whole album of rock'n'roll. Ever since the break-up of the Blue Caps, different producers had been trying to soften Gene's sound and make it more commercial, though completely without success. The only really rockin' track that Gene had cut since then had been *I'm Goin' Home* with Sounds Incorporated. Now he was allowed to cut an album that was more or less a reflection of his frantic non-stop stage act. The result, *Shakin' Up A Storm* on Columbia Records, has been criticized by some rockers as being too rushed, and apparently it was cut in two or three days. But it makes up for this with its abundant energy and the terrific drumming of Victor Clark. Gene did a lot of standards, including Little Richard's *Hey-Hey-Hey-Hey*, *Long Tall Sally* and *Slippin' and Slidin*, Dale Hawkin's *Susi Q* and Sam Cooke's *Another Saturday Night*, as well as some originals. But the highlight of the album is probably Gene's second rendition of his self-penned fifties classic *Baby Blue*, where organ and saxophone are used instead of background vocals. Back in the *Be-Bop-A-Lula* days, Gene's voice had been almost too pure and sweet. Now, after eight years of touring, his voice had become rougher and more soulful, yet his range hadn't suffered, as some of the ballads like *Lavender Blue* and *Someday (You'll Want Me To Want You)* demonstrate. Still, Gene's come-back attempt was not entirely successful. Columbia released a fourth single, *Private Detective* b/w *You Are My Sunshine*, and though Gene and the Shouts did a tremendous version of *You Are My Sunshine* in the film *Don't Knock the Rock*, the record never made the charts.

1964 was definitely the year for the British groups. In August the Beatles had their third Number One hit of the year with *A Hard Day's Night*. That same month the Rolling Stones hit the number two position with *It's All Over Now*, and in December they made Number One with *Little Red Rooster*. Even Presley, who had three singles in the charts that year, failed to get into the top ten. The only American rockers who did well were Chuck Berry, who made the number six position in June with *No Particular Place to Go* (a re-make of his 1956 classic *School Days*), and Roy Orbison, who reached number two with *Pretty Woman*.

Gene, as always, kept on touring. A drummer named Terry Noon played with Gene for some time and saw him at his best and his worst. According to Noon, Vincent was lonely and felt he was being exploited. He was in continuous pain with his leg and often con-sulted specialists. At times he had either a brace on his leg or a thick plaster cast from the knee to the ankle. 'Not many people realized after seeing him going from one end of the stage to another with just the microphone as an aid, that off stage he could hardly walk without the aid of two crutches. He would take codeine tablets to relieve the pain and the daily consumption of these obviously increased.'[1]

Noon wrote in an issue of the *Gene Vincent Fan Club Magazine* that Gene was always polite, but in no way was he a sissy:

One evening after we'd finished playing a gig in the North of England, Peter Grant (Gene's roadie), Gene and myself went to the carpark behind the ballroom to get our car. The car was surrounded by about fifteen youths aged about eighteen who started calling out various names. This would often happen,

---

1. Terry Noon, in the *Gene Vincent Fan Club Magazine*.

especially if some of their girlfriends thought Gene was sexy, etcetera. Gene was between Peter and I and about twenty yards from the car. Peter, who was six foot two and weighed about twenty stone, said he thought it better that we return to the ballroom to get help or the police as there were too many for the two of us. Peter had discounted Gene because he was on crutches, and anyway, there was no way Peter or I could allow someone of Gene's stature to get mixed up in a street brawl. As we turned our backs on the gang, one of them called Gene a 'Yankee coward!' Suddenly, Gene turned on the gang and went after them, swinging one of his crutches over his head, shouting that he was going to take them all on! Within seconds they disappeared, running in all directions, which, for their sakes, was good. He really would have sorted them all out!

Terry Noon particularly remembers a five-night gig at the Olympia in Paris:

Some nights the whole show used to stand in the wings, as enthralled and enthusiastic as the audience over Gene's magic performance. When he was on form, nobody could follow him on stage! It seemed that every young person in the French capital came to see him. They blocked up the main streets outside our hotel and it took the police hours to clear the traffic. All the French recording artists attended the first night's performance, and Gene would often get really excited if the act was going well. Nearly every show would end up with at least one microphone being smashed. At times he'd also attack my drums, and at one concert I was left holding two drumsticks while the rest of my kit was scattered all over the stage where Gene had either thrown it or kicked it. This wasn't very good for my kit, but the audience would go wild!

Noon writes of how performing became harder and harder for Gene:

When I first became his drummer, he did a straight 45 minute act that was full pace from start to finish. We would all sweat buckets. Gene himself would shed more sweat than anyone else and work twice as hard. But towards the end of my stint with him he would sometimes only be on stage for twenty minutes and couldn't continue a minute longer.

About six months after I parted company with Gene, I went to see him at a ballroom in the North of England. The group backing him wasn't very good and his performance was poor. When I went backstage to his dressing room to say 'Hello', he seemed pleased to see me, but I could also sense the embarrassment that he felt. He knew things weren't 'right', but he seemed too tired mentally and physically to do anything about it.

Paris, 1964 (courtesy of Serge Schlawick)

Although Gene was no longer in the top ranks of the music industry, his personal life at least took a turn for the better: he got together with Jackie Frisco, the young singer he'd met in South Africa in 1961. One story has it that she came to London looking for him, found him in rough shape and nursed him back to health. Gene's parents say that Gene was in the hospital and Jackie got her father to get him out. Gene was to spend the next six years with her.

In late '64, Gene and Jackie left London and flew to South Africa. After a short holiday they flew to New York, then to Albuquerque, New Mexico, where the Craddocks and Ed and Evelyn Butler were living. Ed Butler says that Gene came back to retain his American citizenship and/or his naval pension. After visiting with his family, Gene and Jackie flew to Mexico where Gene got a quickie divorce from Margie Russell. He probably married Jackie Frisco in Mexico as well, though he wasn't legally divorced from Margie until March of 1970.

Jackie and Gene (courtesy of Tina Craddock)

In early 1965, Gene and Jackie returned to Britain and Gene began touring with a band called the Puppets. They played in France and Germany as well as the UK, and in June they began a summer-long engagement at the South Pier in Blackpool. Adrian Owlett had seen Gene that spring when he'd been playing around London, and he and some friends would usually try and get to any gigs within about fifty miles: "Gene was very accessible. He might just be standing at the bar. He never acted drunk but he must have been, because no one could drink as much as Gene and not be drunk. He was a veteran drinker; he could put it away and you'd never even know he was intoxicated."

When Gene was in Blackpool, Adrian read in the paper that he might be going into the hospital to have his leg amputated. As yet, Adrian hadn't had a really "in depth" conversation with Gene, but he wrote him and asked about his leg. He also mentioned their mutual interest in motorbikes, and some phoney driving licences that he'd made for Gene when Gene had toured South Africa the previous fall. A letter soon arrived at Adrian's home, written by Jackie and signed by Gene. A few days later Gene phoned and invited Adrian up. He'd rented a large four bedroom house and he and Jackie and the Puppets were all staying there. Adrian and a friend drove up on their motorcycles and stayed for about ten days: "We had just an amazing time. Gene was just great, no finer guy. He confirmed everything I'd ever known about him: the friendliness, the quiet speech, the drinking, the paranoia, and, of course, the phenomenal stage act. It was all there. Gene was clearly very popular with everybody on the show, which included Gerry and the Pacemakers. Gene would get on the bus, or the little railway, and just ride down to the South Pier where he worked. Sometimes he'd stop off at Uncle Tom's Cabin, a big seaside bar, and have a chat with all his friends. Then he'd get back on the bus and later walk down to the pier and sign autographs. He'd check into the theatre and then go to the next building, a big bar, where he'd enjoy a chat with the bartender. He seemed to prefer ordinary people.

"On Sunday he'd do a rock'n'roll charity show and there'd be visiting artists like Manfred Mann, Billy J. Kramer and P. J. Proby. Afterwards they'd all go to Gene's house on the north shore. Gene knew he was being used because there were a lot of flakers and hangers-on and Gene didn't suffer them very well. First of all they'd drink his booze, and that was sacrilege!"

P. J. Proby was a big star in Britain at the time, and though he and Gene were both from the Southern States, they didn't get along. According to Adrian, Proby came over one Sunday and started getting "light-fingered," taking Gene's booze and trying on some of his clothes: "P. J. Proby was a real redneck. He was right out of it and started going through Gene's stuff. So Gene threw him out, physically! Gene had big arms and a massive chest. Gene grabbed him by the scruff of the neck and pushed him to the door. Proby was embarrassed and left. And he wasn't asked to do another show."

Adrian also witnessed some card games: "One time there was a poker school. And Gene was good, but evil. He won everything Karl Denver owned, including his house. Gene didn't cash it in, but he won it. All the neighbourhood thugs showed up. But they didn't come back!"

Every night Gene, Jackie, the Puppets and Gene's entourage would all go down to the South Pier: "The audience would be sitting in deck chairs and Gene only did four songs, *Blue Jean Bop, Dance To the Bop, The Last Word In Lonesome Is Me* and *Be-Bop-A-Lula*. The Puppets had organ, guitar, bass and drums, and they were very average, but quite lively. We'd be standing in the wings with Jackie, and Gene would bring the show to a standstill with *The Last Word In Lonesome Is Me*."

Harry Dodds, who was running Gene's fan club at the time, also spent a week or so at Gene's house in Blackpool. " Gene and Jackie seemed very friendly. Jackie was about eighteen and she never criticized Gene. She seemed a smashing, very nice girl. Gene himself wasn't in a very good mood. He was under pressure. The Puppets were staying at his house and living off him. And there were all these hangers-on and they were all living off Gene. At one time there were about a hundred people there! It was a bit incredible. Gene did fourteen shows a week for twelve weeks and on Sundays he did a charity show for spastics and cripples. Afterwards they'd have a party and Gerry and the Pacemakers and some of the other acts would show up. Gene would have his Sunday dinner at one AM – roast beef and Yorkshire pudding!

"But Gene was strained and tired and he didn't like the Puppets. He had a fight with them one night. He pinned the drummer to the wall with one of his crutches and said, 'I'm gunna kill you!' This was because they took advantage of Gene. There were too many bums coming in. There were cigarettes and beer everywhere. And Gene never locked the doors, though the gold records were upstairs, along with Jackie's fur coats. Gene was drinking, but I never saw him excessively drunk. And he was very obviously looking forward to the end of the season."

When the three-month long gig in Blackpool came to an end, Gene and Jackie moved back to London and stayed briefly at the Madison Hotel in Sussex Gardens. It was known as the Mad Pad, "a time-honoured hotel where all the musos stayed." But Gene didn't plan on staying there long. Margie was demanding money for child support, and Gene was hassling with his manager, Don Arden, about money that should have been paid for taxes but wasn't and the other usual disputes. Adrian comments: "I think that Don Arden was starting to get heavy. Margie was also getting heavy. Don Arden's business methods were *very* suspect. Things weren't going that good. The world started shrinking in on Gene. His creditors and would-be creditors were getting ready to pounce. He'd had a very successful season and if anyone was getting ready to pounce, then now was the time."

In the middle of September, 1965, Adrian Owlett got a call from Jackie saying that Gene had had to leave the country abruptly. A few days later she flew off to join him. This move saddened a lot of British rockers, including Adrian: "That was the virtual end of Gene's British career. From then on there was no rock'n'roll in this country until about 1969."

Hollywood, 1968 (courtesy of Adrian Owlett)

10

I'm Back & I'm Proud

All the audience sing with Gene. Everybody is standing, yelling... It was the finish. But the fans don't care, because now they dream and the dream is all. Several cats said, 'I can die now, because I've seen Gene on stage.' It's the most sensational thing they've seen in their lives.

— Dominique Thura

Gene and Jackie went to South Africa to take a holiday before returning to the States, but as soon as the local promoters found out he was in the country they offered him work and Gene did several gigs. He was interviewed for a South African music magazine called *Pop Gear* and one of Gene's comments sheds light on his hassles with Don Arden. When asked whether he needed his manager's consent to work in South Africa, Gene replied, "Don't talk to me about managers. I don't have a manager any more. Up until a few months ago I had a manager who I trusted – and managers need trusting – but right now this guy's got $28,000 of my money and I can't touch him.... But that's another story."

Before Gene left Britain, his royalty cheques from Capitol Records were going directly to Don Arden, who was handing them over to Margie Russell. And she was allegedly signing Gene's name and cashing them. Capitol Records had released seven albums, 29 singles and nine EP's by Gene, and though they weren't all big hits, they obviously sold steadily and Gene's royalty cheques were no doubt quite substantial.

Financial problems weren't the only reason for Gene's departure from Britain. His left leg had developed osteomyelitis, which is a 'term applied to any inflammation of bone or bone marrow, usually caused by infection by... microorganisms.... Occasionally, osteomyelitis occurs by direct infection after surgery or after a compound fracture (and) especially if systemic infection has been immediately preceded by a blow to a bone. Common symptoms include chills followed by fever, and pain and swelling above the site of inflammation (which) begins in the soft parts of the long bones, often with the formation of pus-containing abscesses, and soon spreads over the entire bone, with consequent death of the hard portions of the bone.... Osteomyelitis is treated by injections of antibiotics such as penicillin, and by concurrent surgery to open the affected bone and drain the pus and dead tissue.... The affected limb is immobilized by traction prior to surgery, and is placed within a plaster cast after surgery to insure immobilization.'[1]

Gene planned to go to Albuquerque where he could be admitted to the Veterans Administration Hospital and have his leg examined, but he and Jackie stopped off in New York where Gene bought a black and white '55 Chevrolet, described by Ed Butler as "the slickest little car in the world." They drove down to Norfolk and visited both Bubba Facenda and Dickie Harrell. Bubba recalls: "Gene came over to my place on his way back from South Africa. He had a girl with him, a cute little girl, and Gene had a bit of an accent. I didn't know whether he was putting it on or not. We talked about doing an album together. I'd drawn a cover for him and he liked it. It had a Union Jack on one side and an American flag on the other. On one side were his American hits and on the other side his British hits. He didn't look bad, but he was heavier. He only stayed an hour or so. He was his same ol' fidgety self."

Gene and Jackie drove to Albuquerque and stayed with the Craddocks, and Gene went into the VA Hospital at the end of February, 1966. At first the doctors thought they could treat Gene's leg with antibiotics, then changed their minds and urged Gene to have it amputated. Gene was going to go through with it, but in the middle of the night before the operation he panicked, left the hospital in his night gown, caught a cab to his parents' place and got his little sister Tina to pay the fare.

1. *Funk & Wagnalls Standard Reference Encyclopedia*, Vol. 18 (New York: Standard Reference Works Publishing Company Inc.)

Gene recuperated at his parents' place, and in the spring of '66 he began thinking about his career again. He got in touch with his old friend Dave Burgess, who'd toured with Gene and the Champs and who was now president of Five Star Music and Challenge Records. Burgess arranged for some sessions, and in May, Gene and his sister Tina drove out to Los Angeles. Gene was drinking beer and speeding and they were chased by the highway patrol, but Gene eluded them by pulling off the highway and into a rest stop. They drove all the way to L.A., stopping only for coffee, and the next afternoon Gene recorded *Bird Doggin'* and *Ain't That Too Much*.

Shortly after this session, Gene and Jackie moved into a duplex on Franklin Street and he continued to record for Challenge. Gene was no doubt aware that lack of good material had been a problem for him the past few years, and he phoned his old pal Jerry Merritt up in Yakima, Washington, and asked him if he had any good songs. Jerry made a demo tape of two songs and one of them, *Born To Be a Rolling Stone*, was written especially for Gene:

> I had me house in Dallas
> A couple of years ago.
> I'd still be livin' in Dallas,
> But I heard a whistle blow . . .
> And I was Born To Be a Rollin' Stone.
> I went over to London,
> And, Lordy, what a swingin' town.
> But a fast talkin' phoney with a big cigar
> Tried to bring me down . . .
> And I was Born To Be a Rollin' Stone!

Gene really put his heart into this recording and he was probably thinking of Don Arden and his $28,000 when he sang that last verse.[2]

At the end of September, 1966, Challenge Records released *Bird Doggin'* b/w *Ain't That Too Much*. In December they released *Lonely Street* b/w *I Got My Eyes On You* and an EP with all four songs was

---

2. Afterwards Jerry complained that Gene had rocked up the song too much and it was meant to be slower.

released in France. None of these made the charts, and there were still no *real* rock'n'roll songs in the top ten: *Cherish*, by the Association, was number one, and the Beatles' hit, *Yellow Submarine*, seemed millennia apart from their early rockers. Even *Devil in a Blue Dress/Good Golly Miss Molly* by Mitch Ryder and the Detroit Wheels was a long way from Little Richard's original version of *Molly*.

Gene had spent most of 1966 recovering from ten years of continual touring, and probably paid more attention to his leg. Aside from a gig in Yakima with Jerry Merritt in January of 1967, Gene stayed away from performing. He had his teeth capped and changed his hairstyle slightly. It had lost a bit of its curl and Gene no longer swept it back into a ducktail or used hair-cream. The developing counter-culture of freaks and hippies were more interested in the San Francisco rock groups such as Country Joe and the Fish, the Grateful Dead, Big Brother and the Holding Company, and Jefferson Airplane. Gene was only 31 years old, yet it seemed he belonged to a different era.

Nevertheless, he still had a large following in Europe and a promoter in France got hold of Gene and began arranging a tour for the coming fall. At the end of July, 1967 Adrian Owlett phoned Gene and asked what was happening in Hollywood. Gene replied, "Ah, it's all a bunch of hippies running around with long hair." Adrian asked what he thought of the hippies and Gene said, "Well, we'll have to talk about that when I get over there. I'm not quite sure what I think about them yet." Adrian and Gene stayed in touch by mail and Gene mentioned that he didn't want any advance publicity on his forthcoming Challenge album because he was sure that Don Arden would try to wreck his career.

Two new albums came out in the fall: the Challenge LP, entitled simply *Gene Vincent*, and EMI's *The Best of Gene Vincent*, though neither was released in the States. It was the first time since 1958 that Gene had two albums out in the same year.

The cover of EMI's *The Best of Gene Vincent* featured a photo from the 1964 *Shakin' Up a Storm* era and Gene looks rather worn-out. But the tracks are almost all from the Blue Caps days and include a number of songs which hadn't yet been on any albums, classics such as '*Lula, Woman Love, Lotta Lovin', Rocky Road Blues, I Got a*

Baby, Say Mama, Wild Cat, Right Here On Earth and *Pistol Packin'*
Mama. (Elvis Presley had a 'greatest hits' LP as early as 1957. Why
Capitol took so long to release one by Gene is still a mystery.)

Back in 1965 when Gene returned to the States, Jackie had no
doubt been thankful for the holiday and wanted Gene to slow
down for a while. But after two years of relatively quiet life in
America, they were probably both eager to return to Europe and do
some touring. On the 11th of September, Gene and Jackie flew to
France and were greeted at Orly Airport by a number of fans
carrying placards heralding his arrival. On his first day he did two
radio interviews, one for Salut les Copains and another for Le Pop
Club. When asked his feelings about '*Lula* he answered, "It's been a
good song for me and we've sold four million. I always include it in
my act. It goes down well and I can't get away without singing it."
The announcer said that his fans considered Gene to be a hero and
Gene replied, "I'm no hero. The fans seem to like me because I've
got my own style. I don't see myself as a hero at all." When asked
about his leg, he said, "It's much better now, thanks to the won-
derful drugs that the U.S. has developed. Actually my leg pains me
about every two months, but in general it's great. I've been in and
out of hospital for tests and operations for some while, but I'm glad
to say I'm much better." Then the French interviewer made a rather
strange statement: "Gene, I have never met you before, and you
seem very nice, but some people I've met have said that you are
mad." Gene was upset and replied, "That's a downright lie. Do I
seem mad at all to you? I can't explain it, but I do notice that when
anything like this is said, I'm never around to hear it. I guess they
wouldn't dare say it if I was."

Gene and Jackie stayed in Paris for six days, then drove to Selon-
court where they began rehearsals with Le Rock'n'Roll Gang, a
French band with two guitars, bass, drums and singer. On the 23rd
of September, Gene and Le Rock'n'Roll Gang played at the town
hall in Rennes, and a fan named Jacques Soules took the train all
the way from Bourdeaux: "They announced 'Here he is, the man
you've been waiting for, from Hollywood, the Great, the King of
Rock... Gene Vincent!' Thunderous applause from the 4,000 fans!
Gene, in black sweater, leathers and his medallion, kicked off with
Bird Doggin'. He put in all the old stage movements and the sound

France, 1967 (courtesy of Steve Aynsley)

was perfect. The applause lasted five minutes! Then *Say Mama, Long Tall Sally* and *I'm Goin' Home*. Gene thanked the audience before doing a fantastic *Hi-Lili, Hi-Lo*. Next came *Good Golly Miss Molly* with the crowd singing along. Gene really let go on this one, dropping to his knees, shaking, stomping and moving in turn to each cat in the group, fixing them with that stare, encouraging them. *Born To Be a Rolling Stone* followed. The crowd kept yelling, 'Baby Blue! Baby Blue!' Gene appeared to be in a trance and wept tears of joy. A chick approached the stage and tendered her hankie. When the number closed, Gene used this to wipe his eyes. In French, spiced with a thick Virginia accent, Gene announced *Be-Bop-A-Lula*, and again the crowd sang along. Later Gene met fans and signed photos. He said the Rennes audience had completely overwhelmed him."

At the gig the following night, in Cherbourg, the promoter, J. C Pognant, booked Gene and Jackie into a "grotty" hotel, "a real flakers joint," and Gene promptly moved into a better place and sent Pognant the bill. This was only the first of Gene's hassles on this tour. Adrian Owlett and a friend showed up, having driven all the way from England on a motorcycle. Gene invited them to the rehearsal at the club, but the manager of the place wouldn't let them in. Gene said, "Oh no! If my friends don't go in, I don't go in!" As Gene turned to go, the manager apologized profusely and they all went in. Gene didn't want the general public admitted, but in ten minutes the club was filled with fans. And the manager had been charging admission! Gene left the stage, furious, and returned to his hotel room.

That night everything went well: "The club was small, but absolutely jam-packed. Gene swung into a fantastic version of *Bird Doggin'* to the delight of the audience. Then he broke into *the* best version of *Say Mama* and the audience went wild. After this, without so much as taking a breath, he began *Long Tall Sally* and rocked it for about five minutes. Then Gene slowed the pace down slightly, but only for a few seconds, with the intro to *I'm Goin' Home*. As soon as it began to rock the fans went wild with excitement. Then Gene said, 'S'il vous plait, *Good Golly Miss Molly*.' He tore into this, rockin' better than I've ever seen him. After *Molly* he spoke to the audience, thanked them and said, 'I'd like to do a song from my new album called *Gene Vincent*. It's a slow song, *Hi-Lili, Hi-Lo*.' Naturally this quietened down the audience, but they went wild again when he bopped into *Born To Be A Rolling Stone*. This, of course, is the favourite of the French cats and they really let Gene know they liked it! Then Gene slid his left leg backwards, put his right arm up and back and gave forth a long 'Weelll, the road is rocky... But it won't be rocky long.'

"After this, Gene turned around and thanked the Rock'n'Roll Gang. They then introduced a groovy beat which heralded *Baby Blue*. It was slower than the record and was the *best* version I have ever heard him do. By now the audience was really swinging and went into complete uproar when Gene went into *Be-Bop-A-Lula*. The effect was electrifying. The old Gene was back with a vengeance. On the floor, mike in the air, head back, shaking, jumping, stomping, it was all there."[3]

Gene went backstage and the manager brought champagne. Afterwards, followed by swarms of fans, Gene made a grand exit on Adrian's motorcycle: "Gene drove back to the hotel and I noticed that he had no trouble with the footbrake – prior to his return to the U.S. he had trouble doing this – Gene, of course, is a great motorcycle fan and he drove like hell away from that club."

Four days later Gene played at the Salle Rameau in Lyons and a young fan named Dominique Thura took a four hour train trip to see him: "The audience begins to yell, 'Gene! Gene!' Lights put out. And the music begins! It's *Bird Doggin'*. I leave my place and go to the front of the stage. I'm on my knees just at Gene's foot. The curtain opens. And Gene appears, Gene Vincent the King! Gene Vincent, God himself! It's great and after *Bird Doggin'* the audience is like crazy. Everybody yells. Gene smiles. And the second song begins. *Say Mama*. It's great too. Gene is wild. He takes the mike-stand, swings it, looks at his group and looks at the audience, but does not see us. He looks upwards, then begins *Long Tall Sally*. It's wild and great too. The Rock'n'Roll Gang back Gene very well. *Long Tall Sally* finished, Gene says, 'Merci beaucoup.' And then he falls to his knees. He crosses his hands and looks upwards. It's the most beau-

---

3. Adrian Owlett.

tiful picture I keep in my mind of this show, this picture I keep of Gene looking like a child who makes a request to God. In the audience nobody yells. Complete silence. Some fans cry as Gene sings *Hi-Lili, Hi-Lo*. It's very pretty and beautiful. After the song the fans yell, scream and howl. Then it's rock'n'roll time again: *Good Golly Miss Molly*. Fans sing along with Gene. A new song follows; it's *Born To Be A Rolling Stone*. It's not exactly like the record. It's better! On the record it's like a pop song, but here on stage it's rock'n'roll. Then begins the best slow song ever: 'Well, I got a brand new baby and I love her, yes, I do. She's my one and only and her name is *Baby Blue*.' Afterwards he does *Rocky Road Blues*, then *Be-Bop-A-Lula*. All the audience sing with Gene. Nobody is sitting. Everybody is standing, yelling. Gene was wild and the cats too.... It was the finish. But the fans don't care, because now they dream and the dream is all.

"Several hours afterwards we ask ourselves if it was real. We just want one thing now: to see another show. Several cats said, 'I can die now, because I've seen Gene on stage.' And I think they're right. It's the most sensational thing they've seen in their lives."

France, 1967 (courtesy of Steve Aynsley)

Gene played Limoges and Toulouse; then on the 6th of October he played in Geneva at the Salle de Reformation. Before the gig he was interviewed on a radio show, and when asked who his favorite artists were, he replied, "Carl Perkins, Chuck Berry, Elvis and Jerry Lee Lewis." When asked what he thought about rhythm 'n' blues, Gene said, "I don't mean the same thing as you when you speak of rhythm and blues. R&B for me comes from the South, the music of the forties and people like Junior Parker, T-Bone Walker, etcetera. And Chuck Berry too. But Chuck doesn't want to be named as a rhythm'n'blues singer, just as a rock'n'roller." When asked to choose one of his favourite R&B songs, Gene chose Chuck Berry's *School Days*, and he chose *Hi-Lili, Hi-Lo* when asked to pick a song from his new album.

Gene, Adrian, Jackie (courtesy of Adrian Owlett)

That night, Gene played at the Salle de la Reformation and he was seen by a young fan named Gabriel Delay: "At about eleven o'clock he appeared – 'The Screamin' Kid', 'The Wildcat', 'The King' himself in his black leather suit, short hair and changed appearance, which seems to make him look younger, a jumpin', singin', screamin' cat. 'Living' all his songs as if in a dream, here is Gene Vincent the *God* of Rock'n'Roll with the most exciting live show in the music world. Six years ago I considered Gene Vincent the greatest (I'm 18 now), but now I admire him a *thousand* times more." Two days later, Gene played Lausanne, Switzerland, then on the 11th of October he was back in France. Gene and Le Rock'n'Roll Gang kept up a steady pace of one-nighters through France and played at Mulhouse, Sens, Enghien, Nevers, Bordeaux, Montbeliard and Montlucon, but apparently there were quite a few hassles, some between Gene and the promoter, and some between Gene and Jackie. At Bordeaux the group apparently showed up late, though Gene was on time. Then at the end of the tour, it was rumoured that Decca (Challenge's distributor in Europe) was organizing a live session at the famous Golf Drouot Club in Paris. Fans travelled miles to be there, but something went wrong. Apparently, neither the band nor the recording equipment showed up. Gene bought drinks for the fans, then borrowed the guitar of his friend Moustique, a well-known French singer, and performed rock and country music by himself for about two hours. At the end of October, Gene and Jackie flew back to Los Angeles.

During the winter of '67/'68, Gene again began working through agent Pat Mason up in Seaside, Oregon. Pat had booked Gene in the fifties, and now he was the manager of Paul Revere and the Raiders. Gene had phoned Pat in Seaside, and while Paul Revere and the Raiders were in LA filming segments for their TV show Where The Action Is, one of the flakier shows of the 60's, Pat visited Gene at his place in Hollywood: "Gene looked fine. Gene always drank a lot, ever since I can remember him. But he seemed to have a good relationship with Jackie and she was into taking care of him. Jackie was a very mellow person, soft-spoken and good-looking. She was a smart girl. Gene was working on a boat at the time, a double-hulled catamaran. His royalties were still coming in and he probably put about $20,000 into that boat."

Gene was looking for work, so Pat got him some gigs in the Northwest. Pat owned a club in Eugene, Oregon, called the Cascade, and Gene would rehearse there during the week, when it was closed. Pat says that Gene would do about two gigs a week and got about $500 a night. This may not seem like much money compared to what Gene had got at the peak of his career, but he hadn't had a hit in years, and in 1968, $500 was a lot of money.

In the spring of 1968, Gene did a tour of the Midwest that included two weeks at the Frontier Club in St. Paul, Minnesota, where he had been so popular in the fifties. DiAnne Kaslow was there: "It wasn't as crowded as the old days at the Prom Ballroom. But Gene looked pretty good. He wasn't as heavy as he was near the end. He did a mixture of songs, rock and country."

In April, Gene was back in Hollywood and did an interview with deejay Jim Pewter. Pewter said that Gene looked great and mentioned that the last time he'd seen Gene was on stage in St. Paul in the fifties. Gene replied, "I just came from Minneapolis and we had... it was packed, every night. And the stuff I done was actually rock'n'roll, the old stuff. They didn't want to hear any of the new stuff." Pewter mentioned that Gene had picked up an English accent, and Gene replied, "Many people has told me that. I was hoping I wouldn't, but I suppose I have." When asked about Eddie Cochran, Gene said, "He was more like a brother to me. We hung around together and we went, you know, almost every place together. And when we were in England, why, you know, we travelled almost constantly together." Gene was asked about the fatal accident and said, "Me and him were coming from Bristol, England, to London. I was supposed to pick up some suits and Eddie had his girlfriend with him. And we hired a car, you see, and we thought that what we hired was a taxi. But on the way back the car skidded and he was killed. And I was busted up. It was a real tragedy. I was upset about it for a long time."

Pewter played Eddie's *C'mon Everybody* and commented that Eddie would be very happy to know that his recordings were still being played. Gene said, "Well, I hope, wherever he's at, I hope he knows they're being played. Because he was a very fun-lovin' fella. He was a *very* good fella. I think if you could have met him you would have liked him very much." Jim Pewter mentioned that he'd seen Eddie live once and asked Gene if Eddie played his own lead guitar: "Yes, he was a *fantastic* lead player. Actually, he started with the lead guitar before he ever started singing. He played for, gee, many record sessions. . . . He played for Capitol and many many recording studios around Hollywood here. Like I said, he was a very fun-lovin' fella. And I've never seen him mad. Never." When asked about his plans for the future, Gene replied, "They've asked me to go back to England on tour again, which I'm not sure I can do as yet because, as you know, I'm in the hospital with my leg."[4]

In May, Capitol Records in Britain re-released the original version of *Be-Bop-A-Lula*, with *Say Mama* as a flip side, a classic and powerful combination. *Say Mama* was picked by a British music magazine as record of the week:

> Possibly the most compelling figure ever to limp into a spotlight, I only ever saw him three times, but the combined image of those occasions is etched as deep in my boogie-box as anything that's happened since. He had an extraordinary appeal. Part hero worship, part sympathy, a false sense of identity – the James Dean syndrome – largely based on a few great records, an original punk personality and one of the most distinctive voices in rock music. Despite his reputation as a greasy demon, Gene was at his peak with cool jive and sentimental ballads, but this one, one of his best shots of energy, is a monster too. Recorded in 1958 and still being attempted by revivalist rock bands the nation over. Let's see it at No. 1!

Gene was supposed to go over to England for a tour at the beginning of June, but he couldn't make it because he was sick. And neither side of the single made the charts. By 1968, the psychedelic bands were enjoying immense popularity and Gene's career was definitely in a tailspin. The tragedy of Gene's career can be seen in the cycles of popular music passing back and forth between England and the U.S.A. The original music of the rockin' 50s, in which Gene had played such an influential role, was driven out of

---

4. From a recorded interview by Jim Pewter, included in the four-record set Rock'n'Roll Legend (Capitol Records).

America and adopted by young British groups who later carried it back to the States. And the popularity of the 'acid' bands was an outgrowth of this 'British invasion', but the connection this time was sociological rather than musical. Unlike the early British groups, the psychedelic bands were not influenced by '50s rock'n'roll but by the British example of self-contained musical groups who wrote and sometimes produced their own material.

At the end of June, Gene was well enough to go into the studio and record two tracks for Playground Productions. One song, *Story of the Rockers*, was written by Jim Pewter, who also produced the session, and its lyrics are worth quoting:

> It started out with Haley's Comets
> A-rockin' 'round the clock
> Then along came Presley
> With some hillbilly rock.
> Mix it in with Carl Perkins,
> Chuck Berry when he's workin'.
> And Little Richard out of Macon
> Inspired Jerry Lee to shakin'.
> Slow down the tempo with the Fat Man
> Bring back the rhythm with Bo's band,
> Don and Phil and Eddie Cochran
> And Buddy Holly kept a-rockin'!
> And that's the Story of the Rockers!

Unfortunately, the lyrics go on to mention various pop stars of the sixties, including such schlockmeisters as Bobby Rydell, the Four Seasons, the Beach Boys and Jan and Dean, but Gene's singing carries it off, and at the end he gets excited and says, "Hit me now... Chuck Willis, lord, ol' Sam Cooke! Sock it to me, yeah! Buddy Knox, Jimmy Bowen, Lloyd Price! Hey, don't touch that dial! I ain't through yet! Bobby Darin, Larry Williams... the Blue Caps!"

The other song, *Pickin' Poppies,* written by Gene and Jackie, also has interesting lyrics:

Poppy as a flower is pretty,
But true, what they do, love,
Do to you, love...
I like to see you when you're only you, love.
What you tryin' to do, love?

No doubt Gene didn't smoke pot or drop acid, but he certainly took prescription drugs, codeine and possibly stronger analgesics, and he at least knew a good deal about opiates and their effects. *Story of the Rockers* b/w *Pickin' Poppies* came out on Forever Records, but they had difficulties finding a distributor, and when it was eventually released it found little success.

In August, Ray Cheetham, an English pro soccer player in Los Angeles for a game, phoned Gene and arranged to meet him the following day: "I arrived at the bar on time, and after a few minutes Gene arrived driving a bright red sports car. He looked pretty fit and said his leg wasn't too bad. We went for a drink in a place called the Brown Derby, a bar in Hollywood that's surrounded by photos of all the stars who've ever been there. Gene's photo was very prominent on one of the walls. We talked for a while and chatted about the music scene in general. Gene said he didn't think much of the present pop scene in America, but was full of praise for the music that comes out of England. He said he liked the Beatles, the Stones and thought Tom Jones was great.

"Leaving Gene after a really memorable few hours (in which, incidentally, Gene never let me pay for a thing), I couldn't help but feel a little depressed. Here was a man with such a great original talent, and it's a tragedy that it is not more widely recognized."

In September, Gene and Jackie moved out of their duplex in Hollywood and into a big house that Gene had bought on Cochran Street in the small town of Simi Valley, a bit north of Los Angeles. It was no coincidence that Gene had picked a home on Cochran Street. In November, due to the efforts of Gene's French fan club, Capitol released *Lucky Star* b/w *Baby, Don't Believe Him*, which had been recorded with Dave Burgess' band back in October, '61. (It came with a photo sleeve that featured a picture of Gene with Sounds Incorporated, but it was only available in France.) In the meantime, Gene's contract with Challenge had expired, and because none of the three singles had made the charts, the album, *Gene Vincent*, wasn't released in the States. Gene looked around for a recording contract, but without any success.

Vancouver, 1969 (courtesy of Rich Hagenson)

In February of 1969, EMI/Capitol of Britain released *The Best of Gene Vincent, Volume Two*, a fine album that featured the best cover on any of Gene's records so far: a black and white picture of Gene in his leathers in 1960. The songs offered a good selection of his work, and some of them, like *The Night Is So Lonely, Yes, I Love You, Baby, I Got It, Crazy Legs, I'm Goin' Home, Right Now, Well, I Knocked, Bim Bam,* and *Race With the Devil,* had never been on an album before. This was Gene's eleventh LP (not counting foreign editions, other than British ones), but Gene still couldn't find a recording contract.

In May, Gene played at the Lamplighter Club in Vancouver, Canada, where he was seen by Rich Hagenson, a local singer and bandleader: "We had his old Capitol LP's and '78's and we gave them to him to autograph. Then he was on: *Be-Bop-A-Lulu, Lotta Lovin', Long Tall Sally*! His voice blasted it out to a full house, just like in the old days! Then he sang several country songs that were beautiful. . . . Later we got to meet him. We talked about rockabilly, Cochran, Perkins, and all the rockers he knew, and he mentioned how influential Bill Haley was in the transition from country to rock'n' roll. . . . Then he was up there again, looking slightly incongruous with a long-haired band behind him. The band didn't do him justice, but he did a great version of *Rocky Road Blues* and his powerful voice shone right through."

Later that month, Gene produced a session of his own and recorded four tracks: *Rainy Day Sunshine, Green Grass, Mister Love* and *Roll Over Beethoven*. They were later released as an EP under the title *Rainy Day Sunshine* on Adrian Owlett's Magnum Force label. Pat Mason says that he wrote *Green Grass* and told Jackie Frisco that she could have it published under her name. According to Pat, this was because Gene and Jackie weren't doing very well financially. These demo tracks undoubtedly made the rounds of American record companies, but without any success. Gene then sent a copy to Adrian Owlett, who couldn't find an interested company either: "I took it to every major company, but nobody was interested. The doors were closed to Gene and he couldn't understand it." Adrian listened to deejay John Peel's radio show, Top Gear, and one night he heard a band called Family doing a whole set of rock'n'roll, including a Buddy Holly song. At the time, Peel was apparently into "hippies and flower power" and rock'n'roll was considered a novelty. Adrian wrote Peel and told him how much he'd enjoyed the show. Later, Adrian was surprised to get a letter from Peel, so he phoned him and asked if he was interested in hearing Gene's demo. Peel had his own record label, Dandelion, and said he'd like to hear Gene's tape. Adrian took it over to Peel's flat and was surprised to find that Peel was a real rock'n'roll fan and had all of Gene's records. Peel heard the demo, then phoned Gene in

North Hollywood, where he'd moved after renting out his home in Simi Valley. After talking with Gene, he said, "We're going to do a rockabilly album!" Peel's partner, Clive Selwood, was the European boss of Elektra Records, so it was easy for him to arrange studio time for Gene in Los Angeles. This was a much-needed break for Gene.

Kim Fowley was the producer, and Skip Battin (who would play with the Byrds) was the bass player and band leader. Before the session started, Gene went to Skip's own studio to go over the arrangements of the songs: "I worked with Gene very closely and we pretty well let him do what he wanted. We got together maybe half a dozen times over a period of about two weeks. Then in August, we went into the studio. Gene was a difficult artist in some ways. He was a bit of a perfectionist, and Kim likes to move pretty quickly. Gene tried very hard, but he was pretty sick at the time. His leg was bothering him and he was in constant pain. But he was a trooper and he suffered through it. Gene was obviously in tune with the times, but I didn't know whether that was a good thing or not. I was familiar with his Capitol records with the Blue Caps and I kind of preferred them. Gene wasn't drinking at the time. Or if he was, then it certainly wasn't a problem because I would have noticed. His wife Jackie was there and their relationship seemed good. They seemed pretty close. The whole session was done in about a week."

Although Skip Battin remembers the session as running smoothly, Adrian Owlett says that Gene was dissatisfied with Kim Fowley and that one time Gene phoned in the middle of the night and said, "They've sent a madman over here. I just can't work with him. He wants to use a Moog synthesizer. He's smoking pot and laying around on the couch!" However, Tom Ayres, who later became Gene's manager, says that Fowley didn't smoke pot and hated synthesizers. (Gene's reference to synthesizers was probably an intentional exaggeration. In any case, the 'piano' on this album is definitely inappropriate and sounds more like a clavichord).

Red Rhodes played steel guitar on the session: "It was pretty loose. Gene was straight and looked fine. But he seemed kind of anxious, like it wasn't going too well." Red remembers that the musicians were drinking, but that Gene was abstaining: "Gene was cleaning up his act. We were drinking beer, but he wasn't. Though he looked like he wanted to."

Johnny Meeks played guitar on the Dandelion session and he says that he was called in because things weren't going too well: "Gene and Kim Fowley had words one day. Gene wanted to cut one of the songs over again, but Fowley said it was all right.... It seems to me, they slaughtered that damn album!"

John Peel hadn't yet met Gene, but during the sessions he talked with him over the phone, usually in the middle of the night as Gene could never remember, or didn't care about, the eight hours difference in time zones. "Gene would call at rather odd times with rather odd requests, like did we know where his wife was and things like that. He seemed rather strange. I just admired him immensely and wanted to be able to say that Gene Vincent had recorded on my label." Gene was probably having one of his alcoholic fantasies and may have thought that Jackie was fooling around. This was a persistent fear of Gene's and whether there was any basis for it or not didn't alter his suspicions.

Gene's Dandelion album, *I'm Back and I'm Proud*, stands up well, especially when compared to some of the crap that was popular at the time. It starts with *Rockin' Robin*, the fifties classic, and Gene does a talking intro:

Say, hey, ladies and gentlemen,
Say, I'm Back and I'm Proud.
Now don't you move another further, mother
'Cause daddy's wise to the rise in your levis.
Laaawd, we're gunna send you out some songs that send,
And we hope we're gunna send you out some songs that swing
And we're gunna do it like this,
Heeeeeeeyyyyyyy! He rocks in the tree-tops all day long...

Gene did covers of his first two hits, *'Lula* and *Lotta Lovin'*, and two other rockers, *Sexy Ways* by Hank Ballard and *White Lightnin'* by the Big Bopper, which Gene had originally recorded with Eddie Cochran in 1960. However, two of the best songs were country tunes that Gene rocked up: Ernest Tubb's *Rainbow at Midnight* and *In the Pines*, where Gene does a talking part in the verses:

211

Then I went to New Orleans and met a woman.
Man, she was a swingin' queen.
She took the number off my car
And gave it to me as a name...
And I shiver when the cold winds blow...
Yes, I walks off from Dallas, ladies and gentlemen,
Just movin' quite fast now.
I kick my side all the time.
Gotta watch out for the police.
Gotta watch out for everybody
Who knows my number and not my name.
Well, I wish I was back In the Pines...
Where the sun never shines,
Where you shiver... when the cold winds blow...
Now let me tell you, I walk south.
I'm movin' toward L.A.,
Movin' fast, with some grass.
I'm talkin' to some people on the way, you know,
But they don't know that it's my number
And not my name...
One of these days they're gunna catch up to me.
The police are gunna hit me with a great big ol' bullet, you
know,
And I'm just gunna lay down.
And I hope someday they're gunna lay me... 'neath the Pines,
And I'll shiver when the cold winds blow.

On the 13th of September, 1969, Gene was in Toronto, playing at
the Rock'n'Roll Revival show at the Varsity Stadium. Jim Morrison
of the Doors had been at the *I'm Back and I'm Proud* sessions and he
and Gene had become friends. It was hoped that the Doors would
back him up, but they were late in arriving so Gene went on with
the Alice Cooper Band.

The Varsity Stadium held an enormous number of fans, and
Gene was overwhelmed by the reception. Jim Christy, a Canadian
novelist and journalist, gives this brief description: "He came out in
his leather jacket and he was overweight, but he went over well. In
fact, his performance was the most touching of the whole festival.

In the middle or end of *Be-Bop-A-Lula* he broke into tears and couldn't finish the song. John Lennon was there to play with the Plastic Ono Band and he came out and embraced Vincent and hugged him. It was really something."

At the end of September, Gene flew to Britain for a European tour. Henry Henroid says that he got a trans-Atlantic call from Gene, who said that he was broke and desperately needed some gigs. Henry promised to get Gene some work, but told him that it would take a few weeks to organize. About a week later, Henry got a call from his friend Chris Hutchins, who was then a promotion manager for Tom Jones, saying that they'd just flown in from Los Angeles and that Gene had been on the flight, drunk, and had caused a big commotion that Tom Jones, an old Vincent fan, had straightened out. Henry didn't yet have a gig for Gene, so he told Hutchins to take Gene to a hotel in Bayswater. Hutchins supposedly booked Gene into the Hyde Park Towers, and when Henry showed up, Adrian Owlett was already there. Henry was surprised at Gene's appearance: "I couldn't believe it when I looked at his face. He was fat and had a beer gut." Gene was no longer the 25 year-old rock idol Henry had met back in 1960; he was 34 and trying to make a come-back.

Adrian Owlett says that he was at John Peel's flat listening to the *I'm Back and I'm Proud* tape and Peel said that he had a tour lined up for Gene. "Who's bringing him in?" asked Adrian.

"Henry Henroid's arranging it."

Adrian was startled: "But he works for Don Arden!"

Peel merely asked, "Does he?" Adrian says that Gene liked Henry personally, but detested him for working for Don Arden. On the 25th of September, Adrian got a call from Gene in L.A. Gene said he'd be over in two days and asked Adrian to meet him at the airport. Adrian also got a call from Jackie, asking him to look after Gene. On the day of Gene's arrival, Jackie sent a telegram to Adrian saying, "Please take care of Gene. I love him more than life itself." Adrian suspects that Gene and Jackie had been quarrelling and that Gene had come over ahead of shedule because "He probably felt a bit hen-pecked."

Adrian had been pledged to secrecy about Gene's new tour, but "unfortunately" Chris Hutchins was on the plane with Tom Jones and Hutchins had phoned Henry. So it's more than likely that Don Arden found out about Gene's return almost immediately, and this may have had a lot to do with the problems Gene was to encounter during his tour.

Adrian's account of Gene's arrival is much different than Henry's: "At first glance, Gene seemed the same as ever, hair beautifully disordered, and actually wearing a suit. He looked very well and the extra pounds he'd put on made him look very powerful. I whipped downstairs and Gene came out of the customs hall with a case, an attache case and guitar. He was pretty tired after the flight, so we made for the bar where I had a beer and Gene (this is true, cats) drank a glass of iced water." Adrian took Gene to his place and Gene slept until late in the afternoon, then he got up and talked with Adrian and a few fans who'd come over. Gene got out his guitar and sang some country songs, then they went to a nearby pub and drank beer. The next day Henry called. Adrian and Gene met him downtown and Gene signed a contract giving Henry 30% of his earnings for the entire tour! Adrian says that Gene signed only because he was desperate for work.

A couple of days later, Harry Dodds, president of the Gene Vincent fan club, came down to London from Newcastle at Adrian's invitation and spent a couple of days at Adrian's place. Adrian was at work, so Harry and Gene spent the days together: "Gene would sit around and play the guitar or else read motorcycle magazines. One time he said, 'I'll play some songs for you that you've never heard me do.' He did *A Million Shades of Blue, Distant Drums, In An English Country Garden, Scarlet Ribbons, I Walk the Line, Mr. Tambourine Man, Louisiana Man, Folsom Prison Blues* and some others. Gene was sober during the day, but he grew a little morose as the night wore on. He'd borrowed some money from Adrian and felt quite bad about that. He gave me some American money to go out and buy brandy. And he was sending flowers to Jackie. He also insisted that I go out and buy chocolates and gift cards for Adrian's mother and the cleaning lady. One night Henry Henroid came over and he and Gene talked privately in another room. He probably gave Gene an advance because he paid for the flowers and gifts with pounds after that. Gene was writing airmail letters to Jackie and I'd go out and post them. Sometimes he'd wake up in the middle of the night and smoke cigarettes in the dark. One time he went through his wallet and showed me various cards, driver's licence and so on, that proved he was still an American. Then he insisted that I parade around in his dressing gown with 'U.S. Navy' on the back. Then, when the gigs materialized and a car showed up to get him, Gene's whole disposition changed. He lightened right up and praised Henry. He'd been bored, just laying around the house."

Henry Henroid had organized a short tour of France, two nights in Paris, Lyon and Grenoble, and one night in Dijon. Adrian couldn't go along so he got a friend, Rob Finnis, to act as Gene's road manager: "The French tour was arranged rather mysteriously and I was sucked into a whirlpool of events beyond my control." In Paris, Gene played at the Rock'n'Roll Circus then at the Golf Drouot Club and he was backed up by Johnny Halliday's band. On the 11th and 12th of October, Gene played at the Palais d'Hiver at Lyon, and, because his scheduled back-up band didn't arrive, the sound was not very good: "The curtain rose and there was Gene wearing dark trousers, but not leathers, and a black leather vest. Gene turned to the group and said, 'Say Mama.' He began to sing, but it was slower than the record 'cause the group was too slow and didn't know exactly what to do. After that, Gene did a new song I didn't know, but later he told me it was *Let's Get Together*. Very good, this. After that came *Baby Blue* on which the backing was very poor. Next Gene did a weird *Good Golly Miss Molly*, and after the first verse the band got lost. At last, Gene, probably thinking that with such a group it was better to end here, sang '*Lula* very fast with a horrible backing and an out-of-tune guitar solo."

The next afternoon, Gene came on again, this time after rehearsing with the Kingbees: "Gene started with *Say Mama*, but much wilder than on Saturday and the band was a bit quicker this time. Then came *Let's Get Together* and *Baby Blue*, which was much better. Gene went wilder and wilder in *Good Golly Miss Molly* and *Long Tall Sally* and towards the end of *Sally* he hoisted the mike up into the air, yelling, 'We're gunna rock'n'roll tonight!' A fantastic '*Lula* closed the act and at the end two girls climbed on stage to kiss Gene... A much better show."

On the 24th of October, the same day that his new single *Be-Bop-A-Lula '69* b/w *Ruby Baby* was released, Gene began a three-day gig at the Drac-Ouest in Grenoble, but *again* the backing band didn't show up and Gene had to use a local group : "Gene sang *Rocky Road Blues*, but the band, even worse than the one in Lyon, didn't seem to react at all. Next was *Let's Get Together*, but the accompaniment was atrocious, and in fact they had to stop due to some technical fault. Gene came off the stage and sat at the bar ... and sighed about the group. The manager asked Gene to have another go and Gene did *Good Golly Miss Molly, Long Tall Sally, Say Mama* and *'Lula*. Then he left the club." Gene was no doubt terribly disappointed and may have had good reason to believe that the long arm of Don Arden had reached across the channel to hinder him.

Gene's last date of this French tour was in Dijon at the Moonlight Club and things finally went a little better according to Gerard Lautrey: "I can tell you this was a real triumph for Gene. He got off to a sensational start by going straight into *Say Mama*, then *Baby Blue*, though the group's knowledge of Gene's material left a lot to be desired. Then he sang *I'm Goin' Home, Long Tall Sally, Good Golly Miss Molly, Let's Get Together* and closed with *Be-Bop-A-Lula*. All the fans were yelling and clapping."

Though this last night may have been all right, overall the tour was a disaster. Adrian explains: "As a natural characteristic, most French promoters are crooks. They have a nasty habit of doing 'runners' after the gig. Poor old Rob Finnis was obviously doing his best to sort things out, but Gene was making outlandish demands, like wanting his money in advance. They'd refuse and Gene would refuse to go on. Then Rob would talk him into going on, and afterwards the promoter would do a runner. One night in Lille, Rob and Gene were in a hotel room and two gangsters arrived, complete with ironmongery. Rob and Gene managed to escape, but they were robbed of all their money. There were a couple of more dates and Henry Henroid went over and sorted it out and the tour ran its length. But Gene came back with no money and was ready to throttle Henry."

The tour had got off to a terrible start right at the beginning, when Air France lost Gene's luggage with all his clothes on the first day of his arrival in Paris. Things just got worse after that and Gene didn't get his clothes back until he returned to England. Henry tells his side of the story: "I got a phone call saying that Gene was causing havoc, so I drove to Paris and Gene was out of it, gone. He was ranting and raving and demanding money, so I drove him back to England and got him a gig at the Isle of Wight."

Actually, Gene flew back to England, and the tour was no longer the least bit secret. There had been a full-page article called 'Gene Vincent Cuts A New LP' in one of the British music magazines. The sub-title was 'John Peel's Label Gets A New Version of Be-Bop-A-Lula': 'Rock'n'roll, which has never been far away since it made its first appearance in the early fifties, is without much doubt about to become all-powerful again. And Gene Vincent, who has stayed closer to the music which made him famous than most other major rock'n'roll singers, is beginning to receive the kind of recognition from the young rock audience which is due to him.' The author had talked with Gene on the phone about his new album and Gene had said, "I have never worked so hard on an LP in my life. It's incredible the effort we've put into this." The author remarked, 'Gene's voice sounded soft and quiet, improbably gentle for a singer with so violent an image.'

The *Record Mirror* ran an article called 'Vincent's Arrival, Hot From Waxie Maxie':

Listen, it's like this... here's a chunk of news to grab those squads of pointy-toed rockers – Ton-Up Teds, and send them hurtling full throttle towards London Airport. Long a favorite here, Gene Vincent will arrive at Skyport on November 5th, 1969. It is hoped to organize a slam-bang 1950's style motorcade to escort Vincent into London. Grapevine whispers indicate booker Graham Wood is bickering with ace promoter Henry Henroid to provide the British rock'n'roll combo the Wild Angels – wearing Wild One caps and studded black leather – as a hefty backing unit for the tour.

Sure enough, not only did a motorcade of rockers show up to escort Gene into town, but the BBC sent a camera crew to shoot an hour-long documentary on Gene. Gene still hadn't got his clothes back and he phoned Adrian to meet him at Customs with something for him to wear. Luckily, the customs officers let Adrian through and he gave Gene a leather jacket and a scarf.

The next day the *Daily Mirror* featured an article called 'Return of the Teddy Boys as Rock Star Gene Flies In':

It was back to the teddy boy era for these pop fans yesterday. They were at London's Heathrow Airport to greet American singer Gene Vincent. . . one of the veterans of the rock'n'roll age. And the fans dressed to suit the occasion. Out of the wardrobes came drainpipe trousers and long jackets complete with velvet lapels. There were shoelace ties to complete the ensemble. And, of course, they wore crepe-soled shoes. Vincent, who was once earning £1,000 a week with records like *Be-Bop-A-Lula* and *Woman Love*, flew in from Paris for two weeks of appearances in Britain. A white Rolls-Royce was to take him into London – but first he had a few minutes with his fans. They chatted to him about the "old days" and then lined up for his autograph. . . on photographs, sleeves and even the inside of jackets.

Disc ran an article called 'The Leather Man Is Back':

Rockers of Britain are once again united by a common hero. Last Wednesday, greeted by members of the Wild Angels, Greasers by the score and a grand motorcycle cavalcade, Gene Vincent flew into Britain for his first tour in six years. The original wild leather man was back among us again!

Actually it had only been four years, but the article at least got some quotes from Gene: "The last time I was here was for a Blackpool summer season with Gerry and the Pacemakers. Then I went on to Africa for a while before my darned leg started playing me up again. I was in hospital in Albuquerque, New Mexico, for a long time under treatment, and eventually the doctors there said I'd have to have it amputated, but I eventually found another hospital in Los Angeles who treated me with a special drug so that things got better. I'm not as young as I used to be – 34 now – and the leg still plays me up every so often. I expect it will have to come off eventually. But it's good to be back in Britain. I didn't even know they were going to put *Be-Bop-A-Lula* out as a single, but anyway they tell me it's selling and I need a doggone hit pretty bad right now."

Melody Maker ran a story called 'Vincent the Great Rock'n'Roller is Back':

There they were in the foyer of a Bayswater hotel, the welcoming committee for rock'n'roll giant Gene Vincent. Complete with bright green socks, bootlace ties and drape jackets, the rockers were there to see the man who first had them rocking an incredible thirteen years ago.

Most of the article consisted of direct quotes from Gene about his music, his career and his new album: "We enjoyed the session very much. It took about a week to record, on and off. I think the album's one of the best I've done. It's the first one for two years, apart from the Best of's which were issued on Capitol. . . . I've always done some country numbers on albums, and this one has got a little bit more. The thing is, what you call country music, I've always called rock'n'roll. It's been rock'n'roll from the old days. The music of today hasn't changed that much. The groups today say they are doing something new, but when I first started you had single singers like Carl Perkins, then the singing groups started coming on strong like the Penguins and the Platters. Then it swung back to the single artists again like Fabian and Avalon. Then the Beatles came out and the groups started again. Now you've got the single artists again like Tom Jones and Engelbert. Nothing's changed really. The groups that are big today aren't really doing anything new. I was sure when I heard Creedence Clearwater that they were playing some Carl Perkins licks. The thing that's really changed is the recording techniques. Now they're really technical, and perhaps that's why people say musicians today can really play. They take care with the recording. Before, we used to go in and rehearse and then take it. . . . Now they do take after take until they get it right. . . . I don't think rock'n'roll has ever gone. The name's just changed. When Chuck Berry arrived, everybody said, 'Man, you're the king of R&B.' He said, 'I play rock'n'roll, but you can call it anything you like.'" The author ended the article with the comment, 'I left Gene to the Wild Angels and to the mercy of the BBC who arrived to film a documentary about one of the greatest rock'n'rollers of all time.'

BBC filmed Gene's arrival at the airport, then they got some footage of him sitting in the back yard at Adrian's house, playing his guitar and singing *Jolie Jacqueline*, an original, and *In An English Country Garden* by Jimmy Rogers. *Jolie Jacqueline* was obviously written and performed for Jackie, and Gene had just received a telegram from her saying, "Gene, please don't desert me. I can't cope. Please contact me. Love, Jackie." Whatever the hassle was between Gene and Jackie, it no doubt related to alcohol.

According to Adrian, the BBC had received threatening phone calls, purportedly from associates of Don Arden, warning them not to do anything on Vincent, but this only made them more eager to continue with the film, which was eventually released under the title *The Rock'n'Roll Singer*. Gene stayed with Adrian for a few days, then on the 8th of November they went with the BBC crew to the Isle of Wight where Gene and the Wild Angels were to appear at the Royal York Hotel in Ryde.

Henry's version of the Isle of Wight gig differs from Adrian's. Henry says, "Gene couldn't make it. He couldn't sing. He was drunk. It was really over. He could only perform for about fifteen minutes. He was just not Gene anymore. I'd had enough."

Adrian says, "Gene and I went over with the BBC crew in their van. Henry and Jimmy Houlihan went to the train, and we met them on the boat. Gene was upset because he wanted to avoid Henry. Then, at the hotel, all the heavies came out of the woodwork. At first Henry seemed very keen. And the club owner, Wilfie Pine, seemed very nice. But it became apparent during the afternoon that Wilf didn't have Gene's best interests at heart. At one point he tried to stop the BBC from filming and said to one of the crew, 'Stop or I'll smash yer fuckin' head in!' They were gangsters. The crew stopped for a few minutes, then re-started and they filmed Wilf grappling with the recordist. The recordist said, 'I'm being paid to do a job.' But Wilf snarled, 'If you carry on, you'll never be paid by anyone again!' The film actually shows the sound recording machine being knocked to the ground! Earlier, Wilf and

Jimmy Houlihan had been coming up to Gene's room with mickey-finned drinks, or at least especially strong drinks, trying to get Gene drunk so he'd lash his own show so that legitimately Gene wouldn't have to be paid. So we just kept tipping the drinks down the sink and Gene, against his nature, let us do it. We told him, 'Gene, these are not nice men and these are not nice drinks!' and he knew. He hadn't played in England in four years and he really wanted to do a good show. And he did. Gene did one or two encores and got tumultuous applause. Even the BBC crew, who'd seen a lot of shows, said that they could feel the electricity."

Part of the BBC film, a very small part, was later included in the film *Blue Suede Shoes*, and it shows Gene and the Wild Angels doing the beginning of *Baby Blue*. Gene puts on a tremendous show. But for some reason, whether copyright hassles or pressure from Don Arden, only about thirty seconds of Gene's performance was shown. BBC radio tapes done on the same tour make evident Gene's undiminished abilities.

According to Adrian, after the gig they went back to their hotel room and Gene said, "We ain't gunna get no money, man!" Adrian tried to collect, but ended up arguing with Wilfie Pine, who tried to get heavy. Henry apparently insisted that Gene owed him money from advances. At this point Gene started drinking. By then it was late in the afternoon and outside their room Jimmy Houlihan was beating up one of Gene's fans. Henry and Adrian started screaming at each other and Henry said, "There's past debts to be settled." Adrian thought he might be killed.

Later, without having been paid, Gene, Adrian and the BBC crew went to an after-hours club: "It was just like a Chicago gangster club in the thirties with guys running around in striped suits, black shirts and white ties." It turned out that the club was owned by Wilfie Pine, so they went straight back to their hotel rooms. In the morning, the BBC people paid for the rooms and the producer, Andy Finney, suggested they take a different route back because otherwise it might be too dangerous. According to Adrian, they were actually chased to the ferry landing by another car and just got on in time.

This must have been very frightening for Gene and no doubt confirmed his paranoid fantasies. He had always thought that agents and managers were using him and trying to do him in. Now he must have felt certain.

Luckily, things soon improved. Two days later, Gene played at a U.S. Airforce base in Suffolk, then on the 11th of November he played at a pub in London called the Northcote Arms and was seen by a fan named Dave Hawkins: "The first thing that struck me was the drapes, hundreds of them. The place was really packed and most of the cats were wearing the great gear. The Wild Angels played for half an hour, then the lead singer said, 'Here's the man himself, Gene Vincent!' The next minute he was standing on the stage and the cats went wild and nothing yet had happened! Gene rocked into *Say Mama* and *Baby Blue* and he was quite overcome by the crowd's reaction. They were going berserk, singing along, bopping, clapping, whistling... As I left you could still hear some of the cats chanting, 'We want Gene!'"

The following night, Gene played at Bligh's Hotel in Sevenoaks, Kent, where he was seen by Dave Bowell: "Gene featured eight numbers and the 500-600 fans gave him a very good reception, yelling for him to do an encore. The show hadn't been advertised, nevertheless there was a fantastic atmosphere. While Gene was singing his shadow moved menacingly at the back of the stage. He was dressed all in black and his movements became more demon-like as he rocked his way through his act."

The next day he filmed a clip for BBC's Top of the Pops, then on the 16th of November he played at the Hampstead Country Club. This gig was written up in a London paper:

Memory Lane took a lot of walking down on Sunday evening at London's Hampstead Country Club where rock'n'roll star Gene Vincent appeared during his British tour. At the entrance to the club there was a poster of Vincent in the old days – hair all greased back, thin-faced and defiant. Today's Vincent has changed. He has grown plump with encroaching middle age, his hair is short and swept forward and the defiance has gone. But he still rocks like mad. Backed by the Wild Angels, Gene went through a whole repertoire of rock'n'roll standards. He was dressed in a black leather waistcoat over a black sweat shirt with a silver medallion hanging from his neck. He held the microphone just like he used to – clinging to it as though it were the only thing keeping him upright. And he bopped around a bit – holding the microphone stand upright in the air and hopping about the stage. The audience screamed for more. It was great old-fashioned rock'n'roll. The Teds in the club had a great time jiving and screaming and chanting that "Rock will never die!" Whether Gene Vincent can keep up rocking and rolling forever is another thing. He's getting on a bit.... But Sunday's performance was a fabulous piece of nostalgia just the same.

On the 20th, Gene and the Angels played a more important club, the Speakeasy, and things went a lot better: "Gene went on and *slayed* the audience. Nearly through the set, Georgie Fame took over on piano.... Gene broke all house box-office records and the audience included many stars such as John and Yoko, George Harrison, some of the Who, and many others.... In the end there were dozens of people who came to congratulate Gene on a brilliant show."[5]

Gene's most important gig was probably at the London Palladium where Gene did two shows and headlined over the Tributes, the Impalas and the Nashville Teens:

Oxford Circus was a hive of activity. The streets began swarming with drapes.... A cheer went up as the curtains parted and there was Gene, completely in black (though minus the gloves), the medallion and chain around his neck, and a belting version of *Say Mama*. Nothing had really changed since I last saw Gene live nearly six years ago. The familiar stance, one leg back, and Gene looking up into the gallery, the mike and stand whipped around him, and pounding the mike-stand on the stage: it was all there in his opening number. After the applause, Gene thanked us and said it was nice to meet lots of

---

5. Adrian Owlett.

friends from a long time ago: 'You've been very kind to me.' He then announced a song from his new album... a fantastic version of *Lonesome Whistle*. It was one of those numbers that proved that as well as putting on a wild rock performance Gene can really *sing*. Gene next announced a song he hoped we'd remember: 'One that Eddie Cochran arranged for me that I picked up after he died.' It could only be *Pistol Packin' Mama*. Then it was a rave-up version of *Rocky Road Blues*. Gene jumped over the stage and the audience clapped in time. It ended up with Gene on one knee with the mike-stand straight up in the air above him for the last verse.... *Good Golly Miss Molly*... more clapping, head shaking and wild hair. Then straight into *'Lula*, the 1969 arrangement, but it was wild and Gene ended the song on one knee with the whole theatre full of hand clapping... The second house audience was more appreciative. During *'Lula*, Gene got down on one knee, his guitarists too, while the drummer went suitably berserk and the pianist courted dire physical injury. All the stalls erupted with a great number of cats boppin' and jivin' in the aisles... A great evening for rock and Gene Vincent fans.

This gig at the Palladium was written up in one newspaper under the headline 'Boos, Then Gene Rocks': 'Gene Vincent must have been the happiest man at London's Palladium on Sunday. Gene turned the boos for the first-half acts—two rock bands and the Nashville Teens... into cheers... Gene looked completely overwhelmed by the Wembley-like applause. His audience... was colourful. Drapes in all colours, string ties, crepe shoes, red socks, DA haircuts—all added authenticity and nostalgia. A night for rockers to remember—two hours of misspent youth recaptured!'

Gene's come-back tour finished with a successful gig in Belfast. Although it had been marred by the problems in France and at the Isle of Wight, the later gigs and the enthusiastic audiences had made up this, and at the end of November, Gene returned to America where Capitol had, at last, released an album that included *Be-Bop-A-Lula*. It was called *Gene Vincent's Greatest*, and though the cover featured only one tiny picture of Gene, taken in 1958, it has some of his best cuts, such as *Race With The Devil*,

Woman Love, Lotta Lovin', Important Words and *She She Little Sheila*.

In January, 1970, Dandelion/Elektra issued *I'm Back and I'm Proud*, and though the press reviews in Britain were lukewarm, Gene got a great feature article in *Rolling Stone* in March of 1970:

Gene Vincent was the most tortured of the Fifties rock stars. I only saw him in concert once and that was weird. He was in pain throughout and sang kneeling, his bad leg stretched out straight behind him. In the faster numbers he gyrated on his knee, swinging his straight leg right round over the microphone, wriggling across the stage, sweat pouring over his leather suit.

He was fat, ugly, and greasier than Joe Cocker. There were no girls in the audience, but for the assembled rockers he was the ultimate in rock'n'roll – offering nothing but music and sacrificing everything to that music, their music. I've never seen another rock star so worshipped and held in such awe by an audience.

The white, drawn, agonized Gene Vincent had entered into myth (he hurt his leg in the crash that killed Eddie Cochran) – but the pain was real enough. It interfered with his career and his music. ... Gene Vincent's music was tough and very edgy, and his best records were extraordinarily tense. The excitement of *Be-Bop-A-Lula* comes less from the beat than from the feeling of suppressed energy and feeling that Vincent and the Blue Caps are holding themselves back.

Gene Vincent had one of the most remarkable voices of the Fifties, with great range and perfect control (most noticeable in slow numbers like *Important Words*), but it always had a neurotic feel, slightly anxious. He used his voice as an instrument (listen to the famous hesitation style in *Woman Love* or his very effective vocal support for the lead guitar in *Race With The Devil*) and the sound of his voice was always more important than the words in giving his songs atmosphere.

The tension was a result of the conflict between Vincent's originality and the demands of the rock'n'roll single. The Blue Caps added to this tension. Both Cliff Gallup and Johnny Meeks... had an extraordinary ability to play all the instrumental-break cliches while still sounding original. On *Blue*

Jean Bop, for example, Gallup sounds as though at any moment he might break out and destroy the record altogether. He never quite does and the results were some of the greatest rock singles.

Long before we worried about the significance of record production, Gene Vincent and the Blue Caps were *issuing* total creations, not just good songs but good *records* with everything going in to make a complete three-minute experience. The best examples on this album [*Gene Vincent's Greatest*] are *Lotta Lovin'* and *Yes I Love You Baby* where the interplay of voices and instruments are perfect, the total effect being built up from the conflict between all the elements. . . . These tracks quite transcended the normal rock'n'roll singles of 1957–58.

The author, Simon Frith, compared *Gene Vincent's Greatest* unfavourably to the English EMI *Best of Gene Vincent*, volumes one and two. Frith picked *Git It* as the best song, as well as *Say Mama* and *Right Here On Earth*, 'which faultlessly sum up rock'n'roll.' Next, Frith went on to review *I'm Back And I'm Proud* and picked *In The Pines* and *White Lightning* as the most interesting tracks. Frith gave the album a good review, but ended it by saying that he preferred the Blue Caps recordings: 'Nobody makes records like that anymore, not even Gene Vincent.'[6]

This article was a full page and included four pictures, one each from '56, '60, '64 and '69. Oddly enough, the story was titled 'Gene Vincent 1956–1970', and it has a slight feeling of eulogy to it, as if Gene were already gone. But it was great publicity, and Gene, no doubt, had great expectations for the future. The sad truth was that, although some of his most creative work lay ahead of him, he now had only a year and a half to live.

---

6. *Rolling Stone,* March 7, 1970. Page 52.

(courtesy of Evelyn Butler)

11

A Million Shades of Blue

After he died, he had the sweetest smile on his face. He wanted to die. He was glad to think he was getting out of the mess he was in.

— Louise Craddock

In the early spring of 1970, Gene got a new manager and a new label and he cut his 14th album. His new manager was Tom Ayres from Shreveport, Louisiana. Gene knew Tom from 1956, when Gene was with the original Blue Caps and Tom played bass with the Johnny Burnette Trio: "I joined after Bob Black quit. We toured through New York State and Ohio. Gene Vincent was just another one of the guys. But he could sing anything. He had one of the best voices in the history of popular music. But the whole pace of rock'n'roll was killing Gene. His leg was super-painful. You could actually bend it like rubber. We wanted to slide him into a sort of Jerry Lee Lewis semi-country style. I wanted Gene to maintain his own permanent band so we could maintain him. We realized that Gene just couldn't continue on the way he was doin'. He was at the age where he couldn't tour the whole country going from club to club anymore."

At the time, Tom was manager of the Sir Douglas Quintet, and after he became Gene's manager he phoned Neil Bogart at Kama Sutra Records in New York and told him, "Look, I've got Gene Vincent and I've got the Sir Douglas Quintet to back him up." Apparently, Bogart was a big fan of both the Quintet and Gene and he told Tom, "Get them into the studio as quickly as possible." This was another big break for Gene. (The details of his previous contract with Dandelion are not known, but it can be assumed that it was a short-term affair, and since neither the album nor the single had

229

sold particularly well, the contract had not been renewed.)

Gene went into the Sound Factory in Los Angeles with the Sir Douglas Quintet, minus Doug Sahm, and recorded ten songs. The session was written up in *Rolling Stone* under the title 'He Sounded Maybe Like He Was Testifying':

When he started recording, Gene was in his teens. He was skinny – all right, lean – and toughlooking and came across three times life-size on record. But the years have not been particularly kind to Gene, and he now sports an obvious paunch. His hair is thinning, and he turns out to be one of the most mild-mannered guys you've ever met. . . . To see him performing a song like *Woman Love* might prove to be a bit embarrassing. On the other hand, it might not. Gene might be fifteen years older, but he sounds better than ever when he wants to. . . . "Let's get on with it," he says. . . . The first song will be *500 Miles*. . . . Things seem to be going well; then Gene stops singing, "I'm sorry, gentlemen. My fault. Let's start over." It always seems to be Gene who senses that a take isn't going well, and he's the one to stop the band. This time it's the inflection of some of the words in the recitation. "Gene," says Tom, "it sounds too preachy, like you're in church. Or maybe like you're testifying."

"That's what I want it to sound like."

Two or three more takes and *500 Miles* is down. . . . The girls were both in the recording booth now, dancing. There was a long instrumental break and the band were cooking hard and heavy. . . suddenly it was over. The audience broke into applause. . . "Wow," someone broke the silence, "have you got a single there!". . . Harvey timed it, just over nine minutes.

"Well, how's it feel to have another gold record?" asks Augie.

"I just don't know," says Gene,. "It's pretty long."

Now everybody's in on the conversation, and it's nine to one, trying to convince Gene that people like long tracks that they can dance to. "Why look at Iron Butterfly, the Doors, *Like A Rolling Stone*. . ." Gene still isn't convinced.

This article is almost incredible. The song in question was *Slow*

Times Coming, possibly the worst recording Gene ever made and Gene obviously realized its faults. Gene sang it well, but then the guitar players go into some of the most idiotic and boring solos ever recorded, complete with wah-wah pedal and fuzz-tone. Years later Tom Ayres confided, "I asked Gene about Johnny Meeks and Cliff Gallup, but he said they were off somewheres. If I could do it again today, I'd keep it to two minute songs and try to get Cliff or Johnny."

Not only did *Slow Times Comin'* clock in at nine minutes and nineteen seconds, but another song, *Tush Hog*, came out at 7:35. The album was released in America as *Gene Vincent*, and in Britain it was called *If Only You Could See Me Today*. It is Gene's poorest album but thankfully it contains three great songs, all of them country ballads: *Sunshine* by Mickey Newbury, *Geese* by Gene, and *500 Miles* by Bobby Bare.

At the end of March, 1970, Gene went to New York where he played at the Felt Forum on a rock'n'roll revival show. The other stars were Little Richard, Bo Diddley, the Drifters, Ruby and the Romantics, Timi Yuro, and the Five Satins. Gene was backed up by Bobby Comstock and the Counts and he did two shows a night, but only did three songs for each show: *Lotta Lovin'*, *Whole Lotta Shakin* and *'Lula*. A fan named James Morfogan saw the gig: "He was good. He was still a great performer." James had a backstage pass, so he went into the dressing room, which Gene shared with the Five Satins. James had originally met Gene at the Toronto Rock'n'Roll Revival Show the previous fall, so he re-introduced himself and congratulated Gene on his performance. James couldn't help but notice Gene's good manners and his soft voice. They talked about rock'n'roll, and when James mentioned Jerry Lee Lewis, Gene said, "I love Jerry Lee Lewis. Trouble is, when we get together, we always fight." Gene asked James if he'd help him find his hotel, the Pennsylvania. James got a taxi and helped Gene with his suitcase, but they couldn't find the right hotel so Gene checked into another place. Another fan, a Vietnam vet, had tagged along, and the three of them chatted for a while. The vet insisted on showing Gene his napalm burn scars. Gene mentioned that he was a Buddhist and that he'd studied yoga. The veteran asked if he knew any pressure points and Gene offered to demonstrate. The vet didn't want to be a guinea pig, so James let Gene squeeze him on the neck with his thumbs. James blacked right out, and when he came to, Gene smiled at him and said, "You know I wouldn't hurt you for the world." James comments: "Gene could be pretty off-the-wall sometimes." (This story is echoed by Adrian Owlett: "Gene was into Buddhism, called himself a Doctor of Metaphysics, and said he had a certificate to prove it. He had the unnerving habit of putting people out by applying pressure to the arteries of the neck. In France one time he put out the whole band! He turned to me and said, 'Look at them. They're at peace. Their souls are leaving them.' I said, 'Gene you've almost killed them!'")

Afterwards, Gene, James and the other fellow all went down to a restaurant in Greenwich Village. Gene had lobster and drank only a couple of beers. Gene and James arm wrestled and Gene won. Later, they went back to the hotel room and James stayed with him. Gene was wearing a black and white shirt and a sheepskin jacket and he opened his case and showed James a picture of Jackie. He showed James his leg injury and said he'd already had eighteen operations. James noticed that Gene had trouble sleeping.

James went to Gene's gig the next night, but didn't stay with Gene afterwards. Gene asked him to come back the following morning and James helped Gene into the cab for the airport. Gene had offered James a job as road manager and told him to call him in L.A. on a credit card number. As Gene sat in the cab, James told him, "I really enjoyed your company. Thanks a lot. See you later."

"I don't think so," said Gene. "Haven't you heard? I've only got a year to live. The leg's got cancer." Then the cab pulled away.

When Gene got back to California, he played a gig at the Avalon Ballroom with Commander Cody and the Lost Planet Airmen as back-up. While he was in the Bay Area, Gene took the time to visit his old friends Johnny and Chuck Wayne who were having a party. Darlene and the kids happened to be there, and Tom Ayres remembers Gene giving Vince Jr. a guitar. Melody Jean Vincent was also there and she looked around the room for her father but couldn't recognize him, though she was familiar with his face from various album covers: "He just wasn't the person I was expecting. I expected a real thin guy, a 'wildcat', but I couldn't see him. Then he came over and introduced himself. Afterwards he took me and Debbie and Vince to Sears and told us to pick out anything we wanted. Debbie got an AM/FM radio and Vince got a punching bag. I got a bike."

A week later, Gene phoned Darlene and asked if the kids could stay with him in Los Angeles for a week or so. Darlene was a little worried that Gene might try to take custody of the kids, but they wanted to go, so she let them: "I kind of felt sorry for Gene 'cause his leg was bothering him a lot. But I didn't have any real deep feelings for him anymore. Just friendship."

Debbie, Melody and Vince flew to L.A. and Gene picked them up in his red sportscar and drove them to his apartment near Santa Monica Boulevard. It was a third floor apartment and Jackie wasn't staying there, though she came over to meet the kids once.

Gene wasn't gigging and had time to spend each day with his kids. He took them to the Capitol Tower and showed them the gold star on the sidewalk with his name beside it. He showed them his gold record of 'Lula and sang to them. He sang *Weeping Willow* to Debbie and told her he had written it for her. He played *Darlene* for them and explained that he'd been angry with their mother when he wrote it. They ate in restaurants every day and nobody came over except the maid, to clean up. At night, when Gene had to relieve himself, he'd get up without bothering to put on his leg brace and simply hop on one leg into the bathroom. Later, the landlady came up to complain about the hopping. None of the kids remember Gene drinking at all. When it was time for them to go back home, Gene drove them to the airport, kissed them goodbye and cried. His children only saw him one more time, later that year. They visited him again in L.A., but only for a few days. Then Gene had to leave town on some tour. Melody says, "I never got to spend that much time with him. But I know one thing. He was a good man."

In April, Gene was interviewed over the phone by a British journalist and some of his comments appeared in an article called 'It's Agony, But I Won't Let Them Amputate My Leg, Says Gene Vincent':

"Rock'n'roll is back," announced Gene Vincent with a smile.

"It's never been away really, but in the last six months I've been so much in demand, you'd never believe it. A new generation has discovered rock'n'roll all over again. It's very exciting for me. . . . The doctors want to take (my leg) off, but I keep saying no. The way medicine progresses every single day, they might find something to cure it, and I'm not willing to take the risk. I have to take morphine to kill the pain when it gets really bad, and the last time I came to England I got really whacked out. My leg is giving me a little problem all right, but I try not to let it beat me. . . . Revival? Rock revival! I don't see that it needed to be revived. It has always been around, even when it was called beat. . . during the Beatles' big period. . . . The Beatles have always been a rock'n'roll group, and John Lennon has said he's just a rocker. . . . A whole new generation has discovered that it's the best pop music there is. . . . I put everything I've got into my stage work. I still love to get out on the road. One day it may kill me, but I'll never stop."

On the 20th of June, Gene flew to Paris for a short French tour and was met at the airport by Adrian Owlett and about fifty French fans. Gene was booked into the Hotel Moderne and another fifty fans were waiting outside for him to arrive. The back-up band was English, the Houseshakers, and their regular singer, Graham Fenton, remembers Gene's arrival: "Fans were asking him for autographs, and Gene looked in pretty good shape. He was fat, but he looked good."

This tour was booked by Michel Thonney: "An absolute amateur, a young guy who was being drafted into the army on the day after the tour. Another bungling amateur."[1] Their first gig was an open air concert at St. Gilbert, and Gene apparently got a raucous reception. That night they played again in Freancaud to a crowd of 2,000 people, but the Houseshakers had been given faulty instructions and couldn't find the venue, so Gene went on with a local jazz band and did some rock standards. They began driving back to Paris, and about two in the morning they got lost. They stopped at a police station to ask instructions and ran into the Houseshakers.

---

1. Adrian Owlett.

They continued toward Paris, but the chauffeur, who looked like the cartoon character Bluto and was nicknamed Gorille, fell asleep at the wheel and nearly drove off the road. Adrian says, "We were very nearly killed." Adrian asked to drive, but Gorille wouldn't let him, so they all crashed out at the side of the road. The House-shakers caught up to them later and Gene said, gesturing toward Gorille, "This guy's fuckin' mad. He's a fuckin' nutcase! He almost killed us!"

Gene decided to go to Moulin with the band in their van: "Gene was in a good mood and he said, 'I wanna go with the boys.' He was wearing a pink jean jacket and big sun-glasses. He was very funny and one time he almost fell out of the open door of the van 'cause he was laughing so much. While he was on tour he drank about five bottles of Martini a day. He got a little wild sometimes, but he never got falling-over drunk. A lot was probably to cover up the pain in his leg. He talked about Jackie a lot."[2] The gig in Moulin was "another triumph," and so was the next one in Strasbourg. The second-to-last gig turned into a disaster. They were supposed to play at Lon-le-Saunier, but the promoter, Michel Thonney, had to leave to join the army. As usual, Gene demanded his money before he went on, but the club manager said he'd already paid Thonney, so Gene refused to go on. He said, "I just feel sorry for the people. But I've been ripped off for years, and I ain't bein' ripped off no more!"

Earl Sheridan, the Houseshakers' manager, went out to explain to the crowd that there was a "financial hitch," but the fans went crazy: "The place exploded with angry fans. The safety curtain fell down, and the fans went crazy and ripped up boxes and seats and started a bonfire. But the building was stone and wouldn't burn. A huge crowd of Frenchmen surrounded the van and let the air out of all the tires."[3] Then the police arrived and escorted the musicians out.

The next day they went back to get the van, only to find it had disappeared. They went to the police, who couldn't find it either. Members of the promoter's family showed up at the train station

2. Graham Fenton.
3. Ibid.

and tried to stop Gene and the hand from leaving, but they managed to push their way through and got on the train to Paris, and when they got back to their hotel they found the van waiting for them.

On the train to Paris, Gene told Graham an interesting story about himself and Eddie Cochran riding the London subway: Eddie saw a sign saying that the fine for pulling the emergency cord was five pounds, so Eddie pulled, the train lurched to a stop, and when the irate conductor showed up, Eddie just smiled at him and handed him a five pound note. Gene said to Graham, "Yeah, Eddie and I sure had some good fun."

They played one last date at St. Étienne: "Gene really slayed them. His voice was really spot on. He left the stage to a standing ovation which lasted several minutes."[4]

At the end of June, Gene flew back to Los Angeles. In August he played three nights at a rock revival series at Harlow's, a night club in New York City. The show was taped and played later on the Mike Douglas TV show and was reviewed favourably by both *Billboard* and *Cashbox* magazines. The single *Sunshine* b/w *Geese* apparently did very well in the New York area, reaching the number ten position, but didn't sell well nationally.

At the beginning of September, Gene did a live radio interview from a restaurant in LA with KCBH deejay Jim Hawthorne, who at one point mentioned that, "Today rock has divided itself in many facets: heavy, commercial, top forty type rock, country rock, soul...."

Gene said, "I think rock'n'roll is rock'n'roll. You may vary certain chords and arrangements, but rock'n'roll is still rock'n'roll.... When it first came out, they said they'd give it six months, 'cause this is just a fad! (Laughter from the audience) Now it's sixteen years later, and they're still giving it six months. (More laughter) They are still saying it's a passing fad!"

In October, after playing at the San Francisco Folk Festival, Gene went back in the studio and recorded *The Day The World Turned*

---

4. Graham Fenton.

Blue. The session started with a Mickey Newbury song, *How I Love Them Old Songs*, and was followed by another hard rocker, Carl Perkins' *Boppin the Blues*. Some ballads followed: *You Can Make It If You Try*, an R&B standard, *Looking Back (On My Life)*, by Brook Benton; and the title track, *The Day The World Turned Blue*, a Gene Vincent original.

> Love is like a window pane,
> The sun shines in, but it stops the rain.
> They say that love is blind,
> For me this is so true;
> The Day The World Turned Blue.
>
> A pill: I thought everything was funny.
> A pill: I thought our walks were sunny.
> God only knows it's true,
> Look what they've done to you
> The Day The World Turned Blue.[5]

Gene did Big Jay McNeeley's *There Is Something On Your Mind*, but Gene's version is totally different from the original. Not only does he change the words and the theme, but the melody as well. Gene begins with a monologue that is repeated between every verse:

> You know, it's so hard to be in love,
> Especially with someone who don't love you,
> Especially when the one she *do* love is your very best friend,
> You know, it takes all the things outa everything when
>   you find this out.
> And the only thing you can do is pack your bags,
> Walk slowly out the door,
> Look over your left shoulder and say, honey,
> (Here he starts singing)

If you ever think about me,
If I ever cross your mind...
Whoaaa... You know I'm yours; God only knows you'll be
mine...
(Here he talks)
And you get tired of all this stuff, you see,
And you walk down to the pawnshop,
And yer as mad as you can be;
And you buy yerself a big ol' 44,
And you go back up there where yer girlfriend and yer very
best friend is now in session.
You kick down the door,
And you shoot him,
And before you can shoot her,
You realize that all your love and everything is in her.
So you say, honey, I forgive you,
And you throw yer arms around her,
And when you do, here comes another one of your very best
friends.
Man, you got some very best friends all over the place when it
comes to a good looking woman.
So you shoot her,
And as she's layin' there she looks up at you and she says,
heh, heh,
(Here he sings)
If you ever think about me....

Our Souls, credited to Jackie Frisco, was actually written by her
father: '*Our Souls* was written and given to Gene by his father-in-
law. It was recorded at Gene's insistence. As you will hear, the
repetitive *Our Souls*, the faster it is repeated it becomes "Assholes"
and at the end of the track he says, "How's that, Mr. Arden." I can
tell you there was no love lost between Gene and [Don]Arden. As
for *The Day The World Turned Blue*, Gene and I discussed it and
agreed to try as closely as possible to simulate Buddy Holly and
what it would have been like if Buddy were still with us. Thus the
similarity of sound."[6]

6. From a letter written by Tom Ayres to the Gene Vincent Fan Club.

Gene also put some country songs on this album, and the strangest track is Gene's own composition, *The Woman In Black*, which is the last professional track that Gene ever recorded. It begins with a spoken intro:

Now I've met my Maker,
Just left the undertaker;
The penalty, you see,
The one who loves you, her face you'll never see. . . .
(Now Gene sings)
Now take me back to the Woman In Black. . . .
Whoaaa, was it the girl from Tennessee
Who I held so tenderly?
Was it the one from Alabam?
When I left I heard the door slam. . . .
Now take me back
To the Woman In Black. . . .
Was it the one from Caroline?
We made love beneath the pines.
Was it the one from Arizona?
Lord, I think her name was Mona. . . .
Take me back to the Woman In Black.[7]

Al Casey, whom Gene knew from the 1957 Rockabilly Spectacular tour when Al was with Sanford Clark, played guitar on this album, as well as the Challenge album, and he comments, "Gene looked pretty good. He wasn't drinking at the sessions, not that I noticed. Actually, I can't remember ever seeing Gene drink on the job. On that rockabilly tour with Perkins and those guys, we were hitting the booze pretty hard. But not Gene. At that Kama Sutra session, Gene was okay. He was a little bit spacey. But then he was always a little bit weird. I played a tour of England with Gene in November '63. Gene had been riding real high over there. I was with Duane Eddy and Gene was on the same bill. We played London, Liverpool and Manchester and Gene went down real good. Then Kennedy got shot and he got really upset. He wanted to go back to the States. But we talked him out of it. We told him there was nothing he could do."

Near the end of 1970, Rob Finnis, who had been Gene's road manager on his tour of France in '69, stayed briefly with Gene and Jackie in their apartment in LA: "Gene would send me across the street to the supermarket in the morning, saying, 'Hey, Rob, go get something for breakfast, some rolls or something.... Oh, and by the way, pick up a bottle of Martini, will you?' Even when he promised to stop drinking, Gene used to sneak down to the garage in the basement and drink in his red sportscar. One time Jackie came up from the basement with about twenty empty bottles and screamed at him, 'You said you were going to stop drinking!' Sometimes he would be pissed before eleven o'clock. One time he was drunk, his whole face almost purple, crawling on his knees in the kitchen, and Jackie stood in the doorway, just before she slammed the door and left she said to me, 'Rob, it's no use trying to help him. He's a hopeless alcoholic!'"

Los Angeles, 1971 (courtesy of Kie and Louise Craddock)

Jackie left, and now Gene's world really turned blue. They had been together for six years and it had been the longest relationship in Gene's life. But Gene never went for long without a woman, and in late January, 1971, when he arrived in England for his penultimate tour, he was accompanied by Marcia Avron, an American singer who Gene had performed with on stage.

Graham Fenton of the Houseshakers showed up at Heathrow Airport in his '59 Chevy to pick Gene up: "Gene had talked about Jackie, so I assumed she was coming. Then Gene showed up with Marcia. And people were whispering, 'Don't call her Jackie. This is Marcia!' She was a slick chick, pretty good looking. She showed up with a tiny suitcase and left with a bloody trunk! Plus new dresses and thigh-length boots. She seemed to do pretty good for herself. My impression was that maybe she was a bit of a goldbricker. But she was rather quiet and I never really got to know her."

Adrian Owlett was also there: "Marcia was okay-looking in an American way. She was a peroxide blond and very soft-spoken. But she thought she knew everything. Gene spent a fortune on her. They bought up shopfuls of clothes, baby clothes for Marcia's kids and stuff."

Gene rehearsed with the Houseshakers, then they drove up to Liverpool and played at the Polytechnic College: "Gene burst straight into *Say Mama*, his voice as forceful as ever, and within seconds the audience was going mad with excitement. *Baby Blue* and *Rocky Road Blues* followed, and the Houseshakers were instantly impressive as a backing group. The next number was *Maybelline* performed at a terrific pace which really had the audience going mad. At the end, Gene tried to speak, but couldn't make himself heard above the cheering crowd. He broke into *Whole Lotta Shakin'*, but was besieged by fans patting him on the back and shaking his hand. I can honestly say that Gene seemed overcome and really rather surprised by the extent of his welcome. Eventually the stage was cleared and Gene continued with *Good Golly Miss Molly*. Then the first chords of *'Lula* had the audience really going berserk once again. Gene left the stage only to be literally brought back from his dressing room by an audience that just would not let the act finish. An encore of *Long Tall Sally* was followed by *The Day The World Turned Blue*. Finally another version of *'Lula*, and amidst really fantastic applause, Gene was allowed to return to his dressing room."

The next evening, Gene played in Bangor, Wales, then they had to drive all the way back to London, a considerable distance by English standards, and late at night Gene demanded that they get some pizza. ("In 1971, in Wales? This was impossible!" says Adrian). Gene said, "Well, if we were in L.A. . . . !" So they changed direction, got on the M1 and stopped at a service station. Adrian was tired and not hungry, so he stayed in the car. This upset Gene and he turned and said, "What? You don't want to eat with us?" A rift was developing between Gene and Adrian who, after all, had got Gene his Dandelion contract and to whom Gene had dedicated *Lonesome Whistle*: "This was the beginning of a radical change in my relationship with Gene, and it was mainly because of Marcia, since she didn't want anybody getting close to Gene. In an amateur way she interfered. Gene's attitude changed. He was spending most of his money on her, and the business suffered a lot because of this."

On the next night Gene played at an all day rock'n'roll festival. He obviously wasn't in a good mood, because when a band manager, eager to meet his idol, burst into Gene's dressing room without knocking, Gene stared at him and said, "There's a door there, a piece of wood. And before you open it, you put your fist like this. . . ." Gene rapped his knuckles against the table. "You know," he continued, "I might be talking about important business."

Gene drank quite a few bottles of wine that day, and after the gig he demanded that they find a Chinese restaurant. Gene was tired and intoxicated and said to Earl Sheridan, the Houseshakers' manager, and Graham Fenton, who was driving, "Goddamnit! You live in England! Don't you know where there's a goddamn restaurant!" Gene was groaning and moaning and going berserk, according to Graham. Then he had a coughing fit and started vomiting. Marcia said, "Gene, it must be your ulcer." Marcia suggested that he go to a hospital, but Gene yelled, "I don't wanna go to no goddamn hospital!" Graham was worried, so he pulled up in front of a hospital. Gene said, "I ain't goin' in no goddam hospital. If you take me in there, then this tour is finished!"

They continued on their way back to London, but Graham started worrying about running out of gas, as his gas gauge wasn't working properly. They couldn't find a gas station, so they stopped at a police station and asked. They were told there was one about seven miles away, but in the opposite direction. They drove there and found it was a 24 hour automatic fuel pump that only took pound notes. Graham and Earl only had a couple of pounds between them. Gene had about two hundred, but he was asleep in the back seat. "Wake him up," Earl said to Graham.

You wake him up!" replied Graham. Finally, Marcia woke Gene up.

"Where's the hotel?" he asked. Graham explained where they were and Gene said, "Gas? I don't believe it, man. You've got a goddamn gauge that tells you when you're out of goddamn gas. Are you some kind of nut?" Gene grabbed a handful of pound notes, handed them over and refused to take a tenner in exchange. "Forget it!" he said. "Just get me home. I'm tired and I wanna go to bed!"

They continued toward London, but by now Graham hadn't slept in about 24 hours, so every half hour or so he would stop and get out and walk around to keep awake. Gene woke up and asked, "What the hell is goin' on?" Graham explained that he was afraid of falling asleep at the wheel and Gene said, "Well, I'm tired too. And I wanna go back to the fuckin' hotel!"

Earl Sheridan had organized the tour, and he was blamed for anything that went wrong, such as the gigs being too far apart, among other things. According to Graham, every once in a while Gene would wake up and moan, "Sheridan, yer a fuckin' asshole!" Gene and Marcia were in the back seat and Graham and Sheridan were in the front. When they got into London, Sheridan was dropped off, but Gene still kept pushing the back of the front seat and saying, "Sheridan, yer an asshole! Why don't you answer me? It only proves yer an asshole!" Graham finally explained that Sheridan had already been dropped off. When they got to Gene's hotel he got out of the car without saying goodbye, but Marcia turned and said, "Gene's tired. He'll be all right tomorrow."

The next day they did a taping session for John Peel's BBC radio program: "That went great. No problems. Gene was in a really great mood. He came over and said, 'I made a bit of a mess in your car last night. You get it cleaned and I'll pay the bill.'" Graham cleaned up the vomit himself, and he was sure that it was at least partially blood.

The John Peel session was extraordinarily good and on *The Day The World Turned Blue*, Gene and the Houseshakers were in top form. A few days later they did another radio show, Johnny Moran's All Our Yesterplays, and on the way to the studio Graham took the corner too fast and Gene yelled at him, "Hey, just remember who yer drivin' with! I've had enough of that shit already!" This was in obvious reference to the car crash with Eddie Cochran. Gene had been drinking all day and he argued with someone at the studio and stomped out. The Houseshakers put down the backing tracks, then Gene returned and added the vocals. He may have been drunk, but this version of *Baby Blue* is as good in its own way as either of his versions with the Blue Caps and the Shouts.

Around this time they did another session, but not for radio, and this apparently landed Gene in trouble with his label, Kama Sutra. B&C Records were doing an album called *Battle of the Bands* and they wanted a name artist like Gene to help it sell. Adrian Owlett advised against it, since it meant that Gene would be breaking his contract with Kama Sutra, but apparently Marcia advised Gene to go ahead, though he was being paid very little. Just before they went into the studio, Gene and Marcia quarrelled and Gene was in a foul mood and began drinking: "I'd known Gene in foul moods before, but not at me. He was in a temper with anything that breathed."[8] Gene and the Houseshakers recorded *Say Mama,* but Gene's voice was rough. He insisted that they do *I'm Movin' On,* though it had never been rehearsed. So they spent another two hours getting that ready. Gene's voice wasn't any better on this cut. At one point the guitar player did something in a very obvious fifties style and Gene told him, "I appreciate what yer doin'. But couldn't you give it a more modern sound? Couldn't you heavy it up a bit?"

Now Gene started doing some more live dates, including one at the Fishmonger's Arms in Wood Green: "Without doubt an outstanding success. Even before the show many people were queing

---

8. Adrian Owlett.

up and approximately 1,000 saw the show. Gene had to sing encores and the audience gave him a very good reception." It may have been a good show, but one thing went wrong: Gene's ex-wife, Margie Russell, showed up with her lawyer and a court order for payment of back alimony. "Some heavies showed up and Gene was served with a writ. But he took it in his stride and said, 'Okay. Fair enough.' Then he went out and did a brilliant show."[9]

Their next gig was at Kingston: 'Enthusiastic fans rolled in to see Gene's performance, mostly Teds and their girlfriends. Gene came on stage to a tumultuous round of applause, cheers and even a few screams. At the end of the show there was much stamping and yelling for more. The Teds were yelling *Blue Jean Bop! Blue Jean Bop!* Another great performance. The leather man rocks on!'

After this show, Gene was served with another writ, this time from the Inland Revenue for back taxes: "So things were starting to heat up and Gene felt under pressure from all sides. At some of his gigs there were people from Don Arden's organization and they were hassling him just by being there, as if to say, 'We're watching you!'"[10]

Gene's last gig, at the Seagull Hotel in Southall, got mixed reactions: 'The crowd there were very lively, mostly Teds in drainpipes and drapes and their girlfriends. But there were quite a few young girls, 16 or 17 who, although they could never remember Gene in his 'good old days', nevertheless knew a lot about him. Gene came on singing *Baby Blue* and had the audience in raptures. He was really terrific, jumping around the small stage and throwing the mike all over the place. It really was a fantastic performance.'

Graham Fenton remembers this gig a bit differently: "There was a big row back stage. Gene complained about the dressing rooms and didn't want to go on. Then Gene and Earl Sheridan had a bust-up. As soon as Gene hit the stage he smiled, but between the songs he made nasty comments about being ripped off. He'd had a bit too much to drink and said something nasty about Sheridan. Then a scuffle broke out in the wings because some bouncer wanted to get Gene off stage. I think Gene was a bit out of order on some points.

---

9. Ibid.
10. Ibid.

Sheridan was a bit un-together, but I don't think he ripped Gene off. The whole tour was on a thread, and on that last gig Gene couldn't hold it back. He had to let his feelings go. And unfortunately it was in front of a live audience."

Adrian Owlett also had a bad impression of this date: "The last gig was a complete shambles. Gene slagged-off Earl Sheridan on stage. It was very unprofessional. There had been money problems, but slagging-off is done in dressing rooms and *not* on stage. And that was the end of the tour. Later I went to Gene's hotel room to see him off, but he was already gone. And this was completely out of character for Gene."

This was Gene's last complete tour of England, and it was written up in at least two articles, one called 'And Gene Is Still Too Much':

Times have changed and black leather and individuality aren't looked upon as weird. Now, in the enlightened seventies, Gene's act can be reviewed for what it is—exciting and marvellous entertainment. Not just a collection of songs, but a tremendous visual performance too. . . . Who can forget a Vincent show with the wild demonic look as he crouched low over the microphone before pounding the stand in wild abandonment, throwing his injured leg over the mike with a silvery blur of speed. . . . Vincent is the most extraordinary eccentric and terrifying spectacle—Gene's voice is the final contradiction, a soft and fluid and beautiful instrument. . . . He's now on the Kama Sutra label and his brilliant first single *Sunshine* augers well for the future. . . . Just give Gene a chance, that's all.

The other article was called 'Gene—He's Still Big All Over':

There is still a strange charisma which hangs around the man who escaped from a car crash involving his best friend Eddie Cochran and occasionally made the headlines in drug, booze and shooting incidents. . . . He is alleged to have taken a baseball bat to a club where an imitator was cashing in on his name as "the British Vincent". . . . The man and the myth are inextricably mixed.

Gene was asked if he liked performing as much as before and answered, "Well, I'm a little older now. . . but you've got to give them an act. That's what they come for." When asked if he'd made much money in his career, he replied, "Making money has never been a problem for me. The problem has been keeping it." He was asked how he'd managed to sustain his career and replied, "Because I've kept with rock'n'roll and not gone into country and western or ballads. I have faith in rock'n'roll. It has excitement and flamboyance."

Although his sisters and parents and his manager all suggested that Gene give up rock'n'roll and become a country singer, Gene steadfastly refused. His sister Evelyn comments: "Gene should have got into country music later on. But he was stubborn. We brought it up to him, but no way! He loved rock'n'roll. It was something special to him." Louise Craddock says, "We begged him to go into country music, but he never did."

Back in the States, Gene continued living with Marcia and her kids in his big house in Simi Valley. Gene loved children, and apparently he treated the kids like they were his own. In May, Tom Ayres got Gene a week-long gig at the Brass Ring in Los Angeles and many celebrities appeared to back him up: "Gene did great. There were thirty or forty people who took turns playing for him. Delaney Bramlett was on guitar, Aynsley Dunbar was one of the drummers and Georgie Fame was on keyboards." Other guests were Del Shannon, Bonnie Bramlett, Kim Fowley, Joe Cocker, the Flames, Melanie, and the Small Faces.

Around this time Gene was hanging around with the lead singer of the Doors, Jim Morrison, as Tom Ayres recounts, "We would go to the Shamrock Bar just around the corner from Gene's place on Santa Monica Boulevard and Jim Morrison would show up and we'd sit and drink and shoot the breeze. We'd sit around and have laughs like blue collar workers. Gene was a soft-spoken gentleman and Jim Morrison would ask him, 'Gene, what's it really like to be a *real* rock'n'roll idol?' And Gene was bewildered! One time he and Morrison were at my place and I mentioned that some German guy in the neighbourhood had been rude to my son. So Gene went looking for him. Gene would always respond with kindness, unless someone was rude. Then he'd go crazy, totally out of proportion. A while later, Morrison came back screaming, 'Do something! Gene's kicking down every door in the neighbourhood!' And Gene did that until he finally found someone with a German accent!"

Gene was getting crazier, and soon the second big crunch came: Kama Sutra cancelled Gene's contract because of the two tracks Gene had cut for B&C Records in London. After Gene's break-up with Jackie Frisco, this was too much to handle and he hit the bottle with a passion.

Sanford Clark, who had toured with Gene in 1957, saw him about this time at a gig in Phoenix, Arizona: "I went up to his hotel room and had a drink with him. But I didn't stay long. Gene was pretty wild and aggressive, talking pretty rough to his girlfriend. His leg was real bad, just the bone was left. He was on crutches and he seemed a little weird, like he was on pills or something. I had a few drinks, then I left."

In September, '71, a promoter arranged for another tour of England. But before Gene left he recorded four tracks for Rollin' Rock Records: *Bring It On Home To Me* by Sam Cooke, *The Rose of Love* by Gene, *Hey-Hey-Hey-Hey* by Little Richard and *Party Doll* by Buddy Knox, and although Gene sings these songs with the husky kind of whiskey-voice that later made Rod Stewart millions, Gene was in bad shape.

When Gene got to London he phoned Adrian Owlett from his hotel in Ealing and invited him over, and Adrian was surprised at Gene's condition: "He looked all right. But his reason was completely gone. He was talking complete gibberish. He was incredibly paranoid. Everyone was against him in his own mind. He said that Jackie's family had attacked him and showed me a bruise that had been caused by Jackie's brother hitting him with a shoe. He was rambling and he sort of broke down and said that he didn't have any friends in the world. I tried to quieten him down and we had a cup of coffee. He said that Capitol Records had put him in the studio and he'd recorded four new tracks. He also said that he'd been served a writ, probably by Margie, as soon as he'd arrived at the airport. He'd been brought over by a guy named Lee Tracey and had been staying with him and his wife. But because of Gene's strange habits, they'd got him a hotel room. The whole tenor of the conversation was extremely sad. I just looked at this man sitting on the bed with his head in his hands and he was utterly depressed and suicidal. I asked him to come home with me, but he had to be in the North of England in the morning and someone was picking him up at the hotel. Gene was obviously dying."

Gene's gig was at the Garrick Club in Leigh, a small town between Manchester and Liverpool, but Gene was in no shape to perform and his contract was cancelled after two nights. Roy Cheetham was there: "Although he was far from well, he still seemed in quite good spirits. I personally thought he gave a reasonable performance, although his voice was not at its best, due to a bad cold and a sore throat. However, as Gene said after the show, 'I have been booked to do a show here and I am going to do it.'" Gene's next gig was in Liverpool at the Wookey Hollow Club, and it too was terminated after only two nights. Apparently Gene's voice could not be heard, although the sound system was adequate.

After appearing on a Lancashire TV program and the Johnny Walker Show on BBC's Radio 1, Gene had to return to London for his court appearance. He showed up late and was arrested by the Tipstaff (sheriff's officer) of the Supreme Court of Judicature. Adrian was at the hearing and saw Margie arriving with her lawyer and some press photographers: "She was going to take Gene to the cleaners. There had been a court order that Gene maintain his child and maybe Margie too. At this point she hadn't re-married. Gene's point, which, rightly or wrongly, he honestly believed, was that the child wasn't his, so he didn't want to pay." The next day, Gene fled the country. He had only a few days to live.

He arrived in Los Angeles to find that Marcia had left his house in Simi Valley, taking her kids with her. Apparently she took all the furniture, including Gene's record player, a Christmas gift from his sisters. Tina Craddock says, "Marcia seemed nice. But when he went to London she took all his money. I told him not to put the bank account in her name. I don't think Gene had any great feelings for Marcia. She was flashy-looking, lots of make-up. But women went in and out of Gene's life so fast. I think it was her kids he loved. When Gene came home from England he found the kids gone and he just gave up. He didn't want to try."

His mother Louise had a premonition that Gene was dying and spent the night praying, "Please, Lord, don't let him die over there all alone." The next morning she phoned Gene's place, even though he was still supposed to be in England. Gene told her, "I just had to come home....But, Mama, she took everything I had, even my record player."

Apparently, Jackie had either picked Gene up at the airport or visited him at Simi Valley, because Mrs. Craddock says that Jackie told her, over the phone, "I was there last night and I know Gene's dying. I saw it on my father's face and I saw it on Gene's. And I don't want any part of it!"

Kie and Louise Craddock were worried and got a friend named Sterling to drive them from their home in Saugus to Gene's house in Simi Valley: "So I went over there and saw it too. His face was grey. It was a nightmare! I knew I had to take him home with me, but at first he didn't want to come." Gene's parents suggested that he check into a Veteran's Administration hospital, but Gene didn't want to go.

The next day, Louise, Kie and Sterling went back to see him and Gene's condition had worsened. He had been drinking steadily and hadn't eaten. This time he decided to go home: "He wanted to come. He kept saying, 'Mama, let's hurry and get home.' He asked me, 'Mama, did you all pray for me last night?' Then he said, 'Mama, if I get through this, I'll be a better man.'" He tripped and fell on the way to the car.

It's a long drive from Simi Valley to Saugus, and Gene was thirsty. When they drove past the Inter-Valley Hospital, Kie and Louise begged Gene to check in, but he refused, saying, "I just want to go home, Mama. I just want to go home."

The Craddocks were staying at a trailer court and as soon as Gene got inside, he tripped again and fell to the floor. While he was on his knees, his ulcer burst and he began vomiting up blood. Louise held his hand and he looked up at her. His last words were, "Mama, you can phone the ambulance now." The ambulance arrived very quickly, but it was too late. Gene died approximately an hour later. Louise Craddock saw his body in the hospital: "After he died, he had the sweetest smile on his face. He wanted to die. He was glad to think that he was getting out of the mess he was in."

A service was held three days later, and according to Evelyn, "That funeral was a joke, really bad." Gene's other sister, Donna, was a member of a religious cult called the Alamo Foundation, and Kie and Louise, understandably being upset, if not in shock, let these people take care of all the arrangements: "People phoned from all over the country, but couldn't get through. Flowers were sent, but didn't arrive. The Alamo Foundation took everything they could get their hands on. Every instrument was gone. And Gene had a bunch. Gene was in a leather jacket and a blue shirt. Then Jackie came in later and raised a fuss about having the casket opened again. It was just too sad."

Few of Gene's friends showed up, but Johnny Meeks was there: "As usual, there was some kind of problem. Jackie was crying and screaming that Gene shouldn't be buried or cremated, but should get a military funeral and be buried at sea. It was crazy. I thought, 'Man, typical Gene! He can't even die right! There's always gotta be some kind of problem!'"

It was a sad end for one of America's most creative artists. Gene was laid to rest in the Eternal Valley Memorial Park, not far from the hospital in Newhall where he died. His grave is right beside the San Fernando Highway. All day long the big semi-trailers and four-wheelers roar past the Black Leather Rebel. And it seems right, because Gene had lived on the road and for the road, with always another show ahead of him. The tours are over, but the music lives on.

(courtesy of britt hagarty)

251

Bibliography

Finnis, Rob and Dunham, Bob. *Gene Vincent and the Blue Caps.* London: Mimeographed edition, c. 1972.

Vince, Alan. *I Remember Gene Vincent.* Prescott: Vintage Rock'n' Roll Appreciation Society, 1977.

Schlawick, Serge. *Gene Vincent Story.* Saulon-la-Chapelle, France: Crazy Times Revue, c. 1978.

Clark, Alan. *The Gene Vincent Souvenir Album.* Los Angeles: Alan Clark Productions, 1980.

Cheland, Jacky. *Gene Vincent: European Tour.* Paris: Les Editions Horus. Undated.

Discography

SINGLES

BE BOP A LULA/WOMAN LOVE, Capitol CL 14599
RACE WITH THE DEVIL/GONNA BACK UP BABY, Capitol
  CL 14628
BLUEJEAN BOP/WHO SLAPPED JOHN?, Capitol CL 14637
JUMPS GIGGLES & SHOUTS/WEDDING BELLS, Capitol
  CL 14681
CRAZY LEGS/IMPORTANT WORDS, Capitol CL 14693
B-I-BICKEY-BI, BO-BO-GO/FIVE DAYS, FIVE DAYS, Capitol
  14722
LOTTA LOVIN'/WEAR MY RING, Capitol CL 14763
DANCE TO THE BOP/I GOT IT, Capitol CL 14808
WALKIN' HOME FROM SCHOOL/I GOT A BABY, Capitol
  CL 14830
BABY BLUE/TRUE TO YOU, Capitol CL 14868
ROCKY ROAD BLUES/YES, I LOVE YOU BABY, Capitol
  CL 14908
GIT IT/LITTLE LOVER, Capitol CL 14935
SAY MAMA/BE BOP BOOGIE BOY, Capitol CL 14974
WHO'S PUSHING YOUR SWING/OVER THE RAINBOW,
  Capitol CL 15000
SUMMERTIME/FRANKIE AND JOHNNIE, Capitol CL 15035
RIGHT NOW/THE NIGHT IS SO LONELY, Capitol CL 15053
WILD CAT/RIGHT HERE ON EARTH, Capitol CL 15099
MY HEART/I GOTTA GET TO YOU YET, Capitol CL 15115
PISTOL PACKIN' MAMA/WEEPING WILLOW, Capitol
  CL 15136
ANNA-ANNABELLE/ACCENTUATE THE POSITIVE, Capitol
  CL 15169
JEZEBEL/MAYBE, Capitol CL 15179
IF YOU WANT MY LOVIN'/MISTER LONELINESS, Capitol

CL 15185
SHE SHE LITTLE SHEILA/HOT DOLLAR, Capitol CL 15202
I'M GOIN' HOME/LOVE OF A MAN, Capitol CL 15215
BRAND NEW BEAT/UNCHAINED MELODY, Capitol CL 15231
LUCKY STAR/BABY DON'T BELIEVE HIM, Capitol CL 15243
KING OF FOOLS/BE BOP A LULA '62, Capitol CL 15264
HELD FOR QUESTIONING/YOU'RE STILL IN MY HEART,
    Capitol CL 15290
CRAZY BEAT/HIGH BLOOD PRESSURE, Capitol CL 15309
WHERE HAVE YOU BEEN/TEMPTATION BABY, Columbia
    DB 7174
HUMPITY DUMPITY/LOVE 'EM LEAVE 'EM KINDA GUY,
    Columbia DB 7218
LA DEN DA DEN DA DA/BEGINNING OF THE END,
    Columbia DB 7293
PRIVATE DETECTIVE/YOU ARE MY SUNSHINE, Columbia
    DB 7343
BIRD DOGGIN'/AIN'T THAT TOO MUCH, London HLH 10079
LONELY STREET/I'VE GOT MY EYES ON YOU, London
    HLH 10099
BE BOP A LULA/SAY MAMA, Capitol CL 15546
BE BOP A LULA '69/RUBY BABY, Dandelion 4596
WHITE LIGHTNING/SCARLET RIBBONS, Dandelion (S) 4974
THE DAY THE WORLD TURNED BLUE/HIGH ON LIVIN',
    Kama Sutra 2013018
STORY OF THE ROCKERS/PICKIN' POPPIES, Spark SRL 1091
ROLL OVER BEETHOVEN/SAY MAMA/BE-BOP-A-LULA,
    Beeb Beeb 001 – Taken from Johnny Walker Radio Show,
    October 1971
SAY MAMA/LOTTA LOVIN'/RACE WITH THE DEVIL, Capitol
    CL 15906

EXTENDED PLAYERS

HOT ROD GANG, Capitol EAP 1-985
Dance In The Street/Baby Blue/Lovely Loretta/Dance To The
Bop (from the film soundtrack)

GENE VINCENT RECORD DATE, NO. 1, Capitol EAP 1-1059
Five Feet Of Lovin'/The Wayward Wind/Somebody Help Me/
Keep It A Secret
GENE VINCENT RECORD DATE, NO. 3, Capitol EAP 3-1059
Look What You Gone and Done To Me/Summertime/Peace Of
Mind/I Love You
IF YOU WANT MY LOVIN', Capitol EAP 1-20173
If You Want My Lovin'/Hey Good Lookin'/Ain't She Sweet/Hold
Me, Hug Me, Rock Me
RACE WITH THE DEVIL, Capitol EAP 1-20354
Race With The Devil/Crazy Legs/Yes, I Love You Baby/Rocky
Road Blues
TRUE TO YOU, Capitol EAP 1-20461
True To You/She She Little Sheila/Little Lover/Weeping Willow
CRAZY BEAT OF GENE VINCENT NO. 1, Capitol EAP 1-20453
Crazy Beat/Important Words/It's Been Nice/Lonesome Boy
CRAZY BEAT OF GENE VINCENT NO. 2, Capitol EAP 2-20453
Good Lovin'/Gonna Catch Me A Rat/Rip It Up/High Blood
Pressure
CRAZY BEAT OF GENE VINCENT NO. 3, Capitol EAP 3-20453
That's The Trouble With Love/Weeping Willow/Tear Drops/
Gone, Gone, Gone
THE LAST WORD IN LONESOME/PRETTY GIRLS
from Saturday Club Radio Show '65/Say Mama from '64 TV Show
/Baby Blue 'live' onstage CHERBOURG '67. Fan Club E.P. only 99
pressed for legal reasons.
RAINY DAY SUNSHINE, Magnum Force MFEP003
Rainy Day Sunshine/Green Grass/Mister Love/Roll Over
Beethoven

LONG PLAYING ALBUMS

BLUEJEAN BOP!, Capitol T764
Bluejean Bop/Jezebel/Who Slapped John?/Ain't She Sweet/
I Flipped/Waltz of the Wind/Jump Back Honey, Jump Back/
That Old Gang of Mine/Jumps Giggles n' Shouts/Up a Lazy River/
Bop Street/Peg O' My Heart

GENE VINCENT AND HIS BLUECAPS, Capitol T8111
Red Bluejeans and a Pony Tail/Hold Me, Hug Me, Rock Me/
Unchained Melody/You Told a Fib/Cat Man/You Better Believe/
Cruisin'/Double Talkin' Baby/Blues Stay Away From Me/Pink
Thunderbird/I Sure Miss You/Pretty Baby
GENE VINCENT ROCKS AND THE BLUE CAPS ROLL, Capitol
T970 Brand New Beat/By The Light of the Silvery Moon/You'll
Never Walk Alone/Frankie and Johnnie/In My Dreams/Flea
Brain/Rollin' Danny/You Belong to Me/Your Cheatin' Heart/Time
Will Bring You Everything/Should I Ever Love Again/It's No Lie
GENE VINCENT RECORD DATE with The Blue Caps, Capitol
T1059 Five Feet of Lovin'/The Wayward Wind/Somebody Help
Me/Keep It a Secret/Hey, Good Lookin'/Git It/Teenage Partner/
Peace of Mind/Look What You Gone and Done to Me/
Summertime/I Can't Help It/I Love You
SOUNDS LIKE GENE VINCENT, Capitol T1207
My Baby Don't 'Low/I Can't Believe You Want to Leave/I Might
Have Known/In Love Again/You Are the One for Me/Ready
Teddy/I Got to Get to You Yet/Vincent's Blues/Maybe/Now is the
Hour/My Heart/Maybelline
CRAZY TIMES, Capitol T1342
Crazy Times/She She Little Sheila/Darlene/Everybody's Got a
Date But Me/Why Don't You People Learn to Drive?/Green Back
Dollar/Big Fat Saturday Night/Mitchiko from Tokyo/Hot Dollar/
Accentuate the Positive/Blue Eyes Cryin' in the Rain/Pretty
Pearly
THE CRAZY BEAT OF GENE VINCENT, Capitol T20453
Crazy Beat/Important Words/It's Been Nice/Lonesome Boy/Good
Lovin'/I'm Gonna Catch Me a Rat/Rip It Up/High Blood Pressure/
That's the Trouble with Love/Weeping Willow/Tear Drops/Gone,
Gone, Gone
SHAKIN' UP A STORM, Columbia 33SX1646
Hey-Hey-Hey-Hey/Lavender Blue/Private Detective/Shimmy
Shammy Shingle/Someday/Another Saturday Night/Slippin' and
Slidin'/Long Tall Sally/Send Me Some Lovin'/Love, Love, Love/
Good Golly, Miss Molly/Baby Blue/Susie Q/You Are My
Sunshine
GENE VINCENT, London HAH 8333

Hurtin' For You Baby/I am a Lonely Fugitive/Born to Be a
Rolling Stone/Hi-Lili, Hi-Lo/Poor Man's Prison/Words and Music/
Bird Doggin'/I've Got My Eyes On You/Love Is A Bird/Ain't That
Too Much/Lonely Street/Am I That Easy To Forget
BEST OF GENE VINCENT VOL. 1, Capitol T 20957
Say Mama/Lotta Lovin'/Wear My Ring/Gonna Back Up Baby/
Rocky Road Blues/Important Words/I Got a Baby/Bluejean Bop/
Woman Love/Pistol Packin' Mama/Little Lover/Right Here On
Earth/Wild Cat/Unchained Melody/My Heart/Be Bop a Lula
BEST OF GENE VINCENT VOL. 2, Capitol ST 21144
B-I-Bickey-Bi, Bo-Bo-Go/Frankie and Johnnie/The Night Is So
Lonely/Git It/Yes, I Love You Baby/Walkin' Home From School/
I Got It/Crazy Legs/I'm Goin' Home/Five Days, Five Days/True
To You/Right Now/Well I Knocked and I Knocked/Over the
Rainbow/Race With the Devil/Be Bop a Lula '62
I'M BACK AND I'M PROUD, Dandelion 63754
Rockin' Robin/In the Pines/Be Bop a Lula '69/Rainbow at
Midnight/Black Letter/White Lightning/Sexy Ways/Ruby Baby/
Lotta Lovin'/Circle Never Broken/I Heard That Lonesome
Whistle Blow/Scarlet Ribbons (for her hair)
IF ONLY YOU COULD SEE ME TODAY, Kama Sutra 2361 009
Sunshine/I Need A Woman's Love/Slow Times Comin'/Danse
Colinda/Geese/500 Miles Away From Home/Listen to the Music/
If Only You Could See Me Today/A Million Shades of Blue/
Tush Hog
THE DAY THE WORLD TURNED BLUE, Kama Sutra 2316 005
How I Love Them Old Songs/High On Life/North Carolina Line/
You Can Make It If You Try/Our Souls/There is Something On
Your Mind/The Day the World Turned Blue/Boppin' The Blues/
Looking Back/Oh Lonesome Me/Woman in Black
PIONEERS OF ROCK VOL. 4 – GENE VINCENT, Starline SRS
5177 King of Fools/Where Have You Been All My Life/Love 'em
Leave 'em Kinda Guy/The Beginning of the End/La-Den-Da-Den-
Da-Da/Spaceship to Mars/Be Bop a Lula '62/You're Still In My
Heart/Held for Questioning/There I Go Again/Humpity Dumpity/
Temptation Baby
GENE VINCENT GREATEST, Capitol Caps 1001
Be Bop a Lula/Race With the Devil/Gonna Back Up Baby/Who

257

Slapped John?/Bluejean Bop/Bop Street/Jump Back Honey/
B-I-Bickey-Bi, Bo-Bo-Go/Lotta Lovin'/Dance to the Bop/Dance in the
Street/Rocky Road Blues/Say Mama/Anna Annabelle/She She
Little Sheila/Wild Cat
THE BOP THAT JUST WON'T STOP, Capitol SM 11826
Be-Bop-A-Lula/Race With the Devil/Woman Love/I Sure Miss
You/Who Slapped John?/Bluejean Bop/Teenage Partner/Cruisin'/
Important Words/B-I-Bickey-Bi, Bo-Bo-Go
ROCK'N'ROLL LEGEND, Capitol 064-82077
Race With the Devil/Be-Bop-A-Lula/Woman Love/Crazy Legs/
Gonna Back Up Baby/Well, I Knocked Bim Bam/Teenage
Partner/Five Feet of Lovin'/B-I-Bickey-Bi, Bo-Bo-Go/Important
Words/Five Days, Five Days/I Got It
Wear My Ring/Lotta Lovin'/True to You/Dance to the Bop/Baby
Blue/Walkin' Home From School/Yes I Love You Baby/Right
Now/I Got a Baby/Dance in the Street/Lovely Loretta/Little Lover
Rocky Road Blues/The Night is so Lonely/Beautiful Brown Eyes/
Say Mama/Be Bop Boogie Boy/Who's Pushing Your Swing/Anna
Annabelle/Over the Rainbow/Darlene/Wild Cat/Right Here on
Earth/Pistol Packin' Mama
Mister Loneliness/If You Want My Lovin'/I'm Going Home/Love
of a Man/Spaceship to Mars/There I Go Again/Baby Don't Believe
Him/Lucky Star/King of Fools/You're Still in my Heart/Held for
Questioning/Be Bop a Lula '62
RHYTHM IN BLUE, Blue Cap BC-2-11-35
Long Tall Sally/What'd I Say/Say Mama/Baby Blue/Pretty Girls
Everywhere/I'm Goin' Home/The Last Word in Lonesome is Me/
Roll Over Beethoven/Be Bop A Lula/Say Mama/Rocky Road
Blues/Baby Blue/Maybelline/Whole Lotta Shakin' Goin' On/
Be-Bop-A-Lula
FOREVER GENE VINCENT, Rolling Rock LP 022
Bring it on Home/The Rose of Love/Hey Hey Hey Hey/Party
Doll/Say Mama/Tribute to Gene Black Leather Rebel/Right Now/
Rocky Road Blues/Dance to the Bop/Be Bop Boogie Boy/Lotta
Lovin'/Important Words
BE-BOP-A-LULA, Koala KOA 14617 1980
Story of the Rockers/Pickin' Poppies/Be-Bop-A-Lula/Pistol Packin'
Mama/Say Mama/Rocky Road Blues/Baby Blue/Whole Lotta

Shakin' Goin' On/The Day the World Turned Blue/Story of the Rockers

ROCK ON WITH GENE, Capitol MFP 50463

Be-Bop-A-Lula/Flea Brain/Lovely Loretta/Maybelline/My Baby Don't 'Low/Rip It Up/Say Mama/Be-Bop Boogie Boy/Darlene/Cat Man/Who's Pushin' Your Swing/Ready Teddy

GENE SINGS VINCENT, Capitol 2C 068-86309

Race With the Devil/Be-Bop-A-Lula/Jezebel/Who Slapped John?/Jumps Giggles and Shouts/Blue Jean Bop/You Told a Fib/Teenage Partner/Cat Man/Hold Me Hug Me/Cruisin'/Important Words

ROCK'N'ROLL HEROES, Rockstar RSR-LP 1004

Say Mama/Summertime/Wildcat/My Heart/Rocky Road Blues/Be-Bop-A-Lula/and 5 tracks by Eddie Cochran

EDDIE COCHRAN & GENE VINCENT: THEIR FINEST YEARS
 — 1958 and 1956, Music for Pleasure MFP 50535

Be-Bop-A-Lula/Woman Love/Race With the Devil/Gonna Back Up Baby/Bluejean Bop/Who Slapped John?/Important Words/Crazy Legs/and 8 tracks by Eddie Cochran

GENE VINCENT with Interview by Red Robinson, Great North-West Records GNW 4016

Story of the Rockers/Be-Bop-A-Lula/Say Mama/Baby Blue/Pistol Packin' Mama/The Day the World Turned Blue/Story of the Rockers

Acknowledgements

The research for this book began with a phone call to Ronnie Weiser of Rollin' Rock Records, who'd recently brought out the album *Gene Vincent Forever*. He gave me the number of Melody Jean Vincent, who in turn led me to Jerry Merritt. Mike and Robbin Fraser paid for my trip to meet Melody and she introduced me to her mother, Darlene, Gene's second wife. Darlene let me stay at her home in San Jose, fed me, sewed my blue jeans, and talked to me for hours. Through Darlene and Melody I got to know Gene's parents, Kie and Louise Craddock, and I visited them in Burbank. One thing led to another and soon I was in Norfolk, Virginia, and Greenville, South Carolina, talking to the Blue Caps. While in Norfolk I was helped by Margaret Van Zandt and Anne Collins, who let me stay at their place and helped me to find Gene's first wife, Ruth Ann. I made this trip with Heather Kelly, who let me use her car and provided me with a cassette player for the Vincent tapes.

My trip through the States was financed by myself, my parents, Karl Siegler of Talonbooks, and Geoff Molyneux of *The Province*, who commissioned me to write an article about the adventure. Karl Siegler also supported my trip to England to meet Henry Henroid and members of Sounds Incorporated.

Henry Henroid bought copies of my novels when I was broke. Alan Holmes supplied me with beer and whiskey and let me sleep on his couch when I missed the train back to North Kensington. In London, Adrian Owlett devoted much time to filling me in on different aspects of Gene's career. Steve Aynsley, president of the Gene Vincent Fan Club, put me up, almost burnt his house down cooking me breakfast, and gave me access to fan magazines, newspaper clippings and many hard-to-get photos. DiAnne Kaslow of St. Paul, Minnesota, also gave me photographs, as did Serge Schlawick, co-author of *Gene Vincent Story* and co-editor of *Crazy Times Revue*, the fan club magazine in France.

Special thanks to the staff of Talonbooks: Mary Schendlinger, who helped type the manuscript and also picked me up at the airport and bought me beer and hamburgers; David Robinson, who did the layout and design; Gary Fisher, who persevered through strenuous editing; and Karl Siegler, who did that most important thing—he believed in the book right from the beginning.

Most of all, thanks to Donna McCallum, who saw me through three long years of work, stayed up all night and danced with me to *Crazy Legs* and *Rocky Road Blues*, and who knows the lyrics to every song.

All the quotes in this book are from interviews by britt hagarty, unless otherwise indicated, with one exception: some of the descriptions of Gene's performances, particularly in Chapter 10, are from the Gene Vincent Fan Club Magazine. Grateful acknowledgement to Steve Aynsley and the Gene Vincent Fan Club (Britain).

Grateful acknowledgement is made to the following for the use of lyrics excerpted from songs:

Acuff-Rose Publishing Inc. for "Born To Be A Rolling Stone" by Jerry Merritt.

Beechwood Music Corp. (Screen Gems-EMI Music) for "Pink Thunderbird" by Paul Peek and Bill Davis; and "Rollin' Danny" by Joe Steen and Paul Edwards.

Big D Music for "Git It" by Bob Kelly.

Bridgeport Music, Inc. for "Crazy Legs" by Donald Austin and Woody Wilson. Copyright © 1973. All Rights Reserved. Used By Permission.

Central Songs (Screen Gems-EMI Music) for "B-I Bickey Bi, Bo Bo Go" by Don Carter, Dub Nalls, and Jack Rhodes; "Cat Man" by Gene Vincent and Bill Davis; "Dance To The Bop" by Floyd Edge; "Important Words", "Race With The Devil" and "Who Slapped John" by Gene Vincent and Bill Davis; and "Woman Love" by Jack Rhodes.

Jackie Craddock for "Pickin' Poppies" by Jackie Craddock.

CBS SONGS for "The Day the World Turned Blue" and "The